Sheffield Hallam University
Learning and IT Services
Adsetts Centre City Campus
Sheffield S1 1WS

D1647300

...RIES

SHEFFIELD HALLAM UNIVERSITY
LEARNING CENTRE
WITHDRAWN FROM STOCK

Tom Stoppard

Rosencrantz and Guildenstern are Dead
Jumpers
Travesties

A CASEBOOK

EDITED BY

T. BAREHAM

SHEFFIELD HALLAM UNIVERSITY
WL
828 Stoppard T
TO
ADSETTS LEARNING CENTRE

Selection, editorial matter and Introduction © T. Bareham 1990

All rights reserved. No reproduction, copy or transmission of this publication may be made without written permission.

No paragraph of this publication may be reproduced, copied or transmitted save with written permission or in accordance with the provisions of the Copyright, Designs and Patents Act 1988, or under the terms of any licence permitting limited copying issued by the Copyright Licensing Agency, 90 Tottenham Court Road, London W1T 4LP.

Any person who does any unauthorised act in relation to this publication may be liable to criminal prosecution and civil claims for damages.

The author has asserted his right to be identified as the author of this work in accordance with the Copyright, Designs and Patents Act 1988.

Published by
MACMILLAN PRESS LTD
Houndmills, Basingstoke, Hampshire RG21 6XS
and London
Companies and representatives
throughout the world

ISBN 0–333–42385–2 hardback
ISBN 0–333–42386–0 paperback

This book is printed on paper suitable for recycling and made from fully managed and sustained forest sources.

A catalogue record for this book is available from the British Library.

Transferred to digital printing 2002

Printed and bound in Great Britain by
Antony Rowe Ltd, Chippenham and Eastbourne

CONTENTS

CONTENTS 7

System of Titling: here and in the Selection, exterior quotemarks are used for editorially devised captions. In other cases, the caption employs the original title of the writer's book, chapter or section of a book, article or essay (in some instances abbreviated from that), and it is displayed without exterior quotemarks.

GENERAL EDITOR'S PREFACE

The Casebook series, launched in 1968, has become a well-regarded library of critical studies. The central concern of the series remains the 'single-author' volume, but suggestions from the academic community have led to an extension of the original plan, to include occasional volumes on such general themes as literary 'schools' and genres.

Each volume in the central category deals either with one well-known and influential work by an individual author, or with closely related works by one writer. The main section consists of critical readings, mostly modern, collected from books and journals. A selection of reviews and comments by the author's contemporaries is also included, and sometimes comment from the author himself. The Editor's Introduction charts the reputation of the work or works from the first appearance to the present time.

Volumes in the 'general themes' category are variable in structure but follow the basic purpose of the series in presenting an integrated selection of readings, with an Introduction which explores the theme and discusses the literary and critical issues involved.

A single volume can represent no more than a small selection of critical opinions. Some critics are excluded for reasons of space, and it is hoped that readers will pursue the suggestions for further reading in the Select Bibliography. Other contributions are severed from their original context, to which some readers may wish to turn. Indeed, if they take a hint from the critics represented here, they certainly will.

A. E. DYSON

INTRODUCTION

I don't write plays for discussion.

I've never felt . . . that art is important.

The playwright who can boldly assert these aphorisms [1] is unlikely ever to be the darling of the academic world. Tom Stoppard's standing with the scholar-critics has never been uniformly high. Nor has the reserve been all on their side. In his *TLS* article of 1972,[2] the author of *Rosencrantz and Guildenstern are Dead*, *Jumpers* and *Travesties* nailed his colours to the mast.* He argued that academic criticism of drama is frequently a self-sustaining game indulged by men who all too often have no practical knowledge of theatre – who very often never even go to the theatre. This throwing about of brains has moments of sharp truth. Some of the professional philosophers who raised hands in horror at the 'defective' philosophy in *Jumpers*, for instance, were funnier even than the bewildered hero of the play himself. This offers a whimsical indictment of scholarly blindness, reminding one of aspects of the great theatre debate between the academics and the professional writers which raged during Shakespeare's lifetime. As the most Elizabethan of all contemporary British playwrights, it may be appropriate that Tom Stoppard has borne this fusty and *mal à propos* nonsense all the way to the bank on his broad and capable shoulders. His is, avowedly, like Noel Coward's 'a talent to amuse'.

Yet this Casebook solemnly sets out to collect criticism of the playwright in order to help students at all levels who are 'set' Stoppard for study. My card-index recording material written about him runs to well over 350 items, the vast bulk of it generated by the academic world. I have leavened this heavy dough with a little of the yeast of 'first night' criticism from the professional reviewers whom Stoppard pointedly exempts from his general strictures on the commentators. It is true that in many cases the academics merely duplicate and elaborate upon the issues first raised in these immediate assessments; the problems posed by the presentation and

* *Rosencrantz and Guildenstern* . . . was first produced in 1966, and appeared in a revised version in the following year. The first production of *Jumpers* was in 1972 and that of *Travesties* was in 1974 [Ed.].

function of Lenin in *Travesties* being but one urgent and obvious example.

Had I believed *all* the scholarly comment to be otiose I would have abandoned the volume. My fine tooth comb has dragged out what I trust is a representative and germane selection of material which may offer guidelines and props to the student. If one of our greatest and most commercially successful modern playwrights must be forced under the microscope of classroom study, I can only hope that the material in this volume illuminates the plays by always remembering that they are scripts for stage enactment, *not* merely case histories for scholarly debate.

One further note of warning This volume deals only with one phase of Stoppard's work. *Travesties* – the last written of the plays included here – was first performed in June 1974, since which time Mr Stoppard has written much, and much that is very different from the work through which this volume represents him. Most of his early interviews (the ones most apposite to this Casebook), find him denying an ostensible intellectual *purpose* to this work. 'Early' and 'middle period' Stoppard, as we may currently allow those designations, is almost peculiarly free of political or directly social message: 'I find it deeply embarrassing when large claims are made for such an involvement', he asserted in 1973.[3] At that juncture he was much opposed to both 'committed' theatre, and to 'pure' art. *Travesties* itself is in part a dramatisation of those reservations. If the truth is 'always a compound of two half-truths'[4] that the artist debates by 'refuting himself, endlessly',[5] the outcome, by way of overt message will naturally lack vehement polemical or political assertiveness.

The later plays do look both less flamboyant and more sober. At first glance *Night and Day* (1978) and *The Real Thing* (1982) are much closer to 'conventional' structure and characterisation than their predecessors, whilst a number of works from the period after *Travesties* dealt four-square with 'the political and social history of Poland during the period which saw the eclipse of Gierek ... (and) ... the rise of Solidarity' (*Squaring The Circle*, 1980–81) or 'have as their theme the quality of private and public life in Eastern Europe' (*Every Good Boy Deserves Favour* and *Professional Foul*, both 1977). We may also note that the first and last of these are television plays, and the second a work for actors and orchestra. Both form and content have made an apparent shift.

The author himself always felt that *Travesties* marked a watershed. The zestful pyrotechnics of language and of action which make *Jumpers* so exciting as theatrical spectacle came to seem dangerous if not dishonest to repeat. What he called 'theatre of audactiy'[6] ceased to be quite so compellingly a forefront pressure upon his sense of craftsmanship. Perhaps this element got released down the 'B' road of translation – among the fireworks of *On The Razzle* (1981), for instance – whilst the main highway led elsewhere, if not towards actual refutation of his earlier stance, then at least towards re-assessment. The same cast of mind is still manifest; the fascination with the eccentric, the delight in puns, the evocation of artistically controlled disorder. But the indulgence of vaudeville routines – the almost wilful desire to lead us into a maze where appearance subverts reality or renders it impotent – has been somewhat subdued.* Thematically the later Stoppard is more socially committed than he used to be; technically he is, perhaps, less charismatic. The three plays covered in this volume belong avowedly and triumphantly to that earlier period of wonderful – sometimes irreverent, but always exciting – discovery of the limits of what is theatrically possible. Critics have speculated about how far Stoppard's own Central European roots† have dictated his more overt political concern in the work since *Travesties*, or how far the unremitting acid despair implicit in the contemporary political climate has eaten its way into his soul. Whatever changes have occurred, he has remained one of the most accomplished and innovative technicians among living British playwrights. The glory of all three works covered in this Casebook surely lies here, regardless of the academic world's quibbles over Stoppard's intellectual credentials, and it is always a celebration of his theatricality that this volume seeks to capture in its selection of material.

It is sometimes asserted that Stoppard is 'cold', that even allowing for the impressiveness of his firework displays, no warmth comes from the sparks. More sensitive critics have seen behind this front. Clive Bigsby embodies this superior perception: 'He creates a series of characters who, although ultimately defeated by social and metaphysical forces, provoke or themselves embrace a human

* The appearance of *Hapgood* since the preparation of this volume has significantly modified the pertinence of these remarks on Stoppard's career. After a ten year gap, *Hapgood* seems to have returned to many of the delightful old tricks and mechanisms of the three plays discussed in this volume: creating a symbiotic relationship with a known genre by standing Le Carré and the byzantine spy-thriller on its head; interweaving literary criticism with an ironic life-view; and playing new versions of the old illusion- and -reality games, both with style and dialogue. The method of teasing and subverting the audience in *Hapgood* is much closer to that employed in the plays covered in this volume than it is to the work of the intervening period.

† Stoppard was born as Tomas Straussler in Zlin, Czechoslovakia, in 1937; he was taken in emigration to Singapore in 1938, and came to England in 1946 [Ed.].

compassion which transcends the relativistic ethics of an absurd universe.'[7] This may take us straight to the centre not only of what constitutes the true nature of Stoppard's drama, but *why*. It manifestly asks us to consider him as someone more valuable and more committed as a writer than the clever but superannuated undergraduate who created precocious party tricks in *Rosencrantz and Guildenstern are Dead* and the work which followed it. Bigsby's perception, I hope, also frees us from the need to pursue the cindery path of Stoppard as disciple, parasite or shadow of Beckett, Ionesco or any other 'Absurdist' guru. A great deal of criticism of *Rosencrantz and Guildenstern are Dead* harps unnecessarily upon this sense of Stoppard's derivativeness, or his place within a movement. The idea of his early masterpiece either as a one-act student prank portentously extended to a full-length play, or of its protagonists as merely Lucky and Pozzo tricked out in doublet and hose, can be demonstrated as callow and jejune. There echoes back to us Stoppard's own assertion that 'a play is not the end product of an idea; the idea is the end product of the play.'[8] If *Rosencrantz and Guildenstern are Dead* is derivative (and how could it be otherwise in one sense, written just when it was, while the author was still developing, and while British theatre was on the crest of a wave of self-discovery?) what matters is the confidence of the particular linguistic dexterity, the imaginative daring of the basic concept, and the sheer zany éclat of the effects. That W. S. Gilbert did an ' *R & G*' eighty years before Stoppard, as one hostile critic waspishly affirms,[9] cannot really make the remotest difference to the organic integrity of Stoppard's effort. One might, equally cogently reply that, if Gilbert's piece had been as memorable as Stoppard's, it too would have survived within the active professional repertory.

Tom Stoppard burst upon the English theatrical world at a critical juncture. As C. W. E. Bigsby points out, it was a time when British theatre had gone 'naturalist' and was showing a slightly heavy-breathing concern for social 'message'.[10] But Stoppard was, particularly in those early years, a 'self-confessed aesthetic reactionary . . . (who) . . . believes in the primacy of words'[11]. 'I burn with no causes', he told the *Sunday Times*, '. . . one writes because one loves writing'[12]. And, avowedly, because 'one' loved Beckett, the Eliot of *Prufrock*, and several other quite recherché authors and styles. But from the outset it was plain that here was an author who also loved the exhilaration of enactment and the challenge of high-wire acts and gymnastics with the elements of live theatre. His position in the revival which characterised the British stage from *Look Back In Anger* onwards is unique, because of this fusion of the intellectual and the visual elements of theatre. Ostensibly there is a huge gulf between, say, the minor Absurdists like N. F. Simpson on the one hand, and the more daring 'message' writers like Joe Orton on the other. It is precisely into this void that the early Stoppard fitted.

His concern with the fusion between medium and ideas is manifest in the range of his early creative activity. A novel, film scripts and very distinguished radio plays broadened his understanding of the problems of communicating through a living and ephemeral medium. The effects run deep. Long set speeches, for instance, are usually anathema in the theatre. Neither actors nor audiences like them. Yet Stoppard is the master of the long speech – most markedly in *Jumpers* and *Travesties*. The wonderful characterisation of Carr in the latter play is entirely founded on Stoppard's ability to let him ramble by the page; nor could George Moore in *Jumpers* exist so convincingly and circumstantially without his long discursive solos. Admittedly it takes a virtuoso performer like Michael Hordern or John Wood to carry these speeches; for a time after *Rosencrantz and Guildenstern are Dead*, Stoppard became a playwright inaccessible to amateur performers (as most noticeably did Peter Shaffer among his contemporaries, in a way which neither Orton, Pinter nor Wesker did). Yet the smaller pieces – his 'nuts and bolts' plays of the same period – *have* remained, justifiably, firm favourites with performers at all levels, particularly *The Real Inspector Hound* (1968) and *After Magritte* (1971).

The more perceptive critics ponder the problem of whether Stoppard should be called an Absurdist at all. Victor Cahn's excellent book is called *Beyond Absurdity* (excerpted in section 2 of Part One, below), and essays on Stoppard's place and genre have titles like 'Absurdism Altered'. This opens the way to genuine perceptions about the uniqueness of Stoppard's art; 'he ends as an Absurdist farceur who has compassion for his characters' affirms Bigsby (op. cit.), and this goes to the heart of his excellence and his permanent value. All his central figures are caught in a bewildering world where absolute values struggle against relativity. This is *Jumpers*, but the presentation of the struggle is always gloriously accessible through his stagecraft. Parodist, wit, ringmaster to a wild troupe of performing words, Stoppard's is a theatre as complete as anything since Ben Jonson, with whom he has much in common, as he does with other great Elizabethan masters as he works for the 'marriage of the play of ideas and . . . high comedy'.[13]

Rosencrantz and Guildenstern are Dead, his first major success, set the critical battle lines in array, and the two armies have remained

entrenched ever since in their chosen positions. For some Stoppard
is a show-off, an overgrown undergraduate, purveyor of callow
jokiness which lacks true substance, and is derivative. Across the
barbed-wire barrier of his puns, his penchant for disorder and his
studied evocation of confusion, helplessness and loss of faith and
identity, are camped the enthusiasts who laud and defend his ability
to contextualise these aspects of the modern *angst* within the confines
of making it all funny. Thus the aim of *Rosencrantz and Guildenstern
are Dead*, he asserts, was primarily to 'entertain a roomfull of people'
with something 'like music-hall, . . . a slightly literate music-hall'.[14]
Perhaps he is occasionally over-defensive. Tom Stoppard/Tomas
Straussler, the Czecho-British ex-provincial journalist who mocks
academicism without having a degree, may formerly have experienced moments of feeling his flank was exposed. The acerbity of
some of the early interviews – particularly 'Doers and Thinkers;
Playwrights and Professors' of 1972 – is heavily self-defensive below
its surface. We must remember, however, that it is the earlier
Stoppard with whom this Casebook is concerned. The tone of the
playwright's self-assessments has shifted latterly, as the style of his
plays has also changed. The Stoppard of *Night And Day* (1978) and
The Real Thing (1982) is altogether less superficially ebullient than
the old Stoppard of *Jumpers* and *Travesties*; he is also less abrasively
anti-intellectual.

The genesis of *Rosencrantz and Guildenstern are Dead* is hinted at in
some of the preliminary extracts reprinted here. The germ was a
blank-verse pastiche about Ros and Guil* who, after their arrival
in England, find King Lear on the throne! This *does* sound like an
undergraduate *jeu d'esprit*, but the piece was quickly re-shaped
towards its present form. The playwright's imagination became
more and more preoccupied with their plight within the confines of
Shakespeare's work: 'these two guys who in Shakespeare's context
don't really know what they are doing. The little they are told is
mainly lies, and there's no reason to suppose they ever find out why
they are killed.'[15] In the early 1960s Stoppard has said, this inevitably
struck a young playwright as being 'a pretty good thing to explore'.[16]
The witty perversity of examining these two archetypal attendant
lords, of inverting normal order, decorum and dramatic expectation,
and of playing the serio-comic metaphysician, strikes one, in
retrospect, as inevitably and inexorably Stoppardian. The admixture

* Many critics have adopted this truncation of names to distinguish Stoppard's
characters from Shakespeare's. This convenient device has been adopted in this
volume [Ed.].

has often been labelled 'existentialist', though the author repudiated this trendy portmanteau label with a characteristically wide-eyed disclaimer of knowledge even of what the word means!

Rosencrantz and Guildenstern are Dead is an essentially theatrical play; the choice of the theatre's most famous work as its jumping-off point is no accident – nor is the careful and brilliantly imaginative building-up of the player-troupe as the battery and the catalyst which provides much of the power and the meaning in the work. It was pleasant to find, in Robert Egan, an academic who had performed the role of the Player Leader, in order to articulate the central importance of this part of the play (see Section 3 of Part Two, below). In the end, the quality and the style of thought in *Rosencrantz and Guildenstern are Dead* are dictated more by the wily, time-worn, infinitely *knowing* old pragmatist who leads the perennially displaced players than it is by Ros and Guil themselves. This opposition of innocence and experience runs right through Stoppard's work. In *Jumpers* George and Archie embody the polarities; in *Travesties* Lenin is set off against all the artists within a cognate framework, and the split personality of Old and Young Carr adds a dimension to it.

Not only is the Player the ideological centre of *Rosencrantz and Guildenstern are Dead* but, in a strange way, this tatty old intellectual down-and-out generates a sense of grotesque poetry. He is richly trenchant on the value of established art (his pragmatism and his evocation of a perennial lowest common denominator are most healthily deflationary), and he is wickedly funny as well. The fleshing-out of Shakespeare's wandering thespian into this germane and timeless study represents an act of creative and imaginative genius of the highest order. One feels that, as much as the original 'Shakespearean' Player, the progenitor of Stoppard's character is Hamlet's gravedigger, with his earthy and grotesque wit, and his appalling ability to outdo his 'betters' at their own word-games. As the Player warns Ros and Guil, 'it costs little to watch, and little more if you happen to get caught up in the action'; and both literally and metaphorically this is what happens to the two bewildered courtiers, summoned to they know not what, by they know not whom, and for a purpose beyond their ken. And through the stylistic and intellectual levels of address to theatricality, role-making and involvement, the audience too is sucked into the work: 'What a fine persecution – to be kept intrigued without ever being enlightened ...', reflects Guil, from way downstage and directly to the audience. The remark is paradigmatic not only of this play, but of Stoppard's consistent attitude to theatrical art. I have chosen to use Thomas

R. Whitaker – again a *practical* academic – to illustrate aspects of *Travesties* for this Casebook, but his critique of Stoppard is also most illuminating on this aspect of *Rosencrantz and Guildenstern are Dead*.[17]

Bewildered innocents, modern anti-heroes, audience within audience: all these are claims for the precise role of Ros and Guil. Each claim contains part of the truth, and repays study. William E. Gruber reminds us, moreover, that the play raises issues of justice, freedom, responsibility; and he rightly stresses the particular qualities of Act Three, once Stoppard has gone beyond – or between the lines of – Shakespeare's controlling script. 'Stoppard here invites his characters to invent their history according to their will. He offers them alternatives, if not absolute choice.'[18]

Their tragedy, according to Gruber, is that they cannot 'transcend their own banality' (perhaps, by extension, their audience-hood). Thus they fail themselves within the new context shaped for them by Stoppard in this 'invented' section of the action. Gruber argues, furthermore, that 'the sudden sweeping reduction of Ros and Guil', intensified by the final convergence of the Shakespeare and the Stoppard plays, makes a vital commentary upon both scripts. If the Jacobean tragedy proposes the tragic dignity of man, the Absurdist parody is intensely reductive, and the interaction at the end of Act Three is a genuine and logical culmination of the ideas propounded throughout: 'together they assert a view of human activity that stresses man's ultimate responsibility.'

It must remain unlikely that any work which elicits intelligent interpretation evoking matters as serious as this constitutes merely an undergraduate frolic. My own experience of directing the play is avowedly of the primary *delight* in the audience at the sparkle of the repartee and the trenchancy and iconoclasm of the sustained parody of a recognised masterpiece. I accept gratefully the playwright's assertion that this was his primary intention – 'to entertain a roomful of people' – but I do equally believe that the critics' case for the ultimate seriousness of the play is a valid one. Stoppard's goal of the marriage of the comedy of ideas and farce seems to me triumphantly consummated in *Rosencrantz and Guildenstern are Dead*, though the process may be pursued with even more sophistication in *Jumpers* and *Travesties*.

Jumpers, then, represents a triumphant extension and development of the elements present in the earlier play. The *mise-en-scène* is more boisterous, revelling in its admixture of vaudeville, detective thriller, political satire, philosophical soliloquy and anti-academic high-jinks. Still acutely conscious of the theatricality of theatre, Stoppard is

here avowedly and overtly intent upon the exposition of ideas. It
has been called 'an oceanic play, with a glistening surface and
profoundly chilling undercurrents'.[19] The condescending hostility it
evoked from some professional philosophers[20] falls into place as an
involuntary footnote to the comic fabric of the work itself –
rather as though Henry Fielding, for example, had persuaded the
unimaginative reactionaries of his own day to write the footnotes to
Tom Thumb, which he so deliciously appends for them. One day
perhaps the variorum Stoppard will include some of the ripe plums
from *Philosophy* as part of its critical apparatus!

Nor is the uncannily prophetic picture of the directions in which
bad universities could actually get worse without interest in the
current catastrophic state of British higher education, particularly
in light of the political overtones which Stoppard foresees as endemic
in the farcical debacle. The gymnastics paradigm is *not* mere whimsy;
it is a sickeningly appropriate symbol of what has come to pass –
and how.

The play is fairly summarised as the work of a 'highly educated
consciousness canalised into hilarious theatricality'.[21] But *Jumpers*
does more than merely provide a farcical depiction of how the
debased pragmatics of cost-effectiveness and trendy but spurious
innovation engorges humanism. It is a wonderfully protean and
broad-based assertion of the need for love, charity and humility in
a crass and mechanistic world. And thus, as Victor Cahn puts it,
Jumpers represents 'a positive step out of the disjointed world of the
traditional Absurdists'. We may go further: 'The most crucial theme
of the play [is] that mankind is not simply a passive victim in this
world but can be an active participant.'[22] This of course is precisely
what Ros and Guil were *not* able to demonstrate.

The attempt to make at least six theatrical styles, modes or genres
intermesh may not work with complete success: Agatha Christie, A.
J. Ayer, Barnum and Bailey, and Robert Falcon Scott, will never
lie easy as bedfellows. But of all living British playwrights only Tom
Stoppard would have dared to try it. Inevitably my constricted
choice of material understates certain elements of the play; even in
production it is difficult to do uniform justice to the richness of
themes present in the script, as was demonstrated in the 1985
Aldwych revival of *Jumpers*, where both Bones and Crouch were
swamped by other strands of the production.

At its centre is George Moore – 'half St George and half a joke
vicar'[23] – struggling to clarify his own sense of values and order
while, *inter alia*, a political coup d'état, a murder mystery, a university
take-over, and the breakdown of domestic harmony all threaten to

swamp him. The ambition of the scheme, and the virtuosity of its execution are breathtakingly ambitious. It is worth noting that the distinguished philosopher A. J. Ayer found the play charismatic, entertaining and valid within its chosen parameters.[24] When the dust has settled there isn't much you can do to redeem the lesser professionals who mistake organic satire for an attempt at verisimilitude. They merely demonstrate the validity of the critique implicit in the act of creativity which conceived Stoppard's George Moore as he is – a victim, among other things, of the cognomen syndrome! It may be better to pass straight to recognition of the actual compendiousness of the erudition required to validate such a skit. Surely no other West End playwright could have attempted the task? The art is to hide the art; in order to be a joke philosopher George actually needs to be thoroughly convincing *on the stage*; whatever happens *on the page* with regard to his 'actual' expertise is of far less moment. Both his language and his style of expression have seemed valid to an impressive array of both scholars and theatre critics through Michael Hordern's marvellous enactment of George in the original production in 1972. As can be seen from our selection in Section 2 of Part Three, below, the more perceptive critics relished this at the outset. B. A. Young points out firmly that 'Mr Stoppard, who is clearly well up in it, invents philosophical discussions with astonishing fertility of ideas and humour of expression', and J. W. Lambert is quick to corroborate this feeling. Conversely, Stanley Kauffman will have none of this, and chooses to see *Jumpers* as juvenile regression even from the antics of *Rosencrantz and Guildenstern are Dead*. The juxtaposition of attitudes collected here is intended to provoke discussion, though, necessarily, it is only professional enactment which can finally arbitrate – and many students will lack this criterion of judgement since the play is enormously demanding of human and technical resources, and thus seldom revived.

If George's serio-comic quest for ultimate justice is at the core of the play, the plight of his wife – admirably named Dotty – is inextricably bound to it. G. B. Crump represents the commentators who have discussed her role and function in the play: 'Dorothy has been psychologically traumatised by the triumph of rationalistic materialism'.[25] Her emotional hinterland as student seduced by an idealisation of George, and as popular singer eviscerated by the rape of the moon, is wonderfully imagined and deftly layered by Stoppard into the comedy and the implicit tragedy of the play. Her disruptively charismatic aura as siren, sex-object and domestic companion manqué neatly draws together the activities of George, Bones, Archie and the 'lunar' sub-plot. Simply, without Dotty, Stoppard could not deploy his outrageous overlap of theatrical genres. Her pathetic human predicament also gives warmth and flesh to the play's necessary intellectualism. Yet, this being high Stoppard, she is also made the vehicle of some of the funniest moments in the play. Subject to George's professional monomania (inspired by fear of the world and the flesh?), to Archie's dermatographical scrutiny (the irresistible force of materialistic pragmatism?), and Bones's gloriously corrupt and spaniel-like devotion (the distracting slush of common sentimentalism?), there seems no chance of her recovery; a predicament at once comic on the surface and deeply disturbing beneath.

The ancillary enrichments of the central anarchic vision in *Jumpers* are brilliantly inventive. Given time to think, they represent for us, and illuminate aspects of, the central themes with fecund and joyous circumstance. Part of the problem is that we are not really given time to think. Sometimes the play works like an engine with the choke out. It runs too rich, floods itself and stalls. The 'Captain Scott' material is of this kind. In production it is sometimes cut or reduced (see the Author's Notes to the 1972 Faber script, p. 11). Ambushes, pits and oubliettes for the audience abound both verbally and situationally. The script is full of distinctive Stoppardisms, from the comic abuse of Zeno's paradoxes (St Anthony dies of *fright* because the arrows fired at him could never logically reach their target!) to the devastating irrefutability that 'if rationality were the criterion for things being allowed to exist, the world would be one gigantic field of soya beans . . .'.

Unlike *Rosencrantz and Guildenstern are Dead*, *Jumpers* is a play about love; love of man for woman, of man for his vocation, of God for man. This is the struggling face of benignity in the play. Greedily asserting itself, however, is the malign love of power over others, represented in a sinister mode by Archie, and with a comic subversion in both Bones and Crouch. The thwarting, corrupting and downgrading of love bring this play as close as any work in the modern canon to becoming that critical impossibility – an Absurdist *tragedy*.

Equally pressing is the problem of Time in the play. 'Then' and 'Now' are constantly juxtaposed: 'then' there was normal government, 'now' we have the sinister Radical-Liberals; 'then' the moon was a symbol of pure romanticism, 'now' it is a raped and degraded piece of cold rock; 'then' Dotty and George were lovers, 'now' they exist across a brittle and unbridgeable void of defensive word-games. When Stoppard suggests that his plays comprise 'convergences of threads', it is easy to see what he means. Also remarkable in retrospect is his description of the genesis of this intricate and complex structure of interlocking styles and theatrical modes.[26]

Whilst most critics admire the energy and the comic *attack* of this mélange – what Ronald Hayman calls his 'architectonic virtuosity', – there is an undertow of reservation about the play's ending. John Weightman (in Section 2 of Part Three) represents this feeling; perhaps the author's own uncertainty about whether to have Captain Scott back in the coda is symptomatic. He was present in the first production, excised from the 'rationalised' published script, and reinstituted for the 1985 revival. This general disquiet about the coda finally homes in upon the closing speech, where radically differing interpretations are offered, ranging from the speculation that Archie is being used inappropriately as the mouthpiece of genuine authorial belief in the future, to a reading of the same words as a last bitter platitudinous irony to mollify the masses under Radical-Liberalism.

The genesis of *Travesties* (1974) – like that of *Jumpers*, which began as a provoking vision raised in an earlier play – is remarkable. During an interview in America at the time of the Broadway launch of *Jumpers*, Stoppard speculated to the critic and theatre commentator Mel Gussow that 'I think it might be nice to do a two act thing, with one act a Dadaist play on communist ideology, and the other an ideological functional drama about Dadaists'.[27] No mention of Carr at this point. From another interview with Gussow we learn that, having managed to acquire John Wood as his leading actor, Stoppard found him physically suited to represent neither Lenin, Tzara nor Joyce.[28] And just at this juncture he stumbled upon the existence of the real-life Carr, who not only became, instantly, the centre of the work, but who uncannily bore some physical resemblance to John Wood. The comic/grotesque incidents actually surrounding Joyce's production of *The Importance of Being Earnest*, and his clash with Carr over tickets and trousers, are documented in the Introduction to the Faber text and in the programme note to the original production (the latter is excerpted in Section 1 of Part Four, below). They represent real life turned into such surreal absurdity that Stoppard's imagination must have been quickly fired. Out of this grew the 'thematic network', the layers of discussion about art and integrity which constitute the structural skeleton of *Travesties*.

In reading assessments of this play it is clear that many critics have had reservations about the role and function of Lenin. In our

selection on *Travesties*, Irving Wardle epitomises the first-night
doubts, while Joan F. Dean articulates the confusion, and Clive
Bigsby ('Lenin remains solidly detached') the positive hostility
which this portion of the play can provoke.

Stoppard himself called it 'rather an exclusive play', and has
revealed his own ambivalent attitudes to the debate on Art which is
customarily seen as its centre. It is very possible to argue that in
Travesties he is coming to the end of a phase of his theatrical
inventiveness. While terms like 'vaudeville' are still partly appropriate to describe its tone and structure, some of the extrovert fun
which created pyramids of gymnasts and trapeze-strippers swinging
across the stage, has been soberised into cerebral and literary
travesty. Benedict Nightingale's disappointment that he couldn't
respond as wholeheartedly to *Travesties* as to *Jumpers* makes overt a
hesitation shared by many critics (Section 2 of Part Four). In Act
One, the Wildean parallels are wittily sustained and are genuinely
germane. After the Interval comes that huge contentious chunk of
undramatised Lenin, and the analogies with Oscar Wilde never
quite recover from it. The *purpose* of the Lenin material is obvious
enough: there is no other ready means for Stoppard to embody the
particular nature of the Socialist Realist ideology of art. And Lenin
was, intriguingly, in Zurich at a date at least close in time to the
Joyce–Carr–Tzara trio. But perhaps Stoppard has here been tempted
to venture one coincidence too far. Intelligent purpose alone does
not justify dramatic practice; 'one has the feeling that the main play
has come to a stop . . .', as Irving Wardle observed.

Despite this one reservation, there are many aspects of the play
which seem logically and triumphantly the culmination of a palpable
stage of Stoppard's development. The character of Carr is a supreme
achievement: rambling, waspish; old quean and charlatan at one
moment, dispassionate chairman of a debate on Art at others. He
evokes pathos and amusement equally.

Though Stoppard once thought of calling the play 'Prism' (itself
a witty and germane conceit), *Travesties* sums it up best. Embodied
in the work are travesties on various kinds of art – Dada anarchy,
Joycean excess, Wildean exquisite esotericism, Shavian polemics
and Soviet social realism. The characters are all travesties of
themselves, as well as being intent upon reducing each other to
travesty, and the joint frames of Carr's untrustworthy memory
within a time-warp, and Wilde's 'pure art' structure from *Earnest*,
offer an ingenious means of holding the individual performances
together. Joan F. Dean, in our selection, discusses the role of Carr
in lending coherence to the 'four distinct views on art' which are at

the play's core. The basic seriousness of the debate is also made
clear in this essay through recognition of Stoppard's ability to be
impartial. ' . . . one doesn't think with one mind on these matters.
One has two or three minds battling with each other' was Stoppard's
own comment;[29] and his ability not to *reduce* views which he
personally suspects (as with Tzara) further than the sympathetic
level of travesty he employs within the overall comic frame for Joyce,
whom he overtly admires – or implicitly for Wilde to whom his
entire construct is indebted – is a sign of his true maturity and
balance as a comic artist.

The play is also the culminating point of a period of verbal
experiment and daring in Stoppard's career. Some critics find the
punning in all the plays of this period excessive. Milton Shulman
hints at this in our reproduction of his first-night reaction to *Travesties*,
and later critics have taken up the theme – particularly Hersch
Zeifman (excerpted in Section 2 of Part One, below). The play could
not exist without its verbal contortions and linguistic travesties, but
they oscillate between the inspired and the excessive. A note of
authorial overkill rather than of dynamic, in-character inventiveness
creeps in, perhaps as Stoppard, consciously intent on writing no
more plays of the kind which he had explored in all three of the
works represented in this volume, bids farewell to an aspect of his
writing which had served him so well in building his reputation.
Even as late as *The Real Thing* (1982) he remains unstoppable when
he does choose to mount the unicycle of trick language, but nowhere
else and never again has a major play of his been quite so dominated
by punning since *Travesties*.

These three plays, then, represent the main stream of Stoppard's
growth from early acclaim to establishment at the centre of contemporary British drama. They evince a distinct pattern of growth and
development within broad boundaries of technique and ideas. Yet
if their similarities and indebtednesses are manifest, their individual
identities are quite distinct too. Inevitable as its termination may
have been – *necessary* as it may have become for the artist himself –
there are many playgoers who regret the passing of pure show-
manship, vaudeville and extrovert daring from the work of this
talented, inventive and witty playwright.

NOTES

1. Both quotations are from an interview of Stoppard's with R. Hudson and others,
called 'Ambushes for the Audience: Towards a High Comedy of Ideas', *Theatre*

Quarterly, IV, 14 (May–July 1974) pp. 3–17. Excerpts from it are included in the relevant sections of this Casebook.

2. Tom Stoppard, 'Doers and Thinkers: Playwrights and Professors', *Times Literary Supplement* (13 Oct. 1972), p. 1219; excerpted in Section 1 of Part One, below.

3. Tom Stoppard, in an interview with Janet Watts, *Guardian* (21 March 1973), p. 12; excerpted in Section 1 of Part One, below.

4. Ibid.

5. See the critique by Mel Gussow, 'Stoppard Refutes Himself, Endlessly', *New York Times* (26 April 1972), p. 54.

6. Ronald Hayman, *Tom Stoppard*, 4th edn (London, 1982).

7. C. W. E. Bigsby, *Tom Stoppard*, (Harlow, 1976), p. 6.

8. Stoppard, 'Doers and Thinkers: Playwrights and Professors', op cit., note 2 above.

9. S. Kaufman, *Persons of the Drama* (New York, 1976); excerpted in Section 2 of Part Three, below.

10. Bigsby, op. cit., p. 3.

11. Ibid., p. 4.

12. Tom Stoppard, 'Something To Declare', *Sunday Times* (25 Feb. 1968), p. 47.

13. Stoppard, 'Ambushes for the Audience', op. cit., note 1, above.

14. Ibid.

15. Ibid.

16. Ibid.

17. Thomas R. Whitaker, *Tom Stoppard* (London 1983); excerpted in Section 3 of Part Four, below.

18. William E. Gruber, 'Wheels Within Wheels' *Comparative Drama*, 15 (1981–82), pp. 291–301; excerpted in Section 3 of Part Two, below.

19. Bigsby, op. cit.

20. E.g. *Philosophy*, 50 & 52, of 1975 and 1977 respectively.

21. Hayman, op. cit., note 6, above.

22. Victor Cahn, *Beyond Absurdity: The Plays of Tom Stoppard* (Rutherford, N.J., 1979); excerpted in Section 3 of Part Three, below.

23. James Morwood, 'Jumpers Revisited', *Agenda*, 18/19 (1981); excerpted in Section 3 of Part Three, below.

24. A. J. Ayer, 'Love Among the Logical Positivists', *Sunday Times* (9 April 1972), p. 16.

25. G. B. Crump, 'The Universe as Murder Mystery: Tom Stoppard's *Jumpers*', *Contemporary Literature*, 20 (1979); excerpted in Section 3 of Part Three, below.

26. Stoppard, in Gussow, op. cit., note 5, above.

27. Ibid.

28. Mel Gussow, 'Playwright, Star Provide a Little Curtain Raiser', *New York Times* (31 Oct. 1975), p. 21.

29. Stoppard, 'Something to Declare', op. cit., note 12, above.

Editor's Notes

It has become increasingly difficult to produce a comprehensive selection for a Casebook on an author about whom all the critical material one wishes to use is still in copyright. The price of permission to use this material has risen desperately. Alongside this runs the Publisher's overall constraint upon the cost of the book. Within this series the Editor bears the cost of payment for permissions fees, which are set against his royalties, and the Publisher imposes a ceiling. Certain critics who have written excellently on Stoppard are not represented here because I could not afford them – some because their publishers' or agents' charges for second use of material already on the market were frankly outrageous.

For conformity certain editorial emendations have been made throughout: I have followed series style in use of inverted commas – viz. single inverted commas except for quotations within quotations. Reference to page-locations of quoted material has been inserted where absent in the original essay and/or made consistently conformable with the following editions of Stoppard's work:

Rosencrantz and Guildenstern are Dead (Faber, London, 1968).
Jumpers (Faber, London, 1972).
Travesties (Faber, London, 1975).

The dates here relate to publication in book form, of course – not necessarily the date of first production on stage. Editorial excisions are, I hope, clear in all cases where I have not used a complete article.

A couple of original misprints have been silently emended.

It is a convention of some writers on *Rosencrantz and Guildenstern are Dead* to make a distinction between Shakespeare's characters and Stoppard's by truncating the names of the latter to Ros and Guil. As indicated in a footnote in the Introduction, above, this distinction has been preserved.

As in all Casebooks, editorial notes are in square brackets. All others are authorial, though some renumbering has been necessary where the essay in question has been excerpted.

I gratefully acknowledge my obligation to the following: to Liz Davis for assistance with some of the latter tidying-up; to Margaret McNulty for tireless effort on the less rewarding parts of the paperchase; to Harry McNulty for use of his office equipment at times when perhaps more obvious sources were inaccessible; and to Messrs Fraser and Dunlop (Scripts) Ltd., Stoppard's professional agents, who made available much otherwise inaccessible material.

PART ONE

Stoppard the Playwright

1. STOPPARD ON HIS OWN ART AND PRACTICE

I INTERVIEW WITH RONALD HAYMAN

. . . At the time when *Godot* was first done, it liberated something for anybody writing plays. It redefined the minima of theatrical validity. It was as simple as that. He got away. He won by twenty-eight lengths, and he'd done it with so little – and I mean that as an enormous compliment. There we all were, busting a gut with great monologues and pyrotechnics, and this extraordinary genius just put this play together with enormous refinement, and then with two completely unprecedented and uncategorisable bursts of architecture in the middle – terrible metaphor – and there it was, theatre! So that was liberating.

It's only too obvious that there's a sort of Godotesque element in *Rosencrantz*. I'm an enormous admirer of Beckett, but if I have to look at my own stuff objectively, I'd say that the Beckett novels show as much as the plays, because there's a Beckett joke which is the funniest joke in the world to me. It appears in various forms but it consists of confident statement followed by immediate refutation by the same voice. It's a constant process of elaborate structure and sudden – and total – dismantlement. In *Travesties*, when John Wood[1] is saying Joyce was this without being that, each sentence radically qualifies the statement before it until he ends up with 'a complex personality'. That sort of Beckettian influence is much more important to me than a mere verbal echo of a line or a parallelism at the end of *Jumpers*. That, if you like, is an open, shy bit of tribute-making, whereas the debt is rather larger than that.

There's an element of coincidence in what's usually called influence. One's appetites and predilections are obviously not unique. They overlap with those of countless other people, one of whom – praise be God – is Samuel Beckett. And it's not surprising if there are fifty writers in England who share in some way a predilection for a certain kind of intellectual or verbal humour or conceit which perhaps in some different but recognisable way is one which Beckett likes and uses.

From play to play Beckett's stage directions progressively give less freedom to the director and actors. How do you feel about that?

I think, truth be told, that were there a language one could do it in, like musical notation, I'd like to notate my plays so that there's only one way of doing everything in them. That's not to say that that would produce the best result. I know from past experience that I've been quite wrong about the way things ought to look and how lines ought to be spoken. One ought to be there for the first production and chance the rest. The first production in France of *Rosencrantz* was a nonsense and I haven't been done in France since.[2]

What about T. S. Eliot and Prufrock?

There are certain things written in English which make me feel as a diabetic must feel when the insulin goes in. Prufrock and Beckett are the twin syringes of my diet, my arterial system. . . .

Generally speaking, are long speeches dangerous?

I always think that they're the safe parts of the play, and they've proved to be so. With *Jumpers* a certain amount of boggling went on when they saw the script. . . . In practice the monologues played themselves, and all the conventionally easy bits – the dialogue – were very difficult indeed to get right. In *Travesties* John Wood, who has the grave disadvantage of being about four times as intelligent as it's good for an actor to be, came in when we were talking about the monologue and he simply said, 'I've looked at it at home. There are no problems in it.' And we didn't rehearse it – just went through it a few times when we were doing the run-throughs and I think I spent two hours with him one day talking about little details of inflection.

What about this question of increasing architectural complexity? It must have the effect of multiplying the unpredictables and the variables and the points where balance will change from one performance to the next.

Yes, I really have a deep desire not to get involved in that kind of play for a long time. . . . One's energy as a writer is going into *theatricality*, and that's okay, but one doesn't want to do that each time, and ideally what I'd like to write now is something that takes place in a whitewashed room with no music and no jumping about, but which is a literary piece – so that the energy can go into the literary side of what I do. I'd like to write a quiet play.

Jumpers and *Travesties* are very similar plays. No one's said that, but they're so similar that were I to do it a third time it would be a bore. You start with a prologue which is slightly strange. Then you have an interminable monologue which is rather funny. Then you have scenes. Then you end up with another monologue. And you have unexpected bits of music and dance, and at the same time people are playing ping-pong with various intellectual arguments.

I can see they have that in common, but the relationship between the abstract ideas and the concrete characters seems different.

Yes, and there are senses in which *Travesties* is a great advance on *Jumpers*, but it's the same kind of pig's breakfast, and I'd really like to abandon that particular paintbox and do a piece of literature for three voices and a dog. One is playing a double game with a play like *Jumpers* and *Travesties:* one is judged as a writer on the strength of what one manages to bring off theatrically, and I'm afraid, with respect to those critics whom I feel to be perceptive, that the chances of a play being judged in isolation from what is done to that play are not great. I was the beneficiary of that happening once, in the case of Ronald Bryden's review of *Rosencrantz*.[3] The play was done in a church hall on a flat floor so that people couldn't actually see it. There was no scenery, student actors. The director didn't show up. Someone else filled in. I turned up for thirty-six hours and tried to put a few things right. It went on in some kind of state or other, and Ronald Bryden, writing for the *Observer*, just saw straight through to the text. . . . It's a nonsense. There's an equation to be got right and there are a number of variables in it. It's not a question of something being right or wrong, it's a question of the variables adding up to the right answer. Things are so interrelated. . . .

I have a love-hate relationship with this mythical figure of the dedicated writer. Isn't there a line in *Man and Superman* about using mother's milk for ink? About 51 per cent of me views this figure with utter contempt and about 49 per cent with total admiration. I also have 51 per cent contempt for the artist who is very serious about himself and ploughs a lonely furrow and occasionally a few pages are released to the millions, and 49 per cent admiration. Conversely, I've got a weakness or a commendable admiration for rather shallow people who knock off a telly play and write a rather good novel and go and interview Castro and write a good poem and a bad poem and give a silly interview and every five years do a really good piece of work as well. That sort of eclectic, trivial person who's very gifted. In a way I catch myself liking those people too much, as if they were sirens on a rock saying, 'Come on, come away from the serious artists'. I never quite know whether I want to be a serious artist or a siren. It's not a condition of good art that you sit in a brown study.

SOURCE: extracts from Ronald Hayman, *Tom Stoppard*, 4th edn (London, 1982), p. 6–8, 11–13, 139.

NOTES

1. [Ed.] John Wood played Carr in the original production.
2. [Ed.] No longer true, but accurate at the time this interview was given.
3. [Ed.] An excerpt from Bryden's review is included in section 2 of Part Two, above.

II Interview with Nancy Shields Hardin

. . .The drafts of my plays would reveal quite banal versions; I just sort of slap down something to remind me what I want to say. I work slowly my productivity is low, as the current jargon has it. I am quite happy if I work a ten hour day and end up with two pages; I am pleased if I end up with one page. I'm pleased – it's ok. It is much easier to work a ten-hour day and end up where you were before.

Q. It is a strange and fascinating thing to me how writers arrive at that energy. I don't mean productivity. But how do you get into the swing of writing? Not how many pages a day, but what is it that finally allows you to produce?

A. I find it quite an alarming way of life when I am into a play because I live in terror of its escaping somehow. You know, each day is a sort of new beginning. I rarely sit down knowing what I want to do next. And I feel that it is something of a miracle to get to the end of a play. I can hardly believe that it all worked out. There is no sense of inevitability about it. I always feel that it is quite scary to sit down in the morning because there is no sense that inevitably something will be added to yesterday's work. I get energized, you know, by finding one good line. It gives me a feeling of optimism which might carry me through to the bottom of the page: I live on these.

Q. Are there other days when you really despair?

A. Oh, I'm afraid more days. I find the despair days are mainly the ones that lead up to page one.

Q. That fearfully empty, blank sheet. That was Mr Moon's problem of *Lord Malquist and Mr Moon* wasn't it?[1]

A. To get to page one – well, let's say to get to page two is almost to reach a point that is downhill. It isn't really, but I find that I get into my deepest despair in that period when I have some rather abstract idea of what I want to write about but no sense of who the people in the play are – where they live. . . .

Q. You don't seem to draw upon any kind of autobiographical information in your writing.

A. No, hardly. Quite true. I've never really had any desire to use myself, even in the case of writing a play about journalism. Somehow my own experience with journalism wasn't what I was after. I think in a way I find it restriciting to write about a world I know. It is almost as though it is a liability to keep to the facts. I think I am much more comfortable where you can invent to your heart's content. Therefore I tend to remove situations from reality – not in *Night and Day*, but in *Jumpers* and *Travesties*. In *Travesties*, once you've decided that the whole thing is happening in an old man's head, you are liberated from the somewhat tedious inconvenience of having to stick to any kind of historical truth. And the same is true of *Jumpers* – except that one does it there by putting it into the future. So again you can make up your world. But I must say that I've no idea whether that applies to my own future at all. I don't know whether I would still be writing with the same instincts this time next year – or whenever I write another play. At the moment I don't feel that I'm going to write another play, including the one I'm in the middle of.

SOURCE: extracts from Nancy Shields Hardin, 'An Interview with Tom Stoppard', *Contemporary Literature*, XXII (1981), pp. 156–7, 162–3.

NOTE

1. [Ed.] This is Stoppard's only published novel, to date; brought out by Anthony Blond in 1966, it was reissued by Faber in 1974.

III   ON CRITICS AND CRITICISM

. . . Probably the best argument for the critic is that he can sometimes send his reader even another critic, as is likely to be the case in academic circles, running to the bookshelf or the theatre to taste the real thing at the fount, but I think this is a more modest role than the critic often visualises for himself and his fellows, for judging by the way they all keep up with each other and continually acknowledge each other with endorsements or rebukes, the real thing is not the Coke but the pffttzzz. And in any case it is a role played more effectively by the biographer: the *facts* about Ibsen whet the appetitie for *Ghosts* much more than the most acute interpretation of the sub-text, which indeed is liable to have the unhappy effect of sending the reader running in the opposite direction.

Because, and this is crucial, an intellectual foray into the substrata of Ibsen, replete with acknowledgements to previous explorers, has got nothing – *nothing* – to do with the experience of watching a performance of *Ghosts*. It is, indeed, unnecessary and probably detrimental for this kind of critic to visit a theatre at all, and there is every reason to believe that most of them know this.

(I hope it is obvious that I am not generally referring to theatre *reviewers*, who are performing a useful public service. Not as obvious, but I trust implicit, is that there is a handful of magisterial figures whose own standing is such that they remove themselves from this particular arena: they speak as equals, and, to take an example, Edmund Wilson on Sophocles is at least as worth reading as Sophocles. In short, we are not talking about the Commercial or the Ecclesiastical branches but the Industrial.)

Thus the general mistake which makes most literary criticism stilted and tautological – the mistake which holds literature to be the end product of the ideas it contains, when in truth the ideas are the end product of the literature – is aggravated in the case of drama criticism which ignores all kinds of purely technical considerations, too: the precise content of a scene is liable to be influenced by the physical limits of a stage, the fire regulations in British theatres, the difficulty of changing the set from a room to a car park and back again, or the length of time for which an audience can be reasonably expected to sit and listen, especially the last, for while a reader can put down a book and return to it another day, when an audience leaves it leaves for good, and it will not be kept in its seats by Ideas. 'Re-read the scenes in *Hamlet* in which R&G appear', instructs an American study guide. 'Explain why Stoppard uses the "sponge" scene but not the recorders scene.' The correct answer is, because we are not sitting in a classroom, we are sitting in a theatre, and we have been sitting here for rather a long time.

SOURCE: extract from Tom Stoppard's article, 'Doers and Thinkers: Playwrights and Professors', *Times Literary Supplement* (13 Oct. 1972), p. 1219.

IV   INTERVIEW WITH R. HUDSON, S. ITZIN, S. TRUSSLER

. . . isn't it true to say that most of your plays have a fascination with the eccentric in human behaviour, at least as a starting point? Aren't you more interested in that than in trying to explore the nuances of ordinary social activity?

What I try to do, is to end up by contriving the perfect marriage between the play of ideas and farce or perhaps even high comedy. Now, whether this is a desirable objective, or why it should be, is a matter which I'm not in the least interested in going into. But it *is* the objective, and to that end I have been writing plays which are farcical and without an idea in their funny heads, and I have also written plays which are all mouth, like *The Gamblers*, and don't bring off the comedy. And occasionally, I think *Jumpers* would be an example, I've got fairly close to a play which works as a funny play and which makes coherent, in terms of theatre, a fairly complicated intellectual argument.

You clearly don't feel yourself part of a 'movement either', and your plays could hardly be called social or political. Does this mean you have no strong political feelings, or simply that they're not what you want to write plays about?

Look, can we clear a few decks to avoid confusion? I'm a professional writer – I'm for hire, if you like – as well as being someone who pursues his own path in his writing. Latterly I have been able to stick to accepting the kind of jobs which happen to lie on my own path, but in the past I've written all kinds of stuff, everything from 70 episodes of a serial translated into Arabic for Bush House, to a one-off spy thing for Granada. Furthermore, the plays which I do from pure choice are not all of a kind either. I find it confusing to talk about 'my plays' as though *Hound* and *Jumpers* were the same sort of thing. . . .

SOURCE: extracts from interview in R. Hudson, S. Itzin and S. Trussler, 'Ambushes for the Audience: Towards a High Comedy of Ideas', *Theatre Quarterly*, IV, 14 (May/July 1974), pp. 7–8, 11.

V   INTERVIEW WITH JANET WATTS

. . . Sitting in on rehearsals is a vital part of the Stoppard operation. 'It cuts a lot of corners. It's always worth trying what the author had in mind, even if you decide not to do it, and if he's not there you can waste a day trying to decide what he's on about.'

There's a deeper participation, too: Stoppard almost directs his plays as he writes. Take a bit of the rubric of *Jumpers*: '. . . She weeps on George's uncomprehending heart. He strokes her hair . . . he really doesn't know what to do. So he plays with her hair for what seems a long time, lifting up her hair, running it through his fingers, looking at it, separating strands of hair. His mind grapples with hair, and then drifts and stops.' [p. 42]

'When I write, I have the production unrolling in my skull', says Stoppard. His plays often begin from an image, and move towards other images. . . .

Stoppard (a true ex-journalist) has a gift for quotable remarks. 'I write fiction because it's a way of making statements I can disown, and I write plays because dialogue is the most respectable way of contradicting myself', he once said on television. He looks wry when reminded of it: 'It seems pointless to be quoted if one isn't going to be quotable . . . it's better to be quotable than honest', he says (doing it again). His plays' dialogue is often 'simply stuff which I've ping-ponged between me and myself', he says this time. He plays a deft game. 'A truth is always a compound of two half-truths, and you never reach it, because there is always something more to say.' After a sequence of Stoppard stone-walling a barrage of interview questions, the words were typed deliberately onto the screen, 'Tom Stoppard doesn't know.'

Yet he never loses control. 'I would think it a personal failure to write a play which is not consistent in every way. – They've got to make absolutely logical sense to me. Otherwise you're drifting over the edge into a kind of artistic anarchy. My plays might have quite unusual things going on within them, but they stick to traditional playwrighting rules. They are much the same sort of play as Terence Rattigan wrote, in the sense that there's a kind of play I don't write and Rattigan doesn't either – a play where one says all these outmoded forms of drama are such a bore, and I'm going to free the whole thing from these fetters – and the result is an absolute boring mess.' So, as he admits, he's a bit of a reactionary in some ways. Not much time for abstract art. He has a handsome collection of eighteenth and nineteenth century watercolours on his sitting-room walls.

His purpose in play-wrighting is purely theatrical, which can disconcert earnest students who want to theorise about his work. 'I don't write plays for *discussion* – plays with secrets in them which are only to be discovered after patient research. I think of a play as an event in the theatre: to look for a kind of cryptogram in a play is to approach it in a way not really to do with theatre. . . .

'There's a line in *Artist Descending a Staircase*[1] that says that, in any community of 1,000 people, there'll be 900 doing the work, 90 doing well, nine doing good, and one lucky bastard writing about the other 999. . . . 'I've always felt that the artist is the lucky man. I get deeply embarrassed by the statements and the postures of "committed" theatre. There is no such thing as "pure" art – art is a commentary on something else in life – it might be adultery in the suburbs, or the Vietnamese war. I think that art ought to involve itself in contemporary social and political history as much as anything else, but I find it deeply embarrassing when large claims are made for such an involvement: when, because art takes notice of something important, it's claimed that the art is important. It's not. We are talking about marginalia – the top tiny fraction of the whole edifice. When Auden said his poetry didn't save one jew from the gas chamber, he'd said it all. Basically I think that the most committed theatre in the land – I suppose that might be the Royal Court – has got about as much to do with events in the political area as the Queen's Theatre in Shaftesbury Avenue. I've never felt this – that art is important. That's been my secret guilt. I think it's the secret guilt of most artists.'

Source: extracts from Janet Watts's interview, *Guardian* (21 March 1973), p. 12.

NOTE

1. [Ed.] *Artist Descending a Staircase* was originally broadcast on BBC Radio 3 on 14 Nov. 1972. It is included in *Four Plays for Radio* (Faber, London, 1984); the line referred to is on p. 46 of that edition.

VI   INTERVIEW WITH MEL GUSSOW (1972)

. . . As a playwright Mr Stoppard is keenly interested in matters of morality. – 'I'm the kind of person who embarks on an endless leapfrog down the great moral issues. I put a position, rebut it, refute the rebuttal, and rebut the refutation. Forever. Endlessly.'

At the same time he believes there is an absolute 'ceiling view of a situation'. Who is looking down from the ceiling? Mr Stoppard leans towards God.

'They found traces of amino acid in volcanic rock – the beginnings of life. – Now a straight line of evolution from amino acid in volcanic rock all the way through to Shakespeare's sonnets – that strikes me as possible, but a very long shot. Why back such an outsider? However preposterous the idea of God is, it seems to have an edge in plausibility.' . . .

About his own plays, he said 'There's stuff I've written I can't bear to watch. They get rotten like fruit, and the softest get rotten first. They're not like ashtrays. You make an ashtray and come back next year and it's the same ashtray. Beckett and Pinter have a lot

more chance of writing ashtrays because they've thrown out all the
potential soft stuff.'

Compared to Beckett Mr Stoppard thinks he writes 'absolutely
traditional straight plays'. . . .

SOURCE: extracts from Mel Gussow, 'Stoppard Refutes Himself, Endlessly', *New York Times* (26 April 1972), p. 54.

VII   INTERVIEW WITH GILES GORDON

. . . GORDON: Who do you feel you've been influenced by as a writer,
or don't you feel it's important?

STOPPARD: It's not important to me, but I suppose it's interesting.
Influences such as appear in *Rosencrantz*, and any play of anybody
else's, are I suppose admirations that have been unsuccessfully
repressed or obscured. I don't mean consciously! But, of the
influences that have been invoked on my behalf, and they have been
Beckett, Kafka, Pirandello of course, I suppose Beckett is the easiest
one to make, yet the most deceptive. Most people who say Beckett
mean *Waiting for Godot*. They haven't read his novels, for example.
I can see a lot of Beckettian things in all my work, but they're not
actually to do with the image of two lost souls waiting for something
to happen, which is why most people connect *Rosencrantz* with *Waiting
for Godot*, because they had this scene in common.

GORDON: Beckett's novels are mainly about one lost soul waiting
for nothing to happen.

STOPPARD: I wasn't thinking so much of what they are about so
much as the way in which Beckett expresses himself, and the bent
of his humour. I find Beckett deliciously funny in the way that he
qualifies everything as he goes along, reduces, refines and dismantles.
When I read it I love it and when I write I just guess it comes out
as other things come out. As for Pirandello, I know very little about
him, I'm afraid. I've seen very little and I really wasn't aware of
that as an influence. It would be very difficult to write a play which
was totally unlike Beckett, Pirandello and Kafka. . . .

GORDON: Do you pay close attention to the work of your
contempoaries?

STOPPARD: I read an enormous amount, at least I used to read an
enormous amount. Now I read less, but of the countless books I've
read and plays I've sat through there are very very few where I feel
that I've been given an experience which differs from all the other
experiences one gets from books and plays. There are very few books

which seem to me to actually get away from what everybody else is doing. I think that a book like *At Swim Two Birds* is going to influence writers for a century. It's influenced writers already. It's certainly influenced B. S. Johnson. How far back can one go? *Tristram Shandy, Ulysses, At Swim Two Birds?* Of plays, of course *Look Back in Anger* had an enormous effect on everybody but it doesn't seem as important now as some others. There are plays which had much less effect at the time which I actually prefer, mainly because of one's own idiosyncrasies. I think *Next Time I'll Sing to You* is one of the best plays written since the war, simply because it's written like music. It's a most beautiful and brilliant use of language. . . .

Source: extracts from Giles Gordon's interview in *Transatlantic Review*, 29 (1968), pp. 23, 24.

2. GENERAL ASSESSMENTS

Victor Cahn   (1979)

Stoppard and the Theatre of the Absurd

The term 'Theatre of the Absurd' has been disparaged in some quarters as but a convenient critical peg upon which to place such disparate playwrights as Beckett, Ionesco, Pinter, Genet and Arrabal. To be sure, these writers have not formalised a common doctrine of principles nor even expressed any artistic accord. Nevertheless, the classification has validity. . . .[1]

Essentially, absurd theatre accepts the absence of a guiding symmetry in the world. God does not exist, nor does any world order normally accepted as a result of his presence. Consequently, it is said, our existence is reduced to a meaningless morass of confusion.

The reader may well ask how this vision of 'absurdity' differs from the philisophical 'absurdity' set forth by such writers as Camus and Sartre. There are crucial points of variance.

First, in the works of Sartre and Camus, man is clearly trapped in such an absurd world. But he is viewed as what might be called a 'tragic–heroic' figure, struggling nobly against an unknowable universe, seeking to inject meaning into his life and thereby to achieve a measure of triumph over the absurdity surrounding him.

In absurd theatre, however, the view of man offered might best be called 'comic-pathetic'. Here man is seen as little more than a clown, bumbling and fumbling his way through the incomprehensible maze that is existence, to both the amusement and the pity of the artist-observer and the audience.

A further distinction can be drawn. The viewpoint here designated 'tragic-heroic' is more properly known as 'existentialist,' and it is essentially one of philosphical origin. The most notable contemporary names in this branch of thought are Sartre, Camus, Heidegger and Jaspers, and, from previous generations, Kierkegaard and Nietzsche. This division of absurdity is concerned primarily with explication and debate. Albeit many existentialists write fiction and drama, at the heart of their output is philosophical argument and the reasoned promulgation of their world vision. . . .

Such intent is precisely opposite the strategy of the playwrights of the absurd. In other words, although the plays of Sartre are clearly of considerable interest, and despite the fact that they are concerned with various aspects of the absurd, they should not be classified as part of the 'theatre of the absurd' tradition.

In purely theatrical terms, the plays of existentialist writers, along with the works of Anouilh, Giraudoux, de Beauvoir and others of the group which Eric Bentley termed the 'theatre of the Resistance', are basically traditional. The existentialist doctrine may be philosophically revolutionary, but the fundamentals of dramatic construction, the settings, the plots, the characterizations, and the dialogue – these are firmly rooted in theatrical convention. . . .

Furthermore, when emotional love is non-existent, physical love becomes no more than a biological urge to be satisfied. In Beckett's plays his decrepit figures are virtually asexual. Ionesco's characters are so trapped in linguistic and circumstantial quandaries that they have little time for either sex or love. In those plays where sexuality is a force, as in the works of Genet or Arrabal, it is often ugly and destructive, intensifying the loneliness each character inhabits.

With the collapse of love and human relationships and the absence of a divinity and therefore of divine justice, moral order breaks down. Values of right and wrong disappear. Horrors may pass unnoticed as characters drown themselves in the pathetic day-to-day sequence of their lives. . . .

Thus absurd theatre presents a world without divine order, without relationships, without sexual fulfilment or genuine love, and without moral awareness. Such a life is hardly precious, and consequently death holds no terror. What frightens Vladimir and Estragon about hanging themselves from the tree is not that they will both die but that only one might die, leaving one alone to live. Survival is the punishment.

Human life is not sacred, and the world is insensible to death. . . .

Thus the transience of human life, its fragility, and its hopelessness, all must be acknowledged. In such recognition is the possibility of salvaging happiness.

These are the intellectual assumptions underlying the theatre of the absurd. However, as indicated, that theatre is not a propagandistic one. These values must be transformed into theatrical form, and therefore the qualities of the *theatre* of absurdist drama must be considered. . . .

. . . inherent in the absurdist consciousness is the chaos of life, the lack of order, symmetry and purpose, which is properly expressed through a dramatic structure also devoid of order, symmetry, and purpose. Therefore first, an absurd play almost always consists of a series of free-floating images. Life does not have a beginning, middle and end; neither does an absurd play. Life does not progress rationally from step to step and culminate in a dramatic climax; neither does an absurd play. In short, the dramatic conventions that have marked absurd theatre have served primarily to shatter the traditional conventions of four walls; sequential plot, dialogue, action and thought; and realistic characters and settings.

Second, playwrights of the absurd generally offer absurdity in some concrete form, often by focusing the action of their dramas on a few objects, whose incomprehensibility and intractability prove overwhelming to the characters. These objects are a manifestation of a world which seems to run riot, beyond the control of man. One thinks of the pinball machine in Adamov's *Ping Pong* (1955), which assumes deistic proportions. Or Pinter's *The Dumbwaiter* (1960), in which the title piece is transformed into a sacrificial altar, a means of submission to a divinity that chooses not to appear.

A third characteristic of absurd theatre is the futility of speech, the inability of man to communicate with others and his failure to understand such plight and its consequences. Perhaps the paradigm of useless speech is to be found in Ionesco's *The Bald Soprano* (1950), which dramatises the banalities that form everyday language – words and phrases that mean nothing and, indeed, block communication. Man flatters himself that language is a force for order. Actually it only adds to the chaos. Furthermore, when speech is useless and communication impossible, the loneliness of the individual is increased. The world is cluttered with words, yet each man is imprisoned within his own thoughts.

Language assumes more insidious dimensions in the plays of Peter Handke, specifically *Kaspar* (1967), in which language is not so much a reflection of human being as a determining force shaping that being. Kaspar is both the product and the victim of the teaching process. He is trained by society but finds himself trapped by the indoctrination he has received. His processes of thought are limited by the extent of his language.

Language in the theatre of the absurd is not a cohesive force, a bond linking civilised man. Rather it is the ultimate entropistic force, isolating each man in a vacuum of words. Man is a prisoner of his own inability to communicate and of society's inability to communicate with him.

Source: extracts from *Beyond Absurdity: The Plays of Tom Stoppard* (Rutherford, N.J., 1979), excerpted from pp. 17–23.

NOTE

1. [Ed.] Cahn in the original here cites two fundamentally important general texts on Absurdism: Martin Esslin, *The Theatre of the Absurd*, (1961; rev. edn, New York and London, 1968); and John Killinger, *World in Collapse: The Vision of Absurd Drama* (New York, 1972).

Hersh Zeifman (1979)

Stoppard's Use of Punning

. . . Puns are both the glory and the bane of Stoppard's critical reputation. On the one hand, his plays are feasts of language; in a time of almost universal famine, it is hardly surprising that audiences have gratefully responded by gorging themselves into paroxysms of delight. The exuberance and inventiveness of Stoppard's puns are difficult to resist, so seductive are they and so starved are we for any kind of verbal elegance in the theatre. On the other hand, there are those 'virtuous' few who wish to abolish theatrical cakes and ale. The truly hostile critics seem to regard punning itself, whatever the merits of any particular pun, as essentially sophomoric: a vaguely shameful adolescent activity that, if indulged in overmuch, results in blindness or insanity. Slightly more sympathetic critics, those who damn Stoppard with faint praise, may acknowledge, if backed into a corner and threatened with unspeakable torture, that his puns are indeed witty and clever, but, oh dear, *merely* clever, too clever by half.

Both of these critical responses seem to me to be almost wilfully blinkered, in that they refuse to look at Stoppard's puns in their wider dramatic context. Stoppard is clearly obsessed with puns, and, like Coward before him, he has an undeniable 'talent to amuse'. But although amusement for its own sake is an honourable theatrical intention hardly deserving the scorn and abuse we sometimes snobbishly and stupidly heap on it, Stoppard's puns are there not only to amuse. Amuse they certainly do, and amuse they were intended to do, but they have other functions as well. Stoppard uses puns, carefully and deliberately, as structural devices in his plays, as an integral part of a play's basic 'meaning'. Just as form invariably mirrors content in Stoppard's drama (indeed, form frequently *becomes* content), so too do patterns of language, and particularly puns. . . .

Puns are a perfect way of conveying, through language, this dialectical structure of Stoppard's drama. For nothing is more

schizophrenic, by definition, than a pun: two or more utterly different
meanings are yoked violently together in the strait-jacket of a single
word (or two words that sound alike). It is language arguing with
itself. And all that is required to set the dialectical ball really rolling
is for one character to assume meaning A while another character
opts for meaning B. A pun is thus quintessentially dialectical,
containing within itself its own thesis and antithesis. On occasion,
some of Stoppard's characters make deliberate use of this 'doub-
leness' of puns, atacking their opponents in a series of punnic wars
which can be fought with relative impunity. It is a deliciously funny
and effective form of aggression, at one and the same time ostensibly
inoffensive and yet teasingly (or viciously) hostile.

In *Artist Descending a Staircase* for example Martello has a go at
Donner's outrageous concept of edible art, represented by a statue
made of sugar ('It will give cubism a new lease of life', Martello
notes sweetly). And sugar is only the beginning:

MARTELLO   Your signed loaves of bread reproduced in sculpted dough, *baked* . . .
  your ceramic steaks carved from meat! It will give opinion back to the intellectuals
  and put taste where it belongs. From now on the artist's palate—
DONNER   Are you laughing at me, Martello?
MARTELLO   Certainly not, Donner. Let them eat art.   [p.29][1]

Along the same lines but far less teasing is Tzara's 'confused'
response to Joyce's poetry in *Travesties*:

TZARA (*to* JOYCE)   For your masterpiece I have great expectorations
(GWEN*'s squeak, 'Oh!'*)
  For you I would eructate a monument.
(*Oh!*)
  Art for art's sake – I defecate!
GWEN   Delectate . . .
TZARA   I'm a foreigner.   [p. 48][2]

But Stoppard's characters do not need to use *deliberate* puns in order
to indicate their opposition to each other. For even when they do
not appear to be arguing, the 'inadvertent' puns they constantly
employ give clear evidence of the wide gulf that inevitably separates
them. The debate format in Stoppard's drama is therefore as much
a linguistic as a structural principle, implicit in the very use of puns
itself. Illustrations of this kind of basic linguistic opposition can be
found in all Stoppard's plays, but perhaps the classic example occurs
in *Travesties*. Thus, Cecily and Carr are poles apart politically and
artistically; Cecily is an ardent socialist and disciple of Lenin,
believing that the 'sole duty and justification for art is social

criticism', whereas Carr is at the extreme other end of the spectrum ('art doesn't change society, it is merely changed by it'). . . .

Travesties, . . . is probably Stoppard's most sustained work of theatrical punning. Henry Carr is a punster's dream (or nightmare, depending on one's point of view); if language is a feast of words, then Carr arrives prepared with fork and knife in tongue, his double-edged and often cutting puns tumbling forth in an unstoppable flow. Some of his puns are outrageous ('What did it do in the Great War, Dada, I am often asked'); some ingeniously subtle ('who'd have thought big oaks from *a corner* room at number 14 Spiegelgasse?' [my italics]); and some sneak up on us so quickly that we are too stunned even to try and categorize them:

TZARA   Eating and drinking, as usual, I see, Henry? I have often observed that Stoical principles are more easily borne by those of Epicurean habits.
CARR *(stiffly)*   I believe it is done to drink a glass of hock and seltzer before luncheon, and it is well done to drink it well before luncheon. I took to drinking hock and seltzer for my nerves at a time when nerves were fashionable in good society. This season it is trenchfoot, but I drink it regardless because I feel much better after it.
TZARA   You might have felt much better anyway.
CARR   No, no – post hock, propter hock.   [p.36]

The cumulative effect of all these puns on an average audience is one of helpless, giddy laughter. But even in *Travesties*, which comes the closest of Stoppard's major plays to using puns for their sheer verve and verbal wit, puns function as more than simply laugh-getters. Once again Stoppard is using puns structurally, to shape our response to the play's larger issues, although the issues have now shifted somewhat. . . .

Stoppard weights the play in favour of Joyce, through various structural stratagems. Thus, for example, Joyce is deliberately given the last word: literally, in his crucial argument with Tzara, and figuratively (and more subtly) at the close of each Act. Act I ends with Carr's devastating reminiscence: 'I dreamed about [Joyce], dreamed I had him in the witness box, a masterly cross-examination, case practically won, admitted it all, the whole thing, the trousers, everything, and I *flung* at him – "And what did you do in the Great War?" "I wrote *Ulysses*", he said. "What did you do?" Bloody nerve'; while the final moments of Act II again remind us of *Ulysses* through Old Cecily's sly echo of Molly Bloom: 'I do remember Joyce, yes you are quite right and he was Irish with glasses but that was the year after – 1918 – and the train had long gone from the station! I waved a red hanky and cried long live the revolution as the carriage

took [Lenin] away in his bowler hat and yes, I said yes when you
asked me . . .'

But perhaps the most effective (because the most insidious)
structural stratagem nudging our sympathies towards Joyce is the
sheer presence of all those marvellous puns in the play. The irony
here is exquisite. Everything Carr says about Joyce is meant to
ridicule and discredit the author of *Ulysses*; but the way in which
Carr says it, the dazzling, exhilarating play with words, betrays his
intentions, having precisely the opposite effect of vindicating Joyce
in our eyes. It is not that, in the debate on art and revolution which
lies at the centre of *Travesties*, Joyce is necessarily given the best
lines: both Tzara and Lenin are allowed equal representation.
Indeed, in terms of the actual substance of its argument, the outcome
of the debate is left, typically for Stoppard, deliberately unresolved.
But because we are so bowled over, so elated by Carr's dizzying
sleight of words, we find ourselves, almost subliminally, identifying
with Joyce, that quintessential punster and wordsmith. . . .

   . . . the point about Stoppard's puns is that they are not simply
comic devices, although there is a marked tendency for many critics
to regard them solely in that light. (Hence the 'My, isn't he
clever' school of response, whether that is meant as compliment or
disparagement.) They are clearly *partly* comic devices, and on that
very important level they succeed brilliantly. Of course, some puns
are weaker than others, and some are very weak indeed; perhaps,
too, there is occasionally the danger of over-bombardment, of failing
to judge when enough is enough. But, in general, Stoppard controls
his puns with dazzling skill. They are meant to make us laugh, and
we do laugh, uproariously; and that is in itself a sufficiently
impressive accomplishment.

But what is even more impressive is the way Stoppard uses his
puns *both* as a comic device *and* as an integral part of what his plays
are trying to communicate. Theatrically, Stoppard's plays are
remarkably all of a piece. In this respect, as in so many others, they
echo the plays of Samuel Beckett. (Beckett has had an enormous
influence on Stoppard's drama, an influence slyly acknowledged by
Stoppard in a lovely pun in the coda to *Jumpers*: 'Wham, bam, thank
you Sam.') Each theatrical element of a Beckett play is 'saying' the
same thing; one can thus pick up the play's 'message' not only from
the words the characters are speaking ('content' in its most obvious
form), but from the way those words are formulated, say, or the
characters' gestures, or the setting, or the very shape of the play.
Much the same thing is true of Stoppard; the dramatic 'message' is
bodied forth in every aspect of the play, as readily apparent in the

kinds of words his characters speak (for example, puns) as in the words themselves. And as the nature of that message shifts from play to play, so the specific implications of what punning can signify (because its range is extremely wide) likewise shift, so as to accommodate the new thematic concern. By thus being an intrinsic part of his plays' very fabric, rather than simply dramatic ornamentation appliqued on some wholly different fabric, Stoppard's puns may be said to constitute a truly theatrical language, in that their presence encapsulates, in a very real sense, the essence of what his plays are all about. Or, to switch the metaphor and end on a suitably outrageous punning note: in Stoppard's drama, punnology recapitulates ontology.

SOURCE: extracts from 'Tomfoolery: Stoppard's Theatrical Puns', in *Yearbook of English Studies*, IX (1979) pp. 204–5, 215–16, 216–18, 219–20.

NOTES

1. [Ed.] Tom Stoppard, *Artist Descending a Staircase*, in *Four Plays for Radio* (London, 1984), p. 29.
2. [Ed.] Tom Stoppard, *Travesties* (London, 1975), p. 48. All subsequent references are to this edition and are designated by page number.

Jill Levenson (1971)

Stoppard, Beckett and the Absurd

. . . Stoppard's debt to the Theatre of the Absurd, particularly to Beckett, is often acknowledged without being analysed. The connection with Beckett is especially important, a means of refuting the general notion that Stoppard is a clever prodigy whose productions do little more than glitter at the surface. For correspondences exist that are far more profound than casual parallels in situation and technique. They have to do primarily with characterization. . . .

Beckett's anguished clowns are barely individualized. Few can articulate their suffering; none can locate its source. It is infrequent that any is lucid enough to pose a significant question, to speculate. Yet we empathize with them and understand their pain. Through symbols, images and key words, we realize not only their despair but also their awareness. For even the least perceptive knows he is afflicted, enduring physical infirmity, hunger, assault, loneliness, impotence, and a sense of the void. . . . All have created games to distract them from hopelessness, games of tyranny and love, of words and memories and logic.

These strange, anonymous characters without history or social milieu are stunningly sympathetic, vulnerable in their naked humanity. They are clearly very different from the unindividualized figures of most Theatre of the Absurd, the grotesques who represent ideas far more often than they represent mortality. Like Beckett's characters, Stoppard's are conceived with compassion. Bewildered and basically gentle people, they struggle to maintain their balance in a world without gravity. In each work, central characters persistently challenge absurdity. Most of these figures are anxious and neurotic, squandering their energy in futile schemes to create order and sense where non exist. Again and again they are exhausted with failure. . . .

While Stoppard's characters are kin to Beckett's, his dramatic structures seem to be based on principles shared by most playwrights of the absurd. Ionesco, a representative spokesman for these principles, has said that the conventional plot in its predictability and resolution is a reassuring distortion of life, whose primary law is unpredictability. A meaningful action, on the other hand, is one that captures and reflects upon the absurd. In Stoppard's plays, plot and theme are correlative. His dramas are all experimental in form. None is strictly linear. To differing degrees they appear arbitrary, unpredictable, and confusing. Yet each is governed by a curious logic, an argument which examines possible solutions to a problem ultimately to reject them all and leave the problem acutely unresolved. The issue is always the same: how can a man live reasonably in a world that makes no sense?

Formally and thematically, *Rosencrantz and Guildenstern are Dead* and *The Real Inspector Hound* are Stoppard's most complex plays. The earlier and more important drama, which depends upon *Hamlet* to define our present *Weltschmerz*, has an intriguing tripartite structure. The foundation is Shakespeare's play, where an intellectual struggle is an heroic endeavour. Superimposed upon this is Stoppard's version of Shakespeare's play, a reduction to absurdity of everything noble and weighty in *Hamlet*. In the rewriting there is no ghost, no bird of dawning, no intimation of a divinity that shapes our ends. Hamlet becomes a slick conniver who drifts in and out of the action, adding to the general confusion. Through a brilliant inversion, the most significant exchanges and soliloquies in the original play have been eliminated, diluted with comedy, or so drastically abridged that they are mere reminiscences of Shakespeare's passages. At the same time, the focus becomes minor characters and incidents, and action that had taken place off-stage. This new *Hamlet* is a disjointed farce without a protagonist. The last component of *Rosencrantz and Guildenstern are Dead* is Stoppard's tale of the two bewildered courtiers who stumble along in a search for direction. Here there are obvious affinities with Beckett's characters, especially the melancholy pairs held together by the peculiar love-hate bred of desperation.

In conjunction, these three actions demonstrate the spiritual disintegration that is Stoppard's major theme. Heroism has degenerated into mock-heroic, and the supernatural has disappeared to leave an irreclaimable void. What could once be viewed with admiration and awe is patronised now as sentimental and futile. This dissolution, so effectively embodied in the general structure, is continually defined by individual situations. When Guildenstern applies the techniques of logic to help him interpret his situation, they cloud comprehension and make him frantic. Rosencrantz's attempt to articulate his questions and fears about death becomes a jerky music-hall routine. Straining to discover their identities, they cannot even remember their names. Efforts to understand why they suffer increase their pain; the elaborate games they play to distract them often daze them. Hope, faith in what is mysterious and beautiful, is again and again disappointed. A man who sees a unicorn quickly learns it is nothing more than a horse with an arrow in its forehead. Meeting the players, Guildenstern is bitterly disillusioned:

It could have been – a bird out of season, dropping bright-feathered on my shoulder.
. . . It could have been a tongueless dwarf standing by the road to point the way.

. . . I was *prepared*. But it's this, is it? No enigma, no dignity, nothing classical, portentous, only this – a comic pornographer and a rabble of prostitutes. . . .

[p. 19][1]

. . .

Finally, language itself disintegrates; the simplest statement or question can become an amazing source of perplexity:

PLAYER: Why?
GUIL: Ah. (*to* ROS.) Why?
ROS: Exactly.
GUIL: Exactly what?
ROS: Exactly why.
GUIL: Exactly why *what*?
ROS: What?
GUIL: *Why*?
ROS: Why what, exactly? [p. 49]

Like Shakespeare's Hamlet, Rosencrantz and Guildenstern are killed trying to understand why they are alive. Emphasizing the fruitlessness of their quest, the troupe of players survive because they have ceased to question. The actors, minor figures in *Hamlet*, are central to Stoppard's play, where they represent an effective way of coming to terms with a capricious universe. They do not analyse, doubt, or worry: 'Relax. Respond. That's what people do. You can't go through life questioning your situation at every turn.' With their roles they have assumed a distance from reality that is comforting and even instructive. The chief player is especially perceptive: 'I extract significance from melodrama, a significance which it does not in fact contain; but occasionally, from out of this matter, there escapes a thin beam of light that, seen at the right angle, can crack the shell of mortality.' That acting is an explicit metaphor is clear from the Player's descriptions of his art, an art which is a way of life and not merely a mirror up to nature. The actors' situation at times is notably similar to Rosencrantz and Guildenstern's; they too cannot function without a sense that someone is watching.

Acting in *Rosencrantz and Guildenstern are Dead* is what novelist John Barth calls Mythotherapy in *End of the Road*, adopting a role consciously or unconsciously to aggrandize or protect the ego: 'The more sharply you can dramatize your situation, and define your own role and everybody else's role, the safer you'll be.' It is an approach not easily dismissed, for it is articulated convincingly by the most coherent and intelligent character in the play. But it is flawed ultimately for Stoppard as it is for Barth. A purely defensive measure, it does nothing to enrich the soul it protects. It leaves little room for real emotion, for compassion and tolerance and love. Like Albert's bridge,[2] it can be dehumanizing; perhaps it too is only a temporary respite. And yet play-acting is the only alternative Stoppard offers to the pointless and fatal pursuits of Rosencrantz and Guildenstern.

The end of the play is a threnody to the values and faith, the incandescent phantoms that once gave life radiance. Juxtaposed with the ludicrous, mimed death of the players and the inconsequential disappearance of Rosencratz and Guildenstern is the last scene of *Hamlet*. Horatio speaks the closing lines of Stoppard's drama, blank verse lines which promise that Hamlet's death and its circumstances will be reported to the world. The contrast is profound. But even as Horatio speaks, his words fade into darkness and music. . . .

SOURCE: extracts from 'Views from a Revolving Door: Tom Stoppard to Date', *Queen's Quarterly*, 78 (1971), pp. 431–2, 435, 436–8.

NOTES

1. [Ed.] Tom Stoppard, *Rosencrantz and Guildenstern are Dead* (London, 1968). All subsequent references are to this edition and are designated by page number.
2. [Ed.] The radio play *Albert's Bridge* is included in *Four Plays for Radio* (London, 1984), pp. 115–50.

Gabrielle Scott Robinson   (1977)

Stoppard and Disorder

... The subjects of Tom Stoppard's theatre are familiar to much of contemporary literature. He writes of the anxiety and confusion of life, of the helplessness of the individual caught up in forces impervious to reason, of the loss of identity and faith. He discusses in philosphical terms the lack of absolute values, the problem of freedom, the uncertainty of all knowledge and perception. Stoppard's world is implausible and irrational and also full of cruelty and pain. His characters are the victims of accidental calamities which threaten and occasionally destroy them.

But to dwell upon his themes alone is to falsify the effect of his plays, for Stoppard adds such farce to his philosophy that the result is more funny than painful. He develops his ideas through a series of comical confusions, leaving the hero in a bewilderment which is both sad and funny. The characters may suffer from the insufficiency of reason, but the farce makes this very lack a cause for enjoyment.

Among Stoppard's principal means of generating both the uncertainty and the laughter is the intermingling of the logical with the absurd: fantastic incidents are made to appear logical, while ordinary and apparently rational occurrences are presented as if they were absurd and inexplicable. . . .

Stoppard expresses his basic sense of disorder in two ways: directly, by making it the subject of his plays and having his characters talk about and be thwarted by it; and indirectly, in the form of his plays, by a lack of development and coherence in his plots, which are constructed episodically of a chain of arguments and counter-arguments. Stoppard himself sees it as the greatest virtue of his plays that they present 'a series of conflicting statements made by conflicting characters, and they tend to play a sort of infinite leap-frog. You know, an argument, a refutation, then a rebuttal of the refutation, then a counter-rebuttal, so that there is never any point in this intellectual leap-frog at which I feel *that* is the speech to stop it on, *that* is the last word.'[1] This working method produces both the farce and the intellectual fireworks, but it also leads to dramatic thinness, to characters who are personifications of ideas, always subordinate to a conceit. . . .

Stoppard's characters are unnerved by uncertainty. They are plagued by the thought of having to 'take everything on trust' – the very words recur in three of his plays – everything, from the existence of a country ('a conspiracy of cartographers') to the truth of their own experiences and even their identity. This troubles them particularly since they all live by their heads, trying to order their world with the power of reason.

GUIL: We only know what we're told, and that's little enough. And for all we know it isn't even true.
PLAYER: For all anyone knows, nothing is. Everything has to be taken on trust; truth is only that which is taken to be true.   [R. & G., p. 48]

. . . in *Jumpers* Stoppard rephrases the questions of *Rosencrantz and Guildenstern* in a more directly philosophical manner while at the same time integrating them better into the farcical plot. Here he achieves his best synthesis so far of ideas, characters, and comedy. Thematically the play revolves around witty exchanges between rival philosophical positions, generally representative of the clash between idealism and materialism. But these discussions are carried on amidst farcical, although frequently fatal, accidents: one of the philosophers is shot – by whom no one knows; the inspector who arrives to solve the case leaves with an autographed record of his favourite singer, but without notebook or solution. Thus all attempts at a rational understanding of existence are overwhelmed by absurdity. . . .

Stoppard's characters are trapped in their roles and are constantly foiled by inexplicable events. It is no wonder that they indulge in dreams of escape. The form of these dreams indicates the condition as well as the secret romanticism of his characters. Driven to the breaking point by having to act in an unknown play, Guildenstern sees his ideal in a boat. 'I like the way they're – contained. You don't have to worry about which way to go, or whether to go at all' [p. 72]. Riley, in Stoppard's *Enter a Free Man*, also feels the strain of performance and dreams of a life away from life. Again a boat symbolises this ideal. 'I sometimes think of myself as a sailor . . . with home as a little boat, anchored in the middle of a big calm sea, never going anywhere, just sitting, far from land, life, everything. . . .'[2]

. . . His plays consist of a sequence of farcical situations and abstract ideas put together in a parodistic and seemingly aimless fashion. There is little development, no evolution of characters and relationships. Stoppard admits that 'I have enormous difficulty in working out plots. . . .'[3] He tells interviewers that he tends to write his plays through a series of small, large, and microscopic ambushes – which might consist of a body falling out of a cupboard, or simply an unexpected word in a sentence. But my preoccupation as a writer, which possibly betokens a degree of insecurity, takes the form of contriving to inject some sort of interest and colour into every line, rather than counting on the general situation having a general interest which will hold an audience.'[4] As a result, Stoppard's plots are episodic rather than linear.

As for the characters, they are vehicles for the ideas, personifying argument and counterargument; they are intellectually rather than psychologically complex. At the same time they are the bewildered victims of hostile circumstances and therefore figures of farce. Take, for example, the figure of the Risen Christ in the novel *Lord Malquist and Mr Moon:* he is introduced to create new situations to keep the farce going and to motivate a discussion of God – again, farce and philosophy – and he is dropped as soon as Stoppard has exhausted his possibilities. The same can even be said of heroes like Rosencrantz, Guildenstern and Joyce.

But on the positive side this structural characteristic of Stoppard's plays is both dramatic and theatrical in its tension between conflicting ideas and its juxtaposition of farce and philosophy. Moreover it is itself part of the theme, or even a necessary consequence of Stoppard's world view. Sustained action would bring some degree of coherence to the chaos of the world and meaning to the absurd lives of his characters. Stoppard allows the plot to unfold in a seemingly uncontrolled manner because the characters have no control over their destinies. They are at the mercy of every situation and, as noted in *Rosencrantz and Guildenstern,* 'without possibility of reprieve or hope of explanation' [p. 88].

Moreover the lack of plot turns the play away from sentiment and melodrama. It works as an alienation effect, preventing the spectator from becoming too involved in any one character's dilemma and keeping the often cruel and depressing circumstances from weighing him down with suffering and despair. It also keeps the spectator alert to the intellectual fireworks of the play, serving to create that crisp, detached and extremely funny effect that is Stoppard's trademark.

All of this may help to explain why Stoppard is so successful with parody. Parody is a way of reducing the stature of characters and events, of destroying a known model and revealing its absurdity, of looking at ideas from an angle which fractures their meanings. But when the great truths can no longer be taken on trust, parody seems the only way of at least approaching them. It makes an indirect statement on life. Stoppard is at his best in parody when he plays with other people's ideas, as in *Jumpers* and *Travesties*, or with plots, as in *Rosencrantz and Guildenstern* and *Travesties*. The pleasure derived from parody is largely intellectual. . . .

Stoppard's ideas may be largely derivative – as can be seen from his preference for parody – but he performs theatrical feats in playing with contemporary concepts; he is sensitively attuned to the ideas of his time. He initiates us into a world in which the commonplace is seen as absurd and absurdity accepted as commonplace. Disorder is the order of the day, which is reflected in the incoherence, the lack of 'sustained action' of his plays. Stoppard portrays this state from the standpoint of the average thinking man who cannot relinquish all hope of a reasonable as well as a moral world. This man struggles to direct his life according to rational principles and higher laws but is frustrated in the attempt. Circumstances invariably defeat him. But – and this no doubt adds to the broad popularity of the plays – Stoppard treats his hero's bewilderment as farce. Metaphysical questions are aired but, like the characters themselves, they are submerged in farcical mishaps. This makes the plays both painful and funny. Furthermore, with his 'intellectual leap-frogging', Stoppard opposes his confused, struggling hero with a man who neither believes in nor cares about anything except 'style'. Whether or not these figures are actually artists like Joyce in *Travesties*, they are all artists and performers in their attitude to life.

It is Stoppard's self-declared aim to find 'the perfect marriage between the play of ideas and farce or perhaps even high comedy'.[5] At his most intense Stoppard is like Moon, overwhelmed by the confusion around him, contriving to force his audience into a moment of recognition with the farcical bomb of his plays.

SOURCE: extracts from 'Plays without Plot', *Theatre Journal*, 29 (March 1977), excerpted from pp. 37–48. At the time Robinson's article was published, the magazine was called *Education Theatre Journal*. The title was subsequently changed to *Theatre Journal*, and both its earlier and later forms are generally catalogued under that name [Ed.].

NOTES

1. [Ed.] Tom Stoppard, 'Ambushes for the Audience: Towards a High Comedy of Ideas', *Theatre Quarterly*, 4 (1974), pp. 6–7.
2. [Ed.] Tom Stoppard, *Enter a Free Man* (London 1968), p. 75.
3. [Ed.] 'Ambushes for the Audience', op. cit., p. 8.
4. [Ed.] Ibid. p. 6.
5. [Ed.] Ibid. p. 7.

Ronald Hayman   (1974)

The Intellectual, the Communicator, the Technician

. . . His working life appears to be ruled partly by a love for formal disciplines, partly by an informal dialectic of contrasts and contradictions. It's characteristic of him that from having regularly read every paper every day, he's whittled his newspaper reading down to an average of forty-five minutes divided between *The Times*, *The Guardian* and *The Daily Mirror*. He hardly ever reads novels but in giving his reason he admits that there's no reason. 'I don't actually move my lips when I read but I do read very slowly, and something quite definite happened to my frame of mind to do with what I wanted to read. My time for reading fiction had been spent. *Your time is up. Come in Number 7.* Because the time I had left was only sufficient to read factual and expository, non-imaginative material. I've no desire at all to read the works of Ibsen, though I have a desire to read Michael Meyer's biography of Ibsen. I've no desire to read Kingsley Armis. I read *Lucky Jim* in 1954 and thoroughly enjoyed it and haven't read a single book of his since. Why not? There's no good reason.'

The plays of Tom Stoppard are above all the plays of a man who enjoys arguing with himself and crystallising the contradictions into characters. . . .

. . . his Rosencrantz and Guildenstern add up to himself in the sense that they're carrying out his private dialogue. The mainspring of *Travesties* is the debate about art which has been going on inside his brain for years. Is art useless? Should it have a social purpose? Anyway, what is it? Does the artist need a special skill, or can anyone produce anything he pleases and then see whether he can con other people into accepting it as art? . . .

The guilt Stoppard himself feels about not having to go out

and get a job is neatly cross-fertilised with his scepticism about commitment. 'One of the impulses in *Travesties* is to try to sort out what my answer would in the end be if I was given enough time to think every time I'm asked why my plays aren't political – or ought they to be? Sometimes I have a complete comical reaction, and I think that in future I must stop compromising my plays with this whiff of social application. They must be entirely untouched by any suspicion of usefulness. I should have the courage of my lack of convictions.' This is reminiscent of George Moore, the philosopher in *Jumpers*, who once insisted on talking to Bertrand Russell about the Theory of Descriptions when he was trying to telephone Mao Tse Tung. 'I was simply trying to bring his mind back to matters of universal import, and away from the day to day parochialism of international politics.'

One of the reasons for the proliferation of interconnections between his plays is that – like all good dramatists but more than most – he is constantly refining on the technique he has developed of allowing his inventive mind to loop freely backwards and forwards within an evolving structure which will finally come to look so complex and so neatly geometrical that audiences will find it almost impossible to believe the original conception left anything open to the inspiration of the moment. 'My experience is that a lot of one's work is the result of lucky accident. When you look at the body of it and see all these lucky accidents all in one go, one assumes there must be some kind of almost premeditated connection between them, but there isn't – only in so far as one might suspect the subconscious of working overtime. The plays seem to hinge around incredibly carefully thought-out structural pivots, which I arrive at as thankfully and as unexpectedly as an explorer parting the pampas grass which is head-high and seeing a valley full of sunlight and maidens. No compass. Nothing.

'The way art seems to work best in an ideal state is that all the meaningful and referential possibilities in a work of art exist in a highly compressed form in the mind of the artist probably before he even begins, and the existence of that nucleus dictates what the tentacles do at the extremities of his conscious gift. What's wrong with bad art is that the artist knows exactly what he's doing.'

The need for intellectual credentials is purely notional, of course, and he has almost freed himself from anxiety on the question of whether a good play needs to be good literature: 'All the way from *Enter a Free Man*, which was 1960, to *Travesties*, I've written what appealed to me, and I've written it with the assumption that it would appeal to everybody else. It's surely true that if you don't actually write from that standpoint, you get into deep trouble. I realised quite a long time ago that I was in it because of the theatre rather than because of the literature. I like theatre, I like showbiz, and that's what I'm true to. I really think of the theatre as valuable, and I just hope very much that it'll remain like that as an institution. I think it's vital that the theatre is run by people who like showbiz. "If a thing doesn't work, why is it there in that form?" is roughly the philosophy and I've benefited greatly from Peter Wood's down-to-earth way of telling me "Right, I'm sitting in J 16, and I don't understand what you're trying to tell me. It's not clear."[1] There's none of this stuff about "When Faber and Faber bring it out, I'll be able to read it six times and work it out for myself." Too late.

'What happens in practice is that after a certain number of weeks elapse, I can't see the play any more. I've lost my view of it, and I'm at the mercy of anybody who nudges me. That can work to my disadvantage because it can make the play unnecessarily broad, when I should have kept faith with the delicacy of it. At the same time, it's meant that Peter has actually saved the play. The speech in which Joyce justifies his art wasn't in the text of *Travesties* that I gave to Peter. It was he who said it was necessary, and I now think it's the most important speech in the play. It's showbiz but the speech is there because of its place in the argument.'

Of all living playwrights there is perhaps none less likely to speak with so much respect and affection for showbiz than Samuel Beckett, yet Beckett has exerted a most important influence on Stoppard, who thanks him for it in a characteristically parodistic way at the end of *Jumpers*, when Archie says:

Do not despair – many are happy much of the time; more eat than starve, more are healthy than sick, more curable than dying; not so many dying as dead; and one of the thieves was saved. Hell's bells and all's well – half the world is at peace with itself, and so is the other half; vast areas are unpolluted; millions of children grow up without suffering deprivation, and millions, while deprived, grow up without suffering cruelties, and millions, while deprived and cruelly treated, none the less grow up. No laughter is sad and many tears are joyful. At the graveside the undertaker doffs his top hat and impregnates the prettiest mourner. Wham, bam, thank you Sam.   [p. 87][2]

Another important influence is T. S. Eliot. Rosencrantz and Guildenstern were wooed out from under the shadow of *Godot* by 'The Lovesong of J. Alfred Prufrock'. 'There are certain things written in English which make me feel as a diabetic must feel when the insulin goes in. Prufrock and Becket are the twin syringes of my diet, my arterial system.'

One of the main features in the development of Stoppard's techniques has been the refinement of his capacity for accommodat-

ing both halves of a contradiction and then making the sparks fly,
vivaciously and funnily, between them. Part of the appeal that puns
have for him may lie in the means they provide of yoking unrelated
meanings by violence together, but as his writing becomes more
sophisticated, the conceits work their way further below the verbal
and visual surface. In *Jumpers* we have verbal puns in George's
monologues when he reminisces about the punctuality of his late
friend Bertrand Russell, and theology and ethics are described as
two subjects without an object. The pun is used rather like a jump-
cut in a film when George, having ignored Dotty's attempts to
engage his attention by shouting 'Murder – Rape – Wolves!'
prematurely shoots the arrow from his bow when she shouts 'Fire!'.
There are the visual puns of the charade game they intermittently
play. Lying nude and apparently lifeless on the bed, she is *The Naked
and the Dead*; a vertical view of her naked back later prompts the
guess '*Lulu*'s back! – in town'.

The title word, *jumpers*, takes on more layers of meaning as the play
progresses. The word is introduced near the beginning, when Archie's
voice announces 'And now! – ladies and gentlemen! – the INCREDIBLE –
RADICAL! – LIBERAL!! – JUMPERS!!' and four of them come on from either
side of the stage, jumping, tumbling and somersaulting. It's important
that the first time we hear the word it is coupled with the name of a
political party and it soon acquires an overtone of expediency. Dotty
drunkenly orders them to jump when she says jump, and George, who
is stubbornly, unfashionably a deist in the materialistic university which
serves as a microcosm for the new society, is the one character in the
play who will not 'jump along with the rest', being temperamentally
incapable of 'jumping through the Vice-Chancellor's hoop'. It's only in
the second act that we find out that the surname of Archie, the Vice-
Chancellor, is Jumper, and when he refuses to let George succeed the
murdered McFee into the Chair of Logic, he says he needs 'someone
with a bit of bounce'. Underneath all this is the root idea for the play's
construction: 'One of the threads was the entirely visual image of the
pyramid of acrobats, but while thinking of that pyramid I knew I wanted
to write a play about a professor of moral philosophy, and it's the work
of a moment to think that there was a metaphor at work in the play
already between acrobatics, mental acrobatics and so on. Actually it's
not a bad way of getting excited about a play. . . .

In *Jumpers* and *Travesties*, the story-telling urge does not seem to
have been predominant among the original pressures, but it does
not follow that these plays are more artificial, more remote from
flesh-and-blood actuality, less dependent on direct observation of
human behaviour than *Enter a Free Man*. Set partly in a pub and

partly in the house of an ordinary family, it looks like a realistic play about a man with an unrealistic image of himself. He believes in himself as an inventor, while his daughter succumbs to equally ill-fated fantasies about escaping from the tedium of her job and her home with a man who turns out to be married already. But, as Stoppard says, 'it was a play written about other people's characters. It appears to be more about real people than *Travesties*, which is a huge artifice, but at least I've got a mental acquaintance with the characters, however much, in one sense, they're two-dimensional dream people. Now *Enter a Free Man* looks as though it's about people who are as real – at least in terms of art – as, say, the people in *Coronation Street*. But to me the whole thing is a bit phoney because they're only real because I've seen them in other people's plays. I haven't actually met any of them myself on any level. It's about an upper-working-class family. They had to be a bit upper because I kept giving them extremely well-constructed speeches to speak at a high speed of knots.

'The main point really is that it's actually impossible to write anything at all unless you're absolutely behind it. Everything I've written, at the time I've written it, I've thought "Oh, this is absolutely accessible, communicable". To qualify that, I hadn't thought that at all. One doesn't think it. One simply writes what one is impelled to write at that time, what one wants to write, what one feels one can write. But when I was writing *Rosencrantz*, I was in no sense engaged in any sort of esoteric work. It was like music-hall, if anything, a slightly literate music-hall, perhaps.' . . .

Like an actor, a playwright may become so accustomed to concealing insecurity by deploying technical expertise that he confuses himself as well as his audience. Such reservation as I have about Stoppard's work so far centre on the way he is liable to be distracted from a serious interest in language by his facility for weaving literary parody into theatrical dialogue. It may be that he is unsure how serious he can afford his comedy to be, but one of the serious themes in *Jumpers* is the connection between immorality and imprecision in the use of language. The unscrupulousness in the behaviour of Archie and the Radical Liberals is proportionate to their unscrupulousness in twisting words to mean whatever they want them to mean, while George's scruples about ethics and language put him into an untenable position. Like a more articulate and logical Lucky, he struggles for semantic clarity as he tries to reason his way backwards towards a First Cause, but the system from which his values and his words derive is disintegrating. Traditional ethics cannot survive in a universe where quarrelsome

jumpers can land on the moon, churches are converted to gymnasiums, an agnostic agriculturist is appointed by the government as
Archbishop of Canterbury and the police can be persuaded to
connive at murder. Meanwhile George's credulity about God is
linked with his naïve willingness to believe in the innocence of
Dotty's relationship with Archie.

How does one know what it is one believes when it's so difficult to know what it is
one knows?

His intellectual awareness of the problem is quite sophisticated, and
it is germane to the kind of comedy that Stoppard is cultivating to
interlace George's verbal confusion with his emotional confusion,
and to let Dotty turn his own brand of analysis against him when
he uses language loosely himself, trying to comfort her by saying
that 'things will get better'.

Bad is not what they can *be*. They can be green, or square, or Japanese, loud, fatal,
waterproof or vanilla-flavoured; and the same for actions, which can be *disapproved
of*, or comical, unexpected, saddening or good television, variously, depending on
who frowns, laughs, jumps, weeps or wouldn't have missed it for the world. Things
and actions, you understand, can have any number of real and verifiable properties.
But good and bad, better and worse, these are not real properties of things, they are
just expressions of our feeling about them.   [p. 41]

Accurate and amusing though it is, the philosophical pastiche
which forms the staple of the dialogue in *Jumpers* hinders the play's
main points from emerging as clearly and forcibly as the equivalent
points in *Rosencrantz and Guildenstern are Dead*, in which the partly
Beckettian language alternates very effectively with the passages of
quotation from *Hamlet*. If Rosencrantz and Guildenstern represent
two Tom Stoppards arguing with each other, the dialectic of
argument has continued into *Jumpers* and *Travesties* without being
supported in either play by a strong enough language, a strong
enough dynamic and a strong enough storyline. Part of the structural
trouble in *Jumpers* seems to derive from the unresolved murder
mystery. In one sense, all that matters is that it doesn't matter who
killed McFee; in another sense the murder is the starting-point of a
story which remains not only unfinished but untold.

    In many ways *Jumpers* and *Travesties* are similar. 'There are many
senses in which *Travesties* is a great advance on *Jumpers*, but it's the
same kind of pig's breakfast, and were I to do it a third time it
would be a bore. You start with a prologue which is slightly strange.
Then you have an interminable monologue which is rather funny.
Then you have scenes. Then you end up with another monologue,
and you have unexpected bits of music and dance, and at the

same time people are playing ping-pong with various intellectual arguments.'[3]

The parodies are woven with great expertise into the argument and there is plenty for the audience to laugh at, but the failure to establish a structural principle of relevance is most obvious at the beginning of Act Two. Judged as an essay or a piece of exposition, Cecily's long monologue is very well written. It is lucid and pithy, but its main function in the play is to provide background information about Marxism and Lenin, while one of Stoppard's main intentions in writing it was to balance the information about Dada provided in the catechism at the end of Act One. 'There are several levels going here, and one of them is that what I personally like is the theatre of audacity. I thought "Right. We'll have a rollicking first act, and they'll all come back from their gin-and-tonics thinking 'Isn't it fun? What a lot of lovely jokes!' and they'll sit down, and this pretty girl will start talking about the theory of Marxism and the theory of capitalism and the theory of value, and the smiles, because they're not prepared for it, will atrophy." And that to me was like a joke in itself. But the important thing was that I'd ended the first act with what at that stage was a lengthy exposition of Dada. I wanted to begin the second with a corresponding exposition of how Lenin got to Zürich, not in geographical but political terms. I chose to do that from square one by starting from *Das Kapital*, Marxian theory of profit, theory of labour, theory of value, and then to elide into the populist movement, the terrorism, Ulyanov's brother and so on. If I could have brought that off, I'd have been prouder of that than anything else I'd ever written. There wasn't a joke in it, but I felt I could get away with it because it was going to be a new set, a new character and a new scene after the interval. I overplayed that hand very badly, and at the first preview I realised that the speech had to be about Lenin only. The second act is Lenin's act really, and I just blue-pencilled everything up to the mention of Lenin. So now it was one page instead of five.'

If anyone came to the play without any knowledge of Joyce, Dada or Lenin, he would learn quite a lot about Dada and Lenin but almost nothing about Joyce. If *Jumpers* had been extremely ambitious, Stoppard was setting his sights even higher in trying to incorporate three such difficult subjects into a single play. The consensus of critical opinion seemed to be that he had succeeded with Joyce and Tzara, failing only with Lenin, and it was with Lenin that he had anticipated the greatest difficulty. 'In my original draft I took the Lenin section out of the play far more radically than in the version you saw. I actually stopped the play and had actors coming down

to read that entire passage from clip boards or lecterns, because I
felt very strongly – and now I believe I was right – that one thing I
could not do was to integrate the Lenins into the *Importance* scheme.
Irving Wardle[4] said he'd have liked to see Lenin as Miss Prism, but
that would have killed the play because of the trivialisation. It would
have been disastrous to Prismise and Chasublise the Lenins, and I
believe that that section saves *Travesties*, because I think one's just
about *had* that particular Wilde joke at that point. I wanted the play
to stop – to give the audience documentary illustration of what
Lenin felt about art and so on, and then carry on the play. Peter
Wood's objection was unarguable: the whole thing is within the
framework of Carr's memory except this bit How do you get back
people's belief if you interrupt it?' . . .

Like a collage artist, Stoppard seems to have selected the most
disparate ingredients he could find, so that his ingenuity should be
taxed to the utmost by the task of pasting them together. Maybe
there will be no fresh observation of human behaviour, maybe the
images of humanity will be wilfully fragmented and distorted, but
at least something will emerge that could not have been created in
any other way.

Glue can't be a satisfying substitute for storyline and organic
growth, but if the jokes are funny and the composition clever, who
cares? To qualify that, glue can be a satisfying substitute for storyline
and organic growth.

Source: extracts from 'Profile 9: Tom Stoppard', *New Review*, I/ix (1974),
excerpted from pp. 15–22.

NOTES

1. [Ed.] Peter Wood directed the first productions of (*inter alia*) *Jumpers* and
Travesties.

2. [Ed.] Tom Stoppard, *Jumpers* (London, 1972). All subsequent references are
made to this edition.

3. [Ed.] From the interview with Ronald Hayman excerpted in section 1, above.

4. [Ed.] Drama critic of *The Times*. Part of his review of *Travesties* is reproduced in
section 2 of Part Four, below.

PART TWO

Rosencrantz and
Guildenstern are Dead

1. STOPPARD'S COMMENTS

I Interview with Giles Gordon

... GORDON: I was lucky enough to see *Rosencrantz and Guildenstern are Dead* when it was done at the Edinburgh Festival of 1966, before it was performed in London at the National Theatre at the Old Vic in 1967. In Edinburgh it was mounted by the Oxford Theatre Group in an austere and slightly musty church hall in the Royal Mile, yet it seemed to me that it was a better play there, for two reasons. First, because it was shorter, the right length for its material; second, because it was more pointed. Seeing the highly professional production in London, I felt that the argument was drawn out unnecessarily. You'd made a joke, a witty remark, but the effect was often spoiled because the dialogue pertaining to it would carry on for a few lines beyond the denouement, after the laughter.

STOPPARD: You're the victim of an illusion. The National Theatre script was in fact a little longer than the Edinburgh one but this was mainly because I wrote an entirely new scene for London. At the same time I cut quite a few things out of the script which was performed in London. I remember a meeting with Sir Laurence Olivier and Kenneth Tynan which went on until five o'clock in the morning and quite a few things went that night. Mind you, I put a lot of them back later. It is also true that we didn't even attempt to do the very last scene at Edinburgh; it was simply unstageable in those circumstances, the circumstances being a stage the size of a ping pong table and a dozen actors instead of 35. The *production* in London certainly went on a great deal longer because there was a great deal more of it. Anyway, there is no question of there having been any extra lines beyond the point where we reached a denouement in Edinburgh. Perhaps the Edinburgh audiences laughed at penultimate rather than ultimate moments, for some gnomic Scottish reason. Not that I heard them do it myself. I was only there for the first two or three days of the production and the play was received, well, politely rather than with hilarity. On the day I left – it was a Sunday – Ronald Bryden wrote in the *Observer*[1] that the play was very funny and I understand that after that people tended to laugh at it rather more.

GORDON: What struck me more about the play than anything else was that of any play written by a British playwright since 1956 and *Look Back in Anger* it was the least personal. One had the impression that nothing was revealed about you as its author. It was objective rather than subjective. It wasn't, in fact, autobiographical.

STOPPARD: That's quite true. It wasn't deliberate in the sense that I take pains – or took pains in that play – not to reveal myself, or that I take pains in my writing not to reveal myself. Or should I immediately contradict that remark, because in point of fact I am sensitive about self-revelation. I distrust it. I've written very little which could be said to be even remotely autobiographical and I've been subsequently somewhat embarrassed by what I have written. On the other hand, I suppose that that play, as well as almost everything else, probably has revealed quite a lot about me without it necessarily revealing it in autobiographical terms.

GORDON: Why do you distrust self revelation? Do you think it tends to result in less good plays than might otherwise be the case?

STOPPARD: No it doesn't, at least not from other people. I think probably the real answer would lie concealed somewhere in my history. I simply don't like very much revealing myself. I am a very private sort of person. But there again one has to distinguish between self-revelation and autobiography. A further point is that of course autobiographical work would tend to be on a realistic level since one's life is lived on a realistic level, and it happens that I am not any longer very interested in writing realistic drama. Now, do I not write realistic drama because I don't like to reveal myself autobiographically, or do I not reveal myself autobiographically because I don't like writing realistic drama? I would say the former. I have after all written a realistic play. I started by writing a realistic play and really there is nothing of me in it, that is to say nothing of my life in it, just perhaps the odd stray remark that I have picked up and wrapped up and saved up and thrown up. I did one or two small things; a few unpublished short stories and a couple of published ones which sprang more obviously from my own life, but I don't much like them as short stories now. And I think probably that if I had written my slab of fiction about a young fellow born in Czechoslovakia, brought up in India, went to school in England, joined a newspaper, started writing his first novel, I would probably hate that too.

GORDON: Why do you choose Hamlet? Why Rosencrantz and Guildenstern?

STOPPARD: They chose themselves to a certain extent. I mean that the play *Hamlet* and the characters Rosencrantz and Guildenstern are the only play and the only characters on which you could write my kind of play. They are so much more than merely bit players in another famous play. *Hamlet* I suppose is the most famous play in any language, it is part of a sort of common mythology. I am continually being asked politely whether I will write about the messenger in *Oedipus Rex*, which misses the point.

GORDON: But in a way it is difficult to see the point. It is all very well for you to say that, but it was brilliant insight on your part to see that you could – or someone could – write a play about Rosencrantz and Guildenstern.

STOPPARD: But as I said they are more than just bit players in another play. There are certain things which they bring on with them, particularly the fact that they end up dead without really, as far as any textual evidence goes, knowing why. Hamlet's assumption that they were privy to Claudius's plot is entirely gratuitous. As far as their involvement in Shakespeare's text is concerned they are told very little about what is going on and much of what they are told isn't true. So I see them much more clearly as a couple of bewildered innocents rather than a couple of henchmen, which is the usual way they are depicted in productions of *Hamlet*. . . .

SOURCE: extract from Giles Gordon's interview in *Transatlantic Review*, 29 (1968), pp. 17–20.

NOTE

1. [Ed.] Bryden's review is excerpted in the following section of this Part Two.

II INTERVIEW WITH R. HUDSON, S. ITZIN, S. TRUSSLER

. . . I began writing *Rosencrantz* in 1964. . . . Charles Marowitz was asked by some Germans if he knew any promising young playwrights, because the Ford Foundation was financing a kind of annual cultural picnic in Berlin – part of the general effort around that time to keep Berlin alive in every sense, I suppose. So between May and October they had this colloquium, which in 1964 was to be for young playwrights. We were fed and housed in great comfort and just asked to get on with it. Of course, it was quite incapacitating. . . .

. . . what I wrote in Germany, if I remember – and I'm trying to forget – was just a sort of Shakespearian pastiche. It was Kenneth Ewing who gave me the idea, driving back from some abortive attempt to get ABC Television to commission a play from me – all my ideas were 'too downbeat', they said. But he suggested that it should take place in England, and I remember writing a version – maybe the one Charles read – in which they got to England, and

King Lear was on the throne – I mean, the whole thing was unspeakable. But it did contain some of the dialogue which still exists in the play.

Can you trace the progress of the play from that embryonic version to the one put on two years later at the National Theatre?

Not very adequately in terms of my intellectual process. What I do remember is that the transition from one play to the other was an attempt to find a solution to a practical problem – that if you write a play about Rosencrantz and Guildenstern in England, you can't count on people knowing who they are and how they got there. So one tended to get back into the end of *Hamlet* a bit. But the explanations were always partial and ambiguous, so one went back a bit further into the plot, and as soon as I started doing this I totally lost interest in England. The interesting thing was them at Elsinore.

Were you still looking on it as a play about a play – Hamlet – *or a play about these two characters?*

By this time I was not in the least interested in doing any sort of pastiche, for a start, or in doing a criticism of *Hamlet* – that was simply one of the by-products. The chief interest and objective was to exploit a situation which seemed to me to have enormous dramatic and comic potential – of these two guys who in Shakespeare's context don't really know what they're doing. The little they are told is mainly lies, and there's no reason to suppose that they ever find out why they are killed. And, probably more in the early 1960s than at any other time, that would strike a young playwright as being a pretty good thing to explore. I mean, it has the right combination of specificity and vague generality which was interesting at that time to (it seemed) eight out of ten playwrights. That's why, when the play appeared, it got subjected to so many different kinds of interpretation, all of them plausible, but none of them calculated.

What was calculated?

What was actually calculated was to entertain a roomful of people with the situation of Rosencrantz and Guildenstern at Elsinore. The chief thing that added one line to another line was that the combination of the two should retain an audience's interest in some way. I tend to write through a series of small, large and microscopic ambushes – which might consist of a body falling out of a cupboard, or simply an unexpected word in a sentence. But my preoccupation as a writer, which possibly betokens a degree of insecurity, takes the form of contriving to inject some sort of interest and colour into every line, rather than counting on the general situation having a general interest which will hold an audience.

So really Rosencrantz and Guildenstern *doesn't embody any particular philosophy but is a process of solving craft problems?*

That's absolutely the case *on a conscious level*, but one is a victim and beneficiary of one's subconscious all the time and, obviously, one is making choices all the time. And the kind of things which I personally enjoy, which I personally judge to be – quirky, and therefore interesting enough or funny enough or resonant enough to do the job of retaining an audience's interest, involve rather more than a simple matter of craft. *Why* do these things appeal to me? What is it about them that I find satisfying? There one starts to get into an area where a more interpretive attitude to the material is not irrelevant. It's difficult for me to endorse or discourage particular theories I mean, I get lots of letters from students, and people who are doing the play, asking me questions about it, which seem to expect a yes-or-no answer. It is a mistake to assume that such questions have that kind of answer. I personally think that *anybody's* set of ideas which grows out of the play has its own validity. . . .

SOURCE: extract from interview in R. Hudson, S. Itzin and S. Trussler, 'Ambushes for the Audience: Towards a High Comedy of Ideas', *Theatre Quarterly*, IV, 14 (May/July 1974), pp. 5–6.

III INTERVIEW WITH JOOST KUURMAN

. . . Critics sometimes find messages in your plays – although 'message' is always a difficult word in this respect. Do you consciously 'put messages in'? Have you got 'a message'?

No, not at all – it's misleading to talk about my plays as if they're the same kind of thing; obviously a play like *Every Good Boy Deserves Favour* is a play with a message in the way that *The Real Inspector Hound* is not, so one has to be careful about talking about 'my plays', because one does different things for different occasions. But taking *Every Good Boy Deserves Favour*, nobody could say there's a hidden message in it, because it is not hidden. It's a play about certain very obvious situations, and it declares itself very openly. Where things get more complicated is in a play which appears to be about one thing and may be suspected of really being another thing: a play like *Rosencrantz and Guildenstern* is a play in which people tend to look for messages and in that case I can say quite categorically that one doesn't write a play and hide something in it to see if people can find it at all. I mean, to me *Rosencrantz and Guildenstern* is a play about two Elizabethan courtiers in a castle, wondering what's going on. That's what it's about. That situation reverberates in different ways to people who see it, obviously, and can suggest various analogies for itself, and the author of the play is not, obviously, unaware of this and I know perfectly well that the situation, the predicament which Rozencrantz and Guildenstern find themselves in is an interesting one in the sense that it can be used or thought of as being a metaphor for other situations. That's a very different matter from deciding to write about a particular kind of predicament, a specific predicament of modern man and look around for some symbolic form in which to convey it, and decide to do it in terms of two characters in *Hamlet*. That's, of course, nonsense. The attraction of the play for the writer is the surface level.

And the rest is a by-product?

The rest is a by-product, but it's not even a very conscious by-product. I mean there's an element of one being the beneficiary of one's subconscious. . . .

SOURCE: extract from Joost Kuurman's interview, *Dutch Quarterly Review*, x (1980), pp. 50–1.

2. REVIEWS OF EARLY PRODUCTIONS

Ronald Bryden (1966)

First Production: 'The best thing at Edinburgh'

... The best thing at Edinburgh so far is the new play by Tom Stoppard staged in Cranston Street Hall by the Oxford Theatre Group, *Rosencrantz and Guildenstern are Dead*. Mr Stoppard has taken up the vestigial lives of Hamlet's two Wittenberg cronies, and made out of them an existentialist fable unabashedly indebted to *Waiting for Godot*, but as witty and vaulting as Beckett's original is despairing.

The play does not pretend to know more of the pair's lives than Shakespeare: its point is, neither do they. While the violent drama at Elsinore unrolls off-stage, occasionally sucking them into its fury, they spin coins endlessly in ante-rooms, wondering what is going on, what will happen next, what will become of them? They sense that they should escape, but what to? The tragedy of Denmark offers them the only significance, the only identities life has held out to them – it offers them roles.

Behind the fantastic comedy, you feel allegoric purposes move: is this our relation to our century, to the idea of death, to war? But while the tragedy unfurls in this comic looking-glass, you're too busy with its stream of ironic invention, metaphysical jokes and linguistic acrobatics to pursue them. ... It's the most brilliant debut by a young playwright since John Arden.

SOURCE: extract from review of the Edinburgh Festival première, *Observer Weekend Review* (28 Aug. 1966).

Philip Hope-Wallace (1967)

First London Production: 'A witty theatrical trick'

... R. and G., like the two clowns in *Godot*, find themselves nonetities, yet sure of their own names (more or less and however

much other people confuse them); they hang about in the suburbs
of the drama, carelessly left as loose ends by Shakespeare,
occupying their time with chop logic and cerebral tricks, until they
are momentarily involved in the action at odd points in the story
we know so well. The joke seems rather protracted in the first
and second acts, in spite of the many amusing lines and patter. I
think a bit of cutting would in fact make the final act even better
theatre for coming more swiftly with less preliminary musing on
identity, existence and non-being. Here the pair, either side of the
same coin, find that they are due (aren't we all?) for extinction, to
be written out of the script with a callous line and a sleight of hand
by the Lord Hamlet on board the transport ship. But, in spite of
temptation, they do not interfere with the destiny which will at least
give them a name the world does not forget, albeit smilingly.

Mr Stride in particular carries us along with him. Even so, I had
a sensation that a fairly pithy and witty theatrical trick was being
elongated merely to make an evening of it. Tedium, even kept at
bay, made itself felt.

SOURCE: extract from review of first London production, at the National
Theatre, *Guardian* (12 April 1967).

Irving Wardle   (1967)

'An amazing piece of work'

Those who saw Tom Stoppard's play as a fringe event at last year's
Edinburgh Festival might be forgiven for taking it simply as a
display of cerebral acrobatics. There was little in that production to
suggest the expressive resources which are now revealed by the
National Theatre. As a first stage play it is an amazing piece of
work.

I know of no theatrical precedent for it, but among other things
it might be called a piece of literary detection. From the labyrinthine
picture of Elsinore Mr Stoppard has blown up a single detail and
wrenched enough material from it to create a drama.

The shadowy history of Rosencrantz and Guildenstern always
sticks in the mind as a classic instance of the fate that befalls little
men who are swept into great events. Much is said against them in

the course of *Hamlet*, but they hardly deserve it: they are too insignificant to escape anonymous servitude.

For most of Mr Stoppard's play they are shown in private – abandoned in an ante-chamber of the palace waiting for the next call, spinning coins and playing word games, desperately latching on to the First Player as the only character who will speak to them.

From time to time the court sweeps on to conduct its incomprehensible business and sweeps out again leaving the interchangeable nonentities stranded like driftwood on the beach.

What emerges is a compound of Shakespearean criticism, Beckett-like cross-talk: and the mathematical nonsense comedy which befits a nonsensical situation involving two cyphers. The couple have no memory of the past, no understanding of the present, and no idea where they are going.

All they have is words, and the endless word games they play represent both a way of passing the time and an indefatigable attempt to make sense of their predicament.

Mr Stoppard manages to relate the material to the Shakespearean action, as where a quickfire question game (as exciting as a tennis match) is used as a preparation for an interview with the prince, who promptly wins the game and set ('We were sent for, you said. I didn't know where to put myself').

But his real triumph is in relating the partners' preoccupation with free will to the players, whose profession insists on fixed destiny and who stage a rehearsal of the *Gonzago* prologue forecasting the fatal voyage to England. On the actual voyage, Mr Stoppard secures an existential conclusion in which the partners discover their death warrant and choose to deliver it so as to emerge, if only for a second, into lives of their own.

There are times when the author, like his characters, seems to be casting about for what to say next. But for most of the time he walks his chosen tight-rope with absolute security.

In its origin this is a highly literary play with frank debts to Pirandello and Beckett; but in Derek Goldby's production, these sources prove a route towards technical brilliance and powerful feeling. . . .

SOURCE: extract from review of first London production, *The Times* (12 April 1967).

John Weightman   (1967)

'A brilliant idea, inadequately worked out'

... Stoppard has walked off into the wings to imagine the extra-textual reality of two characters in *Hamlet*, whose Shakespearian appearances are tantalisingly incomplete. Rosencrantz and Guildenstern never come on to the stage, and are never referred to, except as a couple, as if their psychological charge were too slight to allow them to exist separately. Hamlet greets them warmly as old friends and then, a little later, sends them off without compunction to their deaths. They appear fitfully, do nothing very much, and then disappear. This being so, Mr Stoppard has decided that they can be developed as modern anti-heroes. They are siblings in nonentity, sharing a ridiculous Tweedledum/Tweedledee part; they never fully get the hang of the situation and they are swatted like flies through being accidentally caught up in the tragedy. ...

The idea is brilliant, and produces a certain amount of fun, but I don't think it is worked out with complete success. The action is not a legitimate extension of the minimal identity that Shakespeare gives Rosencrantz and Guildenstern in *Hamlet*, and so Mr Stoppard's play operates at an uncomfortable tangent to Shakespeare's. To reduce, or elevate, his protagonists to the status of 'outsiders' with whom we can sympathise, Mr Stoppard has to curtail their biggest Shakespearean scene, because in it they appear as rather silly time-servers, at the opposite pole from Horatio, the friend of sterling quality. Also, he has to put them into a limbo which is largely gratuitous.

We first see them during a pause in their journey to court, and they are presented as having uncertain memories of their past identity. Of course, Existentialist anti-heroes are frequently amnesiac or semi-amnesiac, since their anguish comes partly from living in the ever-moving present, with the past constantly crumbling into nothingness behind them. But Rosencrantz and Guildenstern cannot come out of the void into the action of *Hamlet*; they would only obey the summons if they understood it, and it seems portentous to surround them with questionings as if they were the Magi en route for an unknown Bethlehem, or Vladimir and Estragon really waiting for Godot. Similarly, once they get to court, they would know what was going on there since, as courtiers, they would be in the thick of the gossip. On this point, Mr Stoppard wobbles; he both shows them as understanding the situation to a certain extent and as deliberately killing time in limbo when they are not taking part in the action. Every now and again, the plot of *Hamlet* swirls in and around them and they fall into their Shakespearean roles in Shakespearean English, whereas before they had been talking in 20th-century voices. But it is as if they were members of the audience seeing only those snatches of *Hamlet* in which they themselves are involved, the rest of the play remaining a closed book ('I don't pretend to have understood. ... If they won't tell us, that's their affair'). If this is meant as a symbol, it can only signify that we see our lives as an intermittent, incomprehensible dream, of which we never grasp the plot. But even those people most subject to *Angst* are never as much in the dark as this, except perhaps about collective, public events beyond their range. It may be true of thorough-going schizophrenics, but Rosencrantz and Guildenstern are not made as pathological as that.

In any case, at one point Mr Stoppard completely contradicts this general impression of ignorance by making Rosencrantz and Guildenstern impersonate Hamlet and envisage the situation very penetratingly from his point of view:

ros.: To sum up: your father, whom you love, dies, you are his heir, you come back to find that hardly was the corpse cold before his young brother popped on to his throne and into his sheets, thereby offending both legal and natural practice. Now why are you behaving in this extraordinary manner?

guil.: I can't imagine! [p. 36]

This is a witty demolition of Shakespeare's plot. There would be no *Hamlet*, if the Prince, instead of feigning madness and complicating all the issues, took the obvious course and denounced his uncle publicly from the start as an arrant usurper, which is what he would have done, had he been a character in one of the historical plays. The Ghost, the Players, the interview with Gertrude, the trip to England are all, strictly speaking, unnecessary, and Shakespeare does nothing to justify them, apart from making them the occasion of splendid poetry. All those marvellous words cover up much ado about nothing. The King should not need Rosencrantz and Guildenstern to tell him why Hamlet is uneasy; his problem is rather to know why, in the circumstances, Hamlet has not already begun to topple him from the throne. However, I don't think we worry about this as we watch *Hamlet*. We take it for granted that neither the Prince nor the King does the straightforward, rational thing, because, if they did, Shakespeare would not have been able to give us this extended lament on the puzzling nature of human existence. But we do worry, or at least I worry, about the fact that Mr

Stoppard's heroes are not properly connected up to *Hamlet*, because *Hamlet* is, after all, where they come from. The other alternative is to say that *Rosencrantz and Guildenstern are Dead* has nothing to do with *Hamlet*, but is a dialogue between two near-Existentialist heroes, occasionally decorated with quotations from Shakespeare in an inconsequential, Pop-art manner.

Even if this interpretation is the correct one, it is still difficult to see at times on what level the author wishes us to understand his text. . . .

Perhaps the whole play is just intellectual fooling around, with occasional stabs at seriousness. Now and again, one suspects that Mr Stoppard is trying to be genuinely poetic and is inviting us to commune with Rosencrantz and Guildenstern in some emotion. Since the performers are attractive, we allow ourselves to be beguiled and then are suddenly let down, because the poetry is spurious. For instance, Rosencrantz and Guildenstern are pleased to meet up with the Players, who offer an unexpected distraction during the initial period of waiting. But the troupe turns out to be a sorry band, scraping a living by doing obscene pantomimes and forcing their least unattractive member to function as male whore. On discovering this Guildenstern, 'shaking with rage and fright', exclaims passionately at the disillusionment of the chance encounter:

. . . it didn't have to be *obscene*. . . . It could have been a bird out of season, dropping bright-feathered on my shoulder. . . . It could have been a tongueless dwarf standing by the road to point the way. . . .   [p. 19]

The bird out of season and the tongueless dwarf are surely *kitsch*, but are we meant to appreciate them as being symptomatic of Guildenstern's camp vibration, or to enjoy them as poetry? I guess that Mr Stoppard is hoping for the latter reaction but would settle for the former, and so the former it inevitably is. When, at the end, Rosencrantz and Guildenstern go wittingly to their deaths 'to give their lives a meaning,' the effect is equally thin and camp.

As the play progresses, we see that the only other characters Rosencrantz and Guildenstern commune with in their limbo are the Players and, in fact, the leading player, Graham Crowden, almost steals the show. This is another Existentialist commonplace; if the average person is so befuddled by contingency that he can only give himself an identity by accepting this or that form of 'bad faith', then the actor can become the modern hero, since he sits loose to all identities and plays with them at will. At the same time, he only becomes 'subject' by deliberately making himself 'object' for contemplation by others; if the others stop watching, his identity as subject/object sputters away like a collapsing balloon. This is beautifully expressed in one of the speeches by the leading Player when he complains about Rosencrantz and Guildenstern asking his troupe to put on a show and then not staying to see it through. These exchanges between the Player and Rosencrantz and Guildenstern seem to me to be the best bits in the work. The Player has a strong presence, because he accepts only two basic forces, greed and lust, and looks upon all the superstructures as provisional and interchangeable; this is a rudimentary philosophy which works up to a point. Rosencrantz and Guildenstern have likeable non-presences; they are comparable to actors who haven't yet been adequately briefed about their parts and who are playing word-games or indulging in random reflections until the playwright or the director makes up his mind. Curiously enough, the newspapers say Mr Stoppard was a journalist until he became a dramatist. He strikes me as being a born man of the theatre, but whether the expression is to be taken in its very good, or its less good, sense, I would not yet like to bet.

SOURCE: extracts from review-article, 'Mini-Hamlets in Limbo', *Encounter*, (29 July 1967), excerpted from pp. 38–40.

3. CRITICAL STUDIES

Joseph E. Duncan: 'Stoppard and Beckett'
(1981)

In the decade after the first productions of Tom Stoppard's
Rosencrantz and Guildenstern are Dead, critics frequently remarked on
the similarities between it and Samuel Beckett's *Waiting for Godot.*
Strong similarities exist, chiefly in characterisation, but Stoppard's
two courtiers encounter a predicament and represent an experience
essentially different from those of Beckett's two tramps. While
Beckett's characters face interminable waiting, Stoppard's face
sudden and inexplicable change. One of the most important dis-
tinctions is that in Stoppard's play Godot (as interpreted by various
of Beckett's critics) comes. . . .

Rosencrantz and Guildenstern are Dead seems to show some strong
influence from *Waiting for Godot.* Both plays present two little men,
lacking knowledge and power, who are trying to grapple with a
universe full of uncertainty. Similarities in characterisation and in
the relationships between the two main characters in each play are
particularly striking. Guildenstern resembles Vladimir, or Didi, who
is more head, while Rosencrantz resembles Estragon, or Gogo, who
is more body. Didi experiences anguish in waiting for Godot
and tells Gogo that he perceives things which his friend misses.
Guildenstern shows great strain and fear at the long run of 'heads'
at the beginning of the play, does most of the philosophising, and is
much more mentally alert than Rosencrantz. Gogo is concerned
with food, his feet, erections and sleep; he has been a poet, has
dreams, but forgets about Godot. Rosencrantz is indifferent to the
run of 'heads,' but is aroused by the players' suggested pornographic
exhibition; he is the first to voice an intuition of his own and
Guildenstern's approaching deaths, and later the first to voice
acceptance. A very poor memory is characteristic of both Gogo and
Rosencrantz. Didi and Guildenstern are the dominant members of
these duos. Both Gogo and Rosencrantz frequently want to leave,
but Didi and Guildenstern think they should remain, waiting for
Godot or waiting on the King. Gogo has difficulty in understanding
how to play at Pozzo and Lucky, and Rosencrantz has even more
difficulty in understanding how to play at questioning Hamlet. The
scenes in which Guildenstern plays the 'nursemaid' to Rosencrantz

are reminiscent of the way Didi comforts and sings to Gogo; and Rosencrantz's plea to Guildenstern, 'Don't leave me!' when the Player steps on his hand, seems an echo of Gogo's 'Stay with me!' after he has been beaten. Didi can become irritated at Gogo's uncertainty and 'whining', while Guildenstern becomes increasingly angry about Rosencrantz's lack of perception and initiative and finally 'smashes him down'. Stoppard has departed from *Hamlet*, where the two friends are virtually indistinguishable, to follow the dominant patterns of the characterisation of the principals in *Waiting for Godot*.

Because Stoppard seems to be following Beckett very closely in some aspects of his play, the differences between *Rosencrantz and Guildenstern are Dead* and *Waiting for Godot* are particularly important. If Stoppard consciously depended on Beckett and expected his audience to be aware of the dependence, he was also presenting thought, action, and a theatrical experience distinctively different from that in *Waiting for Godot*. 'Nothing to be done', 'Nothing ever happens' are the cries of Didi and Gogo, but in Stoppard's play a great deal happens very rapidly. Time hangs very heavy for the two modern tramps, but the two courtiers seldom refer to the passage of time, think time may be an illusion, and at times find 'Never a moment's peace!'. They do resort to games to pass the time and avoid facing their own predicament; however, they are at the same time trapped in the fast-moving, eventful *Hamlet* plot and are becoming increasingly anxious about their entrapment. Didi and Gogo are concerned about guilt and salvation, but make no assured contact with anything beyond themselves. Guildenstern and Rosencrantz are concerned chiefly with freedom of action and are amazed that the 'they' who had it in for them found them so important. Beckett's play, in short, is about the uncertainty and frustration felt by Didi and Gogo in their interminable waiting in limitless time. Stoppard's is about the uncertainty felt by Rosencrantz and Guildenstern in trying to understand the origin and meaning of events which they come to realise are carrying them to their deaths.

If Rosencrantz and Guildenstern have existed in boredom and waiting up to the time of the summons, as the play suggests, with the summons their lives are transformed. The summons, the impossible run of 'heads' in the coin tossing, their being 'caught up' with the players, the entrapment in the action of Hamlet, and the deaths – all are intricately intermeshed and are part of a pattern which they enter, or which encloses them, at the time of the summons. Didi and sometimes Gogo remember fragments of a long

lost past. . . . Rosencrantz and Guildenstern refer to no recollections
from the time before the summons, and Rosencrantz cannot even
remember the first thing he can remember. But they remember
clearly the summons and the ensuing events. In fact, they refer to it
eight times in the course of the play, frequently with vivid detail.
Though the two courtiers were sent for in *Hamlet*, the details of the
summons are Stoppard's. Their names were called and they were
awakened in the dawn – to a new kind of life. They are 'practically
starting from scratch', 'with an extra slice of childhood when you
least expect it'. In *Waiting for Godot* the boy messengers address
Vladimir as Mr Albert, and it is uncertain if they are really from
Godot and if they carry the two tramps' messages correctly, but in
any case the messages result only in continued waiting. However,
in *Rosencrantz and Guildenstern are Dead* the messenger calls the names
of the two courtiers and delivers the 'royal summons'. It results in
their galloping off 'headlong and hotfoot across the land, our guides
outstripped in the breakneck pursuit of our duty. Fearful lest we
come too late!!'. Amidst the uncertainties of Elsinore, Guildenstern
observes, 'That much is certain – we came'.

The summons functions much as a leitmotif in the play and
becomes associated with the run of 'heads', the *Hamlet* pattern
represented by the Tragedians, and the deaths of the principals.
These elements are brought together and their interrelationships
suggested in two key passages. In the first passage, Guildenstern
makes the second reference to the summons in his speculation about
the impossible run of 'heads':

> The sun came up about as often as it went down, in the long run, and a coin showed
> heads about as often as it showed tails. Then a messenger arrived. We had been sent
> for. Nothing else happened. Ninety-two coins spun consecutively have come down
> heads ninety-two consecutive times . . . and for the last three minutes on the wind
> of a windless day I have heard the sound of drums and flute . . .   [p. 12]

The music heralds the Tragedians, the first characters from the
entrapping *Hamlet* plot whom Rosencrantz and Guildenstern meet,
and the plot of course includes the players' production which results
in the two being sent to England and their deaths. Rosencrantz's
next remark to Gildenstern, that the fingernails and beard grow
after death – the first reference to death – is only seemingly a *non
sequitur*.

A second key passage occurs a few minutes later:

> GUIL: Practically starting from scratch . . . An awakening, a man standing on his
> saddle to bang on the shutters, our names shouted in a certain dawn, a message,
> a summons . . . A new record for heads and tails. We have not been picked out

. . . simply to be abandoned . . . set loose to find our own way . . . We are entitled
to some direction . . . I would have thought.
ROS: (alert, listening) I say—! I say—
GUIL: Yes?
ROS: I heard – I thought I heard – music.   [p. 14]

Guildenstern's comment about lack of direction has been cited to
show the loneliness and frustration of absurd man.[1] And indeed the
two characters are generally lonely and frustrated. But the words
are ironic in their dramatic context, for their lives will not be without
direction. The music announces the players and the dramatic pattern
represented by the players in which Rosencrantz and Guildenstern
will be 'caught up' and swept along. They will be directed to
England and their deaths. The 'direction' which they receive includes
the meaning of the direction of actors in a play. As the play
progresses, Rosencrantz and Guildenstern are more bewildered by
the direction which they are receiving than by the lack of it. A
similar linking between the summons and the music of the players
occurs at the court; and on the boat, just as Rosencrantz complains
of lack of help, the sound of a recorder announces the Tragedians.

The coin tossing not only provides a protracted opening scene,
but is referred to frequently in the play, and extends into the first
meeting with the Tragedians. The fantastic run of 'heads' involves
the problem of chance, freedom and determinacy, which is central
to Stoppard's examination of the lives of these two minor characters
from *Hamlet*. . . .

When the play opens, Rosencrantz announces after a few onstage
tosses that the score is seventy-six-love. The game is continued with
the players and the final string of 'heads' comes to one hundred.
This is a change from their past experience. Guildenstern observes
'with tight hysteria': 'We have been spinning coins together since I
don't know when, and in all that time (if it *is* all that time) I don't
suppose that either of us was more than a couple of gold pieces up
or down' [p. 12]. This has happened only after the summons, indeed
on the same day as the summons, and has been continued into the
meeting with the players, who introduce the controlling *Hamlet* plot.
The series is not infinite, since 'tails' finally comes up.

Guildenstern observes that the 'fortuitous and the ordained'
formed 'a reassuring union which we recognised as nature . . . Then
a messenger arrived' [p. 12]. The coin tossing marks the two
courtiers' apparent departure from what they and the audience have
regarded as the normal realm of law, chance, and nature and their
entry into a realm where happenings seem both capricious and
deterministic. The long run of 'heads' is a kind of epiphany, revealing

an absurdist universe and foreshadowing the unbreakable chain of events in the *Hamlet* pattern which will catch up Rosencrantz and Guildenstern and sweep them along to their deaths. The events which will entangle them are as different from their previous eventless existence as this coin tossing is from earlier games. The ambiguous 'they,' who Rosencrantz and Guildenstern feel 'had it in' for them from the beginning, becomes a personification for the order or disorder that causes or permits coins or courtiers to become fixed in unexpected patterns. More fundamental than the seemingly 'natural' laws of mathematical probability is the law that all the world's actor-spectators have no real control. While 'almost anything can happen,' all are caught in whatever happens in the same way. The coin tossing also provides an image of life as a game in which one may lose suddenly and inexplicably; tossing or choosing coins, 'questions', or entering a plot one did not write, far from being monotonous, may be filled with terrifying implications. This opening scene is parodied as Rosencrantz presents both fists empty several times and then holds a coin in both fists so that Guildenstern, again anxious, chooses the 'correct' fist six consecutive times. Rosencrantz may be a parody of the absurdist god revealed in the run of 'heads', but it is also implied that the absurdist god may be like him. The difference between this deity and Hamlet's 'divinity that shapes our ends' [v ii 10] defines the difference between the universe which Shakespeare's Hamlet and Stoppard's Rosencrantz and Guildenstern seek to understand.

The summons and the coin tossing, both with each other and with the Tragedians, lead to the courtiers being 'caught up' in the *Hamlet* pattern. William Babula has pointed out that for Rosencrantz and Guildenstern 'destiny lies in the plot of an Elizabethan revenge tragedy', and that the play becomes a metaphor for life.[2] Formerly nonentities who do not recall anything about their previous existence, they gain their only memorable experience and their only identity through their involvement in the events of *Hamlet*. The players appropriately represent the entrapment which makes them participants in a play they did not write. The Tragedians include sex shows in their repertory and tell Rosencrantz and Guildenstern that 'It costs little more if you happen to get caught up in the action'. Guildenstern understands the implications before Rosencrantz and asks further about being 'caught up' and the players prepare to catch them up. The figure suggests the ambiguous relationship between control and consent and between player and spectator as well as the tenuous distinction between being 'caught up' and 'caught'. Later, in the midst of their efforts to 'glean' from Hamlet,

Guildenstern says, 'We've been caught up. Your smallest action sets off another somewhere else and is set off by it' [p. 29]. When they are practicing the questioning of Hamlet, Guildenstern tells Rosencrantz to 'catch me unawares'. Also the players who are catching them up in the action are catching up with them in the journey. Finally, in a speech that anticipates the conclusion of the pattern in which they are caught, Guildenstern tells the Player that he doesn't 'catch them [the spectators] unawares and start the whisper in their skull that says – "One day you are going to die".' The Player maintains that he does [p. 61]. Three times the entrapment of Rosencrantz and Guildenstern in the play – or the play as life – is revealed by the players. As the Tragedians enter for their fateful performance before the King, Rosencrantz 'breaks for the opposite wing' only to encounter two more approaching Tragedians [p. 55]. Immediately after the two courtiers have discovered the letter ordering their deaths, 'the players emerge, impossibly, from the barrel and form a casually menacing circle round ROS and GUIL.' [p. 89]. Desperately, Guildenstern tries to kill the Player, but discovers that his 'death' was just a competent job of acting.

While at court and on the ship, Rosencrantz and Guildenstern, like Didi and Gogo, experience uncertainty and frustration. Beckett's characters, particularly Didi, are uncertain about what Godot is like, whether he will come, and whether the boys will carry the messages; Stoppard's characters, particularly Guildenstern, are uncertain about the King's motives and intentions, their assignment from the King, their own safety and death. The principal characters in both plays are frustrated because of lack of success. But Rosencrantz and Guildenstern are not bored and are not existing in a void of endless time and space. They are primarily concerned with excaping from the *Hamlet* pattern in which they have been 'caught up.' So much is happening that Rosencrantz repeatedly wants to go home. Guildenstern thinks that they will come through 'all right' if they 'tread warily' and 'follow instructions', but that being 'arbitrary' might cause a 'shambles', and 'If we go there's no knowing'. They are blocked in time by an unbroken series of fast-moving events and in space by other characters. They have some time between *Hamlet* scenes to practice how to act with Hamlet (who always comes), but they are imprisoned within the *Hamlet* plot and within twenty-four hours arrive at Elsinore, receive instructions, try to 'glean' from Hamlet, witness the play (including the foreshadowing of their own deaths) and the King's agitation, become involved in the slaying of Polonius, the arrest of Hamlet, and are sent off to England with

Hamlet. Only for a 'fractional moment' is there a possible escape from this pattern. Along with the confrontations with the Tragedians, Rosencrantz and Guildenstern feel trapped by other characters: 'In and out, on and off, they're coming at us from all sides', and 'As soon as we make a move they'll come pouring in from all sides . . .'. They vaguely hope for not just anything to happen, but for something that would bring an explanation or release. Ironically (very much as when the Tragedians' music is first heard, Guildenstern thinks the sound of a pipe aboard the ship 'could change the course of events'), but the music again heralds the players, who personify the ineluctable pattern of events.

Two young courtiers, then, have been suddenly awakened by a summons from uneventful and directionless lives, coins turn up 'heads' one hundred consecutive times in an absurdist epiphany, and the courtiers become part of a pattern of events – whose cause or purpose they do not understand – which they cannot or will not escape and which both gives them their only identity and carries them to their deaths. In this sense Godot comes in *Rosencrantz and Guildenstern are Dead*. Critics have given numerous interpretations to Beckett's Godot. In one sense, Godot by definition can never come. Godot has been described by Ruby Cohn as 'the promise that is always awaited and never fulfilled',[3] and by David H. Hesla as 'simply Time Future' which is no longer Godot when it passes the barrier into time present.[4] But in another sense, time future, what we have waited for, knowingly or unknowingly, becomes time present, as Guildenstern remarks at Elsinore: 'One is, after all, having it [the future] all the time . . . now . . . now . . . and now . . .'. Esslin has said that 'Godot simply represents the objective of our waiting – an event, or thing, a person, death', or 'the intervention of a supernatural agency'.[5] Other critics have seen Godot as 'the anthropomorphic image of God'[6], a little god, love or death.[7] In some of these forms Godot comes to Rosencrantz and Guildenstern. They experience a 'future' very different from their past; however, most importantly, they experience approaching death and apparent supernatural intervention.

Rosencrantz and Guildenstern have seemingly been waiting in the wings before assuming their roles and being 'caught up in' the *Hamlet* pattern, which leads to their deaths and suggests to them the intervention of some supernatural agency. Hesla has said that if the question of Godot's meaning 'is put in its ancient gnostic form or modern existentialist form – the form that holds that the sin man must repent is, in Gogo's words, "Our being born" – then Godot is simply Death or Nonbeing'[8]; and Esslin has observed that suicide is the favourite solution sought by Didi and Gogo.[9] Rosencrantz and Guildenstern are increasingly preoccupied by death. Not only the title of the play, but the philosophical musings on death as not-being, the word play on 'death', the obsession of the Tragedians with slaying and dying, the dumbshow presenting the death of the two spies – all point to the 'dead stop' which Rosencrantz intuitively perceives when first arriving at Elsinore. In his last words he has 'had enough' and is 'relieved.' As in the dumbshow 'the SPIES die at some length, rather well,' so presumably do Rosencrantz and Guildenstern – probably better than they have done anything else. They gain identity as humans and as individuals in accepting the inevitability of their own approaching deaths, indeed in knowingly delivering their own death-warrants. Keyssar-Franke shows that Stoppard has skilfully manipulated the responses of his audience to bring them unawares to realise that they are actor-spectators like the two courtiers and that their deaths too are inescapable.[10] In some ways *Rosencrantz and Guildenstern are Dead* is a modern *Everyman* in which the principals do not know why they answered the summons and where it is leading them.

After the summons, Rosencrantz and Guildenstern, particularly the latter, feel that they are experiencing an un-, sub-, or super-natural force. In Act One Guildenstern feels afraid because the run of 'heads' seems to mean the end of a natural order and the presence of a deity or force that permits or causes the fantastic to become inescapable. Guildenstern, 'desperate to lose', experiences the same fear when he chooses the fist with the coin six consecutive times – only to learn that Rosencrantz had a coin in both fists. On the ship Guildenstern feels that they are caught in an incredible chain of events: 'And it *has* all happened. Hasn't it?' The two feel more and more that their fate is determined. Guildenstern expresses it best: 'Where we went wrong was getting on a boat. We can move, of course, change direction, rattle about, but our movement is contained within a larger one that carries us along as inexorably as the wind and current . . .' [p. 89].[11] Also, more and more they see the forces controlling them as personified and hostile. They see themselves as intended victims but also as gaining importance. Their lives, they feel, are being directed and ended by an unseen 'they' which sometimes suggests the King and the court, but which increasingly means some un-, sub-, or super-natural agency: 'They don't care', says Rosencrantz. Again, jumping overboard 'would put a spoke in their wheel', Rosencrantz says. 'Unless they're counting on it', Guildenstern replies. Assume, Guildenstern remarks later, 'that they're going to kill him' (i.e., Hamlet). As they near the coast of

England, Rosencrantz sums up the courtiers' perception of 'they':
'They had it in for us, didn't they? Right from the beginning. Who'd
have thought that we were so important?' [p. 89]. Ironically,
Rosencrantz says, 'They'll just have to wait', before he disappears
at the end. Though this agency does not appear in person,
Rosencrantz and Guildenstern are convinced that 'they' have seized
control of their lives and swept them to their deaths. They do not
feel, like Didi and Gogo, that they have been abandoned, but that
they are receiving a disproportionate amount of attention.

In keeping with the different fates of the principals in relation to
their Godots in *Waiting for Godot* and in *Rosencrantz and Guildenstern
are Dead*, the two plays differ structurally in at least two important
respects. The structure of *Waiting for Godot* reflects the process of
waiting and is basically circular and repetitive. Cohn has pointed
out that the dialogue and stage directions of the first act of *Waiting
for Godot* indicate that Didi and Gogo are doing what they have
often done before,[12] and critics have generally recognised that the
play's two acts suggest a repeated rather than a completed action
and that the second act does largely repeat the first. On the contrary,
the first act of Stoppard's play is concerned with sudden change,
and the play presents a completed action within a structure that is
basically linear. The summons leads to the involvement in the *Hamlet*
plot, which leads to the deaths of Rosencrantz and Guildenstern.
Another structural difference is that in *Waiting for Godot* the two
tramps generate their own action of waiting (whether Godot can or
cannot come), whereas in Stoppard's play the two courtiers are
trapped in the *Hamlet* plot through what seems to them to be a
supernatural agency. Rolf Breuer has explained 'that the two tramps'
behaviour generates its own goal' and that the first act gives birth
to the second,[13] while Eugene Webb has described Beckett's play as
'the story of two vagabonds who impose on their slovenly wilderness
an illusory, but desperately defended pattern: waiting'.[14] In Stoppard's play the two central characters are unable to escape from the
pre-existing *Hamlet* pattern.

If we compare *Rosencrantz and Guildenstern are Dead* with *Waiting for
Godot*, we see in Stoppard's play two characters strikingly similar to
Didi and Gogo who find themselves in a predicament essentially
different from that in *Waiting for Godot*. Didi and Gogo, Rosencrantz
and Guildenstern, are all representative of humanity, and feel
uncertain, frustrated and powerless to change their situation. Didi
and Gogo are desperate, but always wait for some resolution
and explanation tomorrow. Rosencrantz and Guildenstern are
bewildered by fast-moving developments – the *Hamlet* pattern, the

revelation of the 'they' who had it in for them, and their approaching deaths. From the run of 'heads' to their plaintive wondering at the end if they had done anything wrong, they cannot understand why these sudden and unforeseen changes have come to them. Whereas Didi and Gogo represent the universal experience of waiting, Rosencrantz and Guildenstern represent the universal experience of feeling caught up by an incomprehensible force in a bizarre tragedy, written by an unknown author, 'where everyone who is marked for death dies' [p. 57].

SOURCE: extracts from essay, 'Godot Comes', *Ariel*, XII, 4 (1981), excerpted from pp. 57–70.

NOTES

1. C. J. Gianakaris, 'Absurdism Altered: *Rosencrantz and Guildenstern are Dead*', *Drama Survey* 7 (Winter 1968–69), pp. 52–8.

2. W. Babula, 'The Play-Life Metaphor in Shakespeare and Stoppard', *Modern Drama* 15 (Dec. 1972), pp. 279–81.

3. Ruby Cohn, *Back to Beckett* (Princeton, N.J., 1972), p. 132.

4. David H. Hesla, *The Shape of Chaos: An Interpretation of the Art of Samuel Beckett* (Minneapolis, 1971), p. 134.

5. Martin Esslin, *The Theatre of the Absurd* (New York, and London, 1969), p. 29.

6. 'They Also Serve' (anonymous article), *Times Literary Supplement*, 55, (10 February 1956), p. 84.

7. Cohn, op. cit., pp. 131–2; and Hesla, op. cit., p. 134.

8. Hesla, p. 134.

9. Esslin, op. cit., p. 36.

10. Helene Keyssar-Franke, 'The Strategy of *Rosencrantz and Guildenstern are Dead*', [*Education*] *Theatre Journal*, 27 (March 1975), pp. 85–97.

11. Hamlet's lines about the 'divinity that shapes our ends' [v ii 10–11] are spoken specifically in connection with his discovering and changing the letter borne by Rosencrantz and Guildenstern. The 'they' to whom they attribute their fate appears as a modern interpretation of – or response to – Hamlet's 'divinity'.

12. Cohn, op. cit., p. 132.

13. Rolf Breuer, 'The Solution as Problem: Beckett's *Waiting For Godot*', *Modern Drama* 19 (Nov. 1976), p. 231.

14. Eugene Webb, *The Plays of Samuel Beckett* (Seattle, 1972.), p. 26.

William E. Gruber   'A Version of Justice'
(1982)

. . . What sort of play is *Rosencrantz and Guildenstern are Dead?* To call the play a burlesque or a parody betrays one's insensitivity to its rich and manifold significances; and 'tragicomedy' is a term grown so vague as to be almost without meaning. Clearly, Stoppard has surrealist longings in him (*After Magritte; Travesties; Artist Descending a Staircase*), but *Rosencrantz and Guildenstern are Dead*, despite its veneer of gimickry, proves instead the lasting power of straightforward theatre. There is a small measure of truth in Brustein's term for the play – 'theatrical parasite'[1] – for it is obvious that Stoppard needs *Hamlet* if his play is to exist at all. Stoppard's play seems to vibrate because of the older classic, as a second tuning fork resonates by means of one already in motion.

Nevertheless, the tone of the modern play is distinct. Properly speaking, Stoppard has not composed a 'play within a play', nor has he written a lesser action which mirrors a larger. The old text and the new text are not simply 'joined'; they exist as a colloidal suspension, as it were, rather than as a permanent chemical solution. Or, to change metaphors to illustrate an important point more clearly, the texts of Hamlet's play and Ros and Guil's play form two separate spheres of human activity which, like two heavenly bodies, impinge upon each other because of their respective gravitational fields. The history of Rosencrantz and Guildenstern swings into line the scattered chunks of *Hamlet;* and the courtiers' story in turn is warped by the immense pull of Hamlet's world. Even though we cannot see much of that world, we may deduce its fullness. Though it exists largely offstage, or on another stage, we nevertheless sense that world's glitter, its nobility and its grandeur, and we feel its awesome power.

This is not to imply that the sum of the two texts results in determinism, or that we leave the theatre pitying Ros and Guil for being victimised. To the contrary: Helene Keyssar-Franke speculates that the juxtaposition of *Hamlet* scenes and invented scenes 'creates a sense of the possibility of freedom and the tension of the improbability of escape'.[2] Such is Stoppard's economy of technique that he chills us with Fate's whisper without a single line of exposition, without an elaborate setting of mood or of theme. Immediately the play begins our attention is mesmerised, as the two courtiers spin their recordbreaking succession of coins. The atmosphere is charged with dramatic potential, tense with impending crisis. The coin which falls 'heads' scores of times in succession defines what has been called a 'boundary situation'; the technique is notably Shakespearean, reminding one of the tense, foreboding beginnings invoked by the witches of *Macbeth*, or, of course, by the ghost of *Hamlet*. Ros and Guil's playing is not the aimless play of Beckett's tramps, with which it has been compared, but a play obviously freighted with imminent peril. We are impressed not by the absurdity of their situation, but by its terrible sense; one senses the chilling presence of *Hamlet*, waiting menacingly in the wings.

But *Hamlet*, as is true of all myths, is what is predicted, not what is ordained. The two courtiers are not snivelling, powerless victims of time and circumstance, and their story does not illustrate the baffling absurdity or the blind fatality that has sometimes been said to arrange their lives. This is the conclusion which many who comment upon the play have reached, guided, in part, by the anguish of Guil: 'No – it is not enough. To be told so little – to such an end – and still, finally, to be denied an explanation –' [p. 89]. We are wrong here to view events wholly through the eyes of the characters, and our pity for them must be conditioned with a little judgement. It is necessary to recognise that the Ros and Guil whom we see in the final scene are in no important way different from the Ros and Guil of the opening scene, and that such implied insensitivity to their world – puny though that world may be – bespeaks a deeper, mortal insensitivity to humanity and to themselves. Facing death, speaking his final lines of the play, the burden incumbent upon him to touch the shape of his life and so give it meaning, Ros one last time chooses to evade responsibility: 'I don't care. I've had enough. To tell you the truth, I'm relieved' [p. 91]. Nor is the more speculative Guil alive to his context: 'Our names shouted in a certain dawn', he ponders; '. . . a message . . . a summons. . . . There must have been a moment, at the beginning, where we could have said – no. But somehow we missed it.'

The context of men's action remains forever a mystery. It was a mystery for Hamlet, it is a mystery for Ros and Guil, it is a mystery for us. Yet between the two plays there exists an important difference in the quality of the characters' responses to what must remain forever hidden from their sight. We do not here – as we did in the closing scenes of *Hamlet* – discover new men. Hamlet, it is true, submits to his world with weary resignation. But Hamlet acknowledges human limitations without lapsing wholly into despair. The difference is between Hamlet, who accepts an ambiguous world while yet believing in the need for human exertion at critical junctures in time, and Ros and Guil, who quail before their world's haunting mysteries, wishing never to have played the game at all. Guil despairs, groping for his freedom 'at the beginning', when he might – so he reasons – have refused to participate. He wishes – there is no other way to put it – to avoid human responsibility. Thus his undeniably moving cry must be understood in the light of our clearer knowledge that his real opportunity came not at the beginning, but near the end of the play, when he accidentally discovered that his mission was to betray Hamlet. He misunderstands, in other words, the nature of his freedom, misunderstands as well the meaning of his choice. Too, we must not overlook the fact that Guil's misreading of his life provokes one final confusion of names: unaware that Ros has silently departed – died – Guil asks, 'Rosen – ? Guil?' In a play in which the floating identities of the two central characters has steadily deepened in seriousness, this final misunderstanding is especially important. Guil's fate is never to know who he is. Ultimately, as Robert Egan has pointed out, 'Guildenstern does die the death he has opted for'.[3]

To insist on Ros and Guil's freedom, and therefore on their responsibility, may seem wrongheaded, particularly because one is reluctant to condemn them for being confused by a script which they had not read. The courtiers are baffled by offstage events; hence it is not surprising that critics and playgoers have been tempted to draw parallels between this play and *Waiting for Godot*. Yet in truth the dramaturgy of Stoppard does not simply grow out of the theatre of Beckett. True, Stoppard employs elements of that theatre; but the effect of this is to call the validity of Absurdist theatre into question. Stoppard uses Absurdist techniques, as he uses the *Hamlet* material, to frame questions concerning the efficacy and significance of these diverse ways of understanding human action.

Evidence for this may be found by examining Stoppard's handling of the *Hamlet* material, and by noting how this handling varies over the course of the three-act structure of *Rosencrantz and Guildenstern are Dead*. Act One first poses the dilemma, defining, as it were, the conflict of the play as a struggle between two plots, between the story an individual (here, two individuals) wills for himself and the story the myth tells about him. Here the two texts seem most at odds, for *Hamlet* intervenes in two large chunks, each time unexpectedly, almost forcing its way on stage. In the second act, however, the compositional pattern shifts: here Shakespeare's text intrudes more frequently, and in shorter bits, as if the completed play were being broken down and assimilated by – or accommodated to – the play in the making. In this second act we feel the maximum presence of *Hamlet*, the increased pull of the myth. Structure here may be clarified by reference to classical terminology: in this act we witness the *epitasis*, the complication, or the tying of the knot. Between the growing design of *Hamlet* and the intertextual freedom of Ros and Guil's discussions there develops maximum tension, maximum interplay. . . .

Then, in the final act, the process whereby *Hamlet* is accommodated to *Rosencrantz and Guildenstern are Dead* seems completed. Here is staged the famous sea voyage of Hamlet, for which no dramatic precedent exists. No lines from Shakespeare's play can here intrude, for none is available. In *Hamlet*, we learn of the events of the voyage only in retrospect, during a subsequent conversation between Horatio and Hamlet. So, even though those of us who know the play remember what happened at sea, we know nothing of the causes of that action. Even knowledgeable playgoers, then, assume that the events at sea had resulted from chance, or, as Hamlet later suggests, from heaven's ordinance. This is an important point: most of Act Three of *Rosencrantz and Guildenstern are Dead* exists between the lines, as it were, of *Hamlet*, in what has always represented an undefined, unwritten zone. Stoppard here invites his characters to invent their history according to their will. He offers them alternatives, if not absolute choice. This is confirmed by the courtiers' imaginings concerning their arrival in England. Ros mourns:

> I have no image. I try to picture us arriving, a little harbour perhaps . . . roads . . . inhabitants to point the way . . . horses on the road . . . riding for a day or a fortnight and then a palace and the English king. . . . That would be the logical kind of thing. . . . But my mind remains a blank. No we're slipping off the map. [pp. 77–8]

The passage chills us, and invites us to recall that for Rosencrantz and Guildenstern there will be no future. Yet does it not invite us equally to reflect upon the courtiers' imaginative shortcomings, their own sinful – not too strong a word – despair? Indeed, soon afterwards they are graced with the opportunity to devise their own script, but they fail to do so because they cannot transcend their own banality, cannot for one moment rise out of their slough. Upon reading the letter which discloses the King's intent to have Hamlet executed, Guil lapses into an empiricism so bland, so callous as to lack utterly moral context:

> Assume, if you like, that they're going to kill him. Well, he is a man, he is mortal, death comes to us all, etcetera, and consequently he would have died anyway, sooner or later. Or to look at it from the social point of view – he's just one man among many, the loss would be well within reason and convenience. And then again, what is so terrible about death? As Socrates so philosophically put it, since we don't know what death is, it is illogical to fear it. It might be . . . very nice. Certainly it is a release from the burden of life, and, for the godly, a haven and a reward. Or to look at it another way – we are little men, we don't know the ins and outs of the matter, there are wheels within wheels, etcetera – it would be presumptuous of us to interfere with the designs of fate or even of kings. All in all, I think we'd be well advised to leave well alone. Tie up the letter – there – neatly – like that. – They won't notice the broken seal, assuming you were in character. [p. 79]

Only by considering Guil's comments in full can we appreciate their

slowly deepening repulsiveness. They are spoken, recall, while our
hearts are yet moved by Ros's intuitive reaction to the letter ordering
Hamlet's death: 'We're his *friends*'. As Guil speaks, the stage grows
quiet, empty: we feel the crisis, feel the awful pressure of a thing
about to be done, feel that (in Brutus's words 'between the acting
of a dreadful thing and the first motion, all the interim is like a
hideous dream'. Given the opportunity for meaningful action, Guil
(and thus, by way of tacit compliance, Ros) refuses to act. Given
suddenly – one is tempted to say beneficiently – ample room and
time to define their selves, the courtiers cannot swell to fit their new
roles. For a moment, *Hamlet* is swept away, suspended powerless;
for a brief interim we sense that the fate of the prince and his play
rests in Ros's and Guil's hands. That interim is theirs alone; it does
not belong to *Hamlet*. And they refuse to act. To choose not to
choose, of course, is a manner of choosing. Ros and Guil fill their
moment of time, their *season*, with emptiness – until the text of
Shakespeare's *Hamlet* rushes back to fill the vacuum. Scarcely has
Ros concluded, 'We're on top of it now', than Shakespeare's text
looms to meet them.

In this light, then, Guil's desperate attempt to slay The Player
who brings the courtiers the news of their deaths seems triply ironic.
Guil is wrong about death, in that it *can* be counterfeited by a
successful actor. And he is wrong about the shape of his life, too,
and about the meaning of human action. No one – not Fate, not
Shakespeare, and not Tom Stoppard – 'had it in for them'. Where
Guil and Ros erred was not in getting on a boat; they failed when
they chose freely to be cowards, chose freely, that is, to be themselves.
Stoppard stresses their cowardice, not their ignorance, and his irony
here flatly contradicts those who see Ros and Guil as powerless
victims. And Guil is wrong, finally, in his desperate attempt to
murder The Player. Guil seems here to hope to win dramatic stature
by an act of violence, to gain identity from a conventionally heroic
act of will. In fact, Stoppard seems to be saying, such conventional
heroism is not necessary; all that was required of Guil was the
destruction of a single letter.

Thus it is inevitable that the stage lights dim on Ros's and Guil's
play and shine in the end on *Hamlet*: 'immediately', Stoppard directs,
'the whole stage is lit up, revealing, upstage, arranged in the
approximate positions last held by the dead tragedians, the tableau
of court and corpses which is the last scene of *Hamlet*' [p. 91]. The
text of Shakespeare's play suddenly appears to overwhelm its modern
analogue, as the old play and the new play here converge in a
genuine *coup de théâtre*. Yet the point here is more than mere theatrics,

more, too, than weary fatalism or anguish at the absurdity of human life. The sudden sweeping reduction of Ros and Guil completes Stoppard's play at the same time it affirms unconditionally the morality of Shakespeare's. On this crucial point, Stoppard is unequivocal: in rehearsals, and in all published editions of the play after the first, Stoppard excised a bit of action which brought his drama full circle, so that it ended with someone banging on a shutter, shouting two names.[4] Stoppard's alteration moves his play away from the cultivated theatricality and ambiguity one finds often in Absurdist drama; and we are left with the clear knowledge that Ros and Guil, despite their being given an entire play of their own, have not advanced beyond the interchangeable, nondescript pair who took the boards more than three hundred years ago. Just as he disappears from view, Guil quips, 'Well, we'll know better next time'. But the evidence from *two* plays, now, suggests that they won't. Oddly, Stoppard is here not following Shakespeare's script so much as he is redefining and reasserting its tragic validity: *Rosencrantz and Guildenstern are Dead* proves that Shakespeare had it right after all. For this reason, Ros and Guil are not permitted to 'die' on stage; they merely disappear from view. Is this not one final demonstration of Stoppard's consistent dramatic technique? – for he merely whisks the courtiers off the stage, lest their corpses – visible proof that they had lived – convince an audience of their dramatic substance.

   Wheels within wheels: *Rosencrantz and Guildenstern are Dead* is deeply ironic, yet the irony is not at all the mocking, ambivalent irony we have come to expect of the modern theatre. To be sure, to rank the orders of reality in this haunting play is to invert *mimesis*, for here the admitted fiction – the world of *Hamlet* – possesses most substance. It turns out, in fact, that even The Player is more real, that is, of more worth, than Ros and Guil. But this does not mean that The Player – whose essence is his artifice – forms the play's thematic centre. Like *Hamlet, Rosencrantz and Guildenstern are Dead* brings into conjunction a number of states of being, examines from a variety of perspectives some modes of human action. What the play *means*, it means largely by virtue of these numerous contrasts and resulting tensions. No one perspective is so broad as to embrace the whole; each, by itself, is faulty, both intellectually and morally. Nevertheless, together they assert a view of human activity that stresses men's ultimate responsibility – whether prince or actor or lackey – for what they do, and so for who they are.

   It is simply incorrect, for this reason, to call *Rosencrantz and Guildenstern are Dead* an example of Absurdist drama, even to call it

'post-Absurdist' drama (in all but the literal sense). In the first
place, we do not find here a 'sense of metaphysical anguish at the
absurdity of the human condition,' a theme which Martin Esslin
long ago defined as central to Absurdist playwrights. Certainly, Ros
and Guil die without knowing what their lives were all about. But
the whole point of the *Hamlet* material is to define for the audience –
if not for Ros and Guil – a knowable logic that shapes men's fortunes,
even as it permits them a part in the process. We must distinguish
here the difference between two varieties of offstage material, such
as one finds, say, in *Waiting for Godot* or in *The Birthday Party*, on the
one hand, and in *Oedipus Rex* and in *Rosencrantz and Guildenstern are
Dead*, on the other. In the former plays, the offstage material
functions exclusively to deepen the audience's awareness of human
ignorance; it is mockingly obscure, purposely baffling to characters
and to spectators. But in the latter plays, the offstage material
functions both as mystery *and* as myth, the myth with its powerful
implications of logic, design, even – in the right circumstances –
knowability.

In other ways, too, *Rosencrantz and Guildenstern are Dead* rejects
much of the Absurdist canon. It is not 'anti-literary'; it does not
'abandon rational devices and discursive thought', but instead
depends upon them; and finally, it does not lament the loss of
opportunities for meaning, even for heroism, because Ros and Guil
enjoy, albeit briefly, such potential.[5] This play is . . . 'comfortingly
classical'. It testifies to the informing aesthetic power even today of
a tragic dramatic form far older than the Elizabethan play which
inspired it. *Rosencrantz and Guildenstern are Dead* offers its audience the
vision of two characters caught in the agony of moral choice. At a
moment when they least expect it, and in a place they had never
forseen, they must decide the shape of their lives. To be sure, the
information upon which they must base their decision comes to
them in the form of riddles, half-truths, things only partly-known;
but when has it ever been otherwise? Like other tragic protagonists
before them, Ros and Guil must choose, and they choose in error.
Leading up to and away from this moral crisis which forms the
dramatic centre of his play, Stoppard constructs a linear plot, set in
time, and moved by a group (or, if you will, two groups) of characters
who are consistent in both motive and response. Behind the play
stands an ancient way of ordering experience, a way which is both
mythic and ritualistic. And for his theme, Stoppard (with the aid of
Hamlet) offers a version of justice: all the characters get what they
deserve. So simple, so moving, so regrettable, but, finally, so
consoling: what, in the end, could be more like classical tragedy
than that?

SOURCE: extract from essay, 'Wheels Within Wheels', *Comparative Drama*, xv (1981–82), pp. 291–310.

NOTES

1. Robert Brustein, *The Third Theatre* (New York, 1969). [This essay is excerpted as the following item in this section 3 of Part Two – Ed.]
2. Helene Keyssar-Franke, 'The Strategy of *Rosencrantz and Guildenstern are Dead*', [*Education*] *Theatre Journal*, 27 (March, 1975), p. 87.
3. Richard Egan, 'A Thin Beam of Light: The Purpose of Playing in *Rosencrantz and Guildenstern are Dead*', [*Education*] *Theatre Journal*, 31 (March 1979), pp. 58–69 [excerpted in this section, below – Ed.].
4. Robert Hayman, *Tom Stoppard* (London, 1977), p. 46.
5. Esslin cites these characteristic features of Absurdist drama. See *The Theatre of the Absurd*, pp. xv – xxiv.

Robert Brustein   'Something Disturbingly Voguish and Available'   (1969)

Tom Stoppard's *Rosencrantz and Guildenstern are Dead* is obviously giving considerable pleasure to large numbers of people, so I advance my own reservations feeling like a spoilsport and a churl: the play strikes me as a noble conception which has not been endowed with any real weight or texture. The author is clearly an intelligent man with a good instinct for the stage, and his premise is one that should suggest an endless series of possibilities. But he manipulates this premise instead of exploring it, and what results is merely an immensely shrewd exercise enlivened more by cunning than by conviction.

As is now generally known, *Rosencrantz and Guildenstern are Dead* is a theatrical parasite, feeding off *Hamlet*, *Waiting for Godot* and *Six Characters in Search of an Author* – Shakespeare provides the characters, Pirandello the technique, and Beckett the tone with which the Stoppard play proceeds. Like Pirandello, Stoppard tries to give extradramatic life to a group of already written characters, introducing elements of chance and spontaneity into a scene previously determined by an author. His object is to discover what happens to people whose lives are completely fixed and formalised when they are allowed to meditate, self-consciously, upon their own predestination.

To do this, he borrows a pair of secondary figures from *Hamlet*, and examines their behavior when they are not playing one of their seven written scenes. Summoned by a messenger to the court of Elsinore, Rosencrantz and Guildenstern await the completion of their roles in an action whose outcome they cannot divine, passing the time in small talk, exits and entrances, verbal games, coin flipping, philosophical disputations, and various meetings with other characters from the play. Like Beckett's two tramps in *Waiting for Godot*, Rosencrantz and Guildenstern are baffled characters imprisoned in a timeless void where they alternate between brief vaudeville routines and ruminations on the vacancy of life in general and theirs in particular. . . .

In outline, the idea is extremely ingenious; in execution, it is derivative and familiar, even prosaic. As an artist, Stoppard does not fight hard enough for his insights – they all seem to come to him, prefabricated, from other plays – with the result that his air of pessimism seems affected, and his philosophical meditations, while witty and urbane, never obtain the thickness of *felt* knowledge. Whenever the play turns metaphysical, which is frequently, it turns spurious, particularly in the author's recurrent discourses upon death: 'Death is not romantic . . . and death is not a game which will soon be over . . . death is not anything . . . death is not. It's the absence of presence, nothing more . . . the endless time of never coming back.' This sort of thing is squeezed out like toothpaste throughout the play, the gravity of the subject never quite overcoming the banality of its expression: 'The only beginning is birth, and the only end is death – if you can't count on that, what can you count on?' Compare this with Pozzo's lines in *Godot:* 'One day we were born, one day we shall die, the same day, the same second, is that not enough for you? They give birth astride a grave, the light gleams an instant, then it's night once more' – and you will see how much Stoppard's language lacks economy, compression, and ambiguity, how far short it falls of poetry.

There is, in short, something disturbingly voguish and available about this play, as well as a prevailing strain of cuteness which shakes one's faith in the author's serious intentions: 'Eternity's a terrible thought', reflects one character, 'I mean where's it going to end?' Hamlet spits into the wind, and receives his spittle back in his eye. There is a good deal of innuendo about the ambiguous sexual nature of the boy playing the Player Queen. And the two central figures are whimsical to the point of nausea.

It is, in fact, the characters of Rosencrantz and Guildenstern that account for a good deal of my queasiness about the play. In

Shakespeare, these characters are time servers – cold, calculating
opportunists who betray a friendship for the sake of a preferment –
whose deaths, therefore, leave Hamlet without a pang of remorse.
In Stoppard, they are garrulous, child-like, ingratiating simpletons,
bewildered by the parts they must play – indeed, by the very notion
of an evil action. It is for this reason, I think, that Stoppard omits
their most crucial scene – the famous recorder scene where they are
exposed as spies for Claudius[1] – for it is here that their characterolog-
ical inconsistency would be most quickly revealed. Since the author
is presumably anxious to demonstrate the awful inevitability of a
literary destiny ('We follow directions – there is no *choice* involved.
The bad end unhappily, the good unluckily. That is what tragedy
means'), it hardly serves his purpose to violate the integrity of
Shakespeare's original conception. But I suspect the author has
another purpose here – that of amusing the audience with winning
heroes – and the necessity to be charming is not always easily
reconciled with the demands of art.

Mr Stoppard doesn't bother to settle the problem either. Worse,
he does not seem aware that it exists or that he has a certain
responsibility to work out the deeper implications of his choices. We
are left wondering why this admittedly entertaining play has found
such ready acceptance on Broadway when *Waiting for Godot* – without
which it would not exist – still awaits a sustained New York
production thirteen years after it was written. I do not think it is
too much to say that Stoppard is benefiting from a *Zeitgeist* created
by authors whose works nobody wants to see, and is achieving his
success by offering a form of Beckett without tears. *Waiting for Godot*
is the creation of a poet, *Rosencrantz and Guildenstern are Dead* the
product of a university wit. Will the poets ever have their day as
well as the wags?

SOURCE: extracts from *The Third Theatre* (New York, 1969), pp. 149–50,
151–3.

NOTE

1. [Ed.] But on this see Stoppard's own comment, p. 32, above.

Robert Egan   'The Importance of the Player
and His Troupe'   (1979)

. . . *Rosencrantz and Guildenstern are Dead* does not present us . . . with
figures in a Beckettian vacuum, at liberty to wait for a Godot who
does not arrive. But neither is the play an ironic account of human
marionettes, utterly without access to hope, insight or meaningful
action. In this study, my chief point of focus will be the Player and
his Tragedians. My contention is that the actions of the Tragedians
and the comments of the Player together constitute a source of
meaning that counterweights the play, significantly offsetting what
would otherwise be its closed, fatalistic perception of existence. My
perspective is a slanted one, having been shaped by my experience
of performing the role of the Player. Consequently, much of the
interpretation that follows derives from a view of the play as seen
by one actor through the eyes of one character. Yet, such a bias
may prove helpful to the central concerns of this essay. For the
essence of the Player's philosophy lies in a particular concept of
play; and I would hope that what I learned in playing the role
afforded me a practical hint, at least, of what that philosophy is.

    For some ten minutes of stage time Rosencrantz and Guildenstern
have been tossing coins and waiting, confined '*in a place without any
visible character*' . . . . Guildenstern, the intellectual of the two, feels
a frustrated suspense that mounts with each call of 'Heads'. Then,
'on the wind of a windless day', they hear 'the sound of drums and
flute' [p. 12]. Thus, the approaching music of the Tragedians seems
to promise relief from their predicament. Guildenstern, in fact, hopes
for a mystical encounter of some sort. When Rosencrantz stolidly
refuses to believe that the music is real, Guidenstern relates a fable
in which a succession of men who see a unicorn deny the truth of
their miraculous experience by convincing themselves that they have
seen 'a horse with an arrow in its forehead' [p. 15]. This parable is
far more applicable to his situation than Guildenstern himself can
know. He does not offer a moral to his little tale; yet in a sense, all
that occurs between him and the Tragedians will point up that
moral.

    When the Player and his band finally straggle onstage, Guil-
denstern is bitterly disappointed: 'it could have been – it didn't have
to be *obscene*. . . . It could have been – a bird out of season, dropping
bright-feathered on my shoulder . . . It could have been a tongueless
dwarf standing by the road to point the way . . . I was *prepared*. But

it's this, is it?' [p. 19]. He has hoped for an omen, such as the hero of a romance might receive at the outset of his quest. Bad enough, given his expectations, to be confronted by 'a comic pornographer and a rabble of prostitutes' [p. 19]; but worse still is the implication that the Tragedians do indeed constitute a kind of obscene anti-omen, a grotesque reflection of Guildenstern's worst fears about his and his friend's place in the order of things. At the outset, the Player hails them both 'as fellow artists', and this seems to be a kind of jeering *tu quoque* jest. Shabby and unheroic, travelling in a random direction toward an unknown goal, the Tragedians play out the roles predetermined for them by the gory melodramas of their repertoire. We immediately sense a metaphor here for the plight of Rosencrantz and Guildenstern, soon to enact the parts dictated to them by Shakespeare's script. Guildenstern himself senses a connection: 'You said something – about getting caught up in the action' [p. 18]. The Player replies by presenting them with an even more explicit and tawdry emblem of their condition: poor Alfred, whose role, no matter what the script, must be that of the helpless and used victim. What happens to Alfred literally in *The Rape of the Sabine Women* reflects figuratively what will happen to Rosencrantz and Guildenstern as they are 'caught up in the action' of *Hamlet*.

Yet Guildenstern, in his aversion to the Tragedians, misses the full significance of what they do and what they are. For, despite their sorry condition, the Player and his troupe are that very hint of magic for which Guildenstern has been looking. Of course, we as audience are in no way disappointed or disturbed by the Tragedians. For us, they are a welcome addition to the show; their incessant slapstick and mock histrionics infuse the stage with playfulness. In fact, in all their onstage moments they call attention to and celebrate the practice of dramatic play itself. The Player's entering cry, 'An audience!' [p. 15] not only expresses the character's response to finding Rosencrantz and Guildenstern; it affords the actor playing the Player an opportunity to voice all the joy, fear and anticipation that accompany his first step into our presence. In the course of my own performance, I found that Stoppard repeatedly provides the role of the Player with such moments, when character and performer intersect in a common testimony to the nature of the theatrical experience.

The behavior of the Tragedians, however, runs beyond the boundaries of what we normally consider theatrical circumstances; and this pertains to more than the services they are prepared to render. Their playing is all-encompassing and nonstop. Always in character, never out of costume, they recognize no limits to the time and place appropriate to dramatic play, and in this they profess 'a kind of integrity, if you look on every exit being an entrance somewhere else' [p. 20].

More than a profession, then, the acting of the Tragedians is in effect a way of living. Thus, the importance of their metaphoric relationship to Rosencrantz and Guildenstern runs deeper than the ironic joke it has seemed to be. Like them, the Player and his band are doomed to act in scenarios not of their own devising. Yet unlike the protagonists, who at this point fear to recognize, let alone come to terms with, the truth of their situation, the Tragedians accept from the outset their dislocated and unfree condition. Acknowledging that they exist within a dramatic plan over which they 'have no control', they 'take [their] chances where [they] find them', playing their roles as best they can, wherever and whenever they must play them: 'Tonight we play to the court. Or the night after. Or to the tavern. Or not' [p. 18]. And they do so in full knowledge that their drama, like that of Rosencrantz and Guildenstern, can have one ending only. Despite their *lazzi* and comic banter, they call themselves Tragedians.

This first encounter with the Player and his company ends in a flourish of stage magic. The Player agrees to perform number 'thirty-eight' in their repertoire and then follows his men offstage, after indicating entrances and a playing area. Rosencrantz picks up the coin the Player has just been standing on and discovers that it has come up heads. Immediately afterward, a lighting change transforms 'a place without any visible character' to the interior of Elsinore, and Ophelia runs on, pursued by Hamlet. There is a two-fold implication here. One one level, our attention is being called to the power of play in the theatre: through their art, actors on a stage *can* change one place into another, end one action and begin a new one. But within Stoppard's fiction, the fact that they have so totally transformed the conditions of reality as Rosencrantz and Guildenstern have known it until now gives the Tragedians new authority and attaches a special significance to their playing. Like the sign Guildenstern had hoped to find by the road, the Tragedians do indeed 'point the way'. The greeting of 'fellow artists' has in fact been an invitation, in which the Player has held out to Rosencrantz and Guildenstern, for the first of several times in the play, a valid mode of action and being.

In the course of Act Two, the Player and his troupe progressively clarify and demonstrate the approach to existence they represent. Late in the first act, however, Rosencrantz and Guildenstern themselves begin to experiment with the key to that approach, with play as a means of ordering and coping with reality. As Guildenstern puns idly on the subject of the King's memory, Rosencrantz, repeating an earlier line of the Player's, asks, 'What are you playing at?' The reply: 'Words, words. They're all we have to go on'. The notion that language itself is a form of play, a system of artificial counters that can be manipulated and rearranged to improvise meanings, leads them to explore its possibilities as such in the competitive game of 'Questions and Answers'. Subsequently, they go on to another game, in which Guildenstern plays the role of Hamlet while Rosencrantz interrogates him. Thus, from word-association to dialogue to dramatic *mimesis*, they explore progressively more sophisticated modes of play, and in the process they manage not only to remember their own names but to anticipate and rehearse their approaching encounter with Hamlet.

Of course, they forget their names again moments later, and their actual interview with Hamlet is a shambles (Rosencrantz scores it twenty-seven to three in Hamlet's favour). The point is that they are not yet experienced players; repeatedly, their attempts break down in confusion, and they are left to ask, 'What's the game? What are the rules?' Nevertheless, their very lack of success at meaningful play prepares them to recognize the authority of the Player, and on their second encounter Guildenstern pays him that recognition, however reluctantly:

GUIL: You're evidently a man who knows his way around.
PLAYER: I've been here before. . . .
   . . .
   And I know which way the wind is blowing.
GUIL: Operating on two levels, are we? How clever! I expect it comes naturally to you, being in the business so to speak.   [p. 47]

Being in the business, he is a past-master of playing, both as a theatrical art and a way of existing, and he proceeds to educate them in what is interchangeably an aesthetic and a philosophy. Nearly all his maxims do indeed operate 'on two levels', since they rest on the assumption that truth onstage is indistinguishable from truth offstage:

GUIL: I'd prefer art to mirror life, if it's all the same to you.
PLAYER: It's all the same to me, sir.   [p. 58]

The Player's instruction begins, properly enough, with a dialogue on the subject of acting:

GUIL: But for God's sake what are we suppoed to *do*?!
PLAYER: Relax. Respond. That's what people do. You can't go through life questioning your situation at every turn.
GUIL: But we don't know what's going on, or what to do with ourselves. We don't
know how to *act*.
PLAYER: Act natural. You know why you're here at least.
GUIL: We only know what we're told, and that's little enough. And for all we know
it isn't even true.
PLAYER: For all anyone knows, nothing is. Everything has to be taken on trust; truth
is only that which is taken to be true. It's the currency of living. There may be
nothing behind it, but it doesn't make any difference so long as it is honoured.
One acts on assumptions. What do you assume?   [pp. 47–8]

The verb 'to act', of course, is used here in both its senses, the
histrionic and the literal. Either way, the principle is the same: if
we are cast irrevocably in a scenario over which 'we have no control',
a dramatic plan whose inherent significance and purpose we can
neither know nor be certain exist, our only valid option is to accept
our roles within that plan and act them 'on assumptions'. For all
anybody knows, nothing is true, but if, in our acting, we honour
what we assume to be true, what in other words we decide *ought* to
be true, we can, in effect, create that truth through the artistry and
conviction of our performances. Through playing, we can endow
the script that confines us with a meaning of our own devising.

Yet any assumptions which are to be acted into truths must be
measured against the single, absolute certainty that circumscribes
all acting; and the Player holds out no optimistic illusions as to what
that certainty is: 'It never varies – we aim at the point where
everyone who is marked for death dies. . . . We're tragedians, you
see. We follow directions – there is no choice involved. The bad end
unhappily, the good unluckily. That is what tragedy means' [pp.
57–8]. Whatever actors may do, everyone who is marked for death
dies, and everyone, like Rosencrantz and Guildenstern, is marked
for death. It follows that a valid attempt to create meaning through
play must take death into account; death itself must be made an
object of play. And playing at death is precisely what the Tragedians
concentrate on doing. Death, as the Player says, 'brings out the
poetry in them'; 'It's what the actors do best. They have to exploit
whatever talent is given to them, and their talent is dying. They can
die heroically, comically, ironically, slowly, suddenly, disgustingly,
charmingly, or from a great height.' Their craft is thus a literal *ars
moriendi*, and like its medieval counterpart it is an *ars vivendi* as well;
by incorporating death into their playing, they can also incorporate
and give meaning to life.

The option that the Player represents is not, as some critics have suggested, a form of self-defence, a retreat from reality into empty histrionics.[1] The playing of the Tragedians in no way insulates them from the pain and fear of existence as Rosencrantz and Guildenstern experience it. On the contrary, playing lays greater demands on the Tragedians and renders them that much more vulnerable. They must enact every aspect of their lives on 'the single assumption which makes [their] existence viable – that somebody is *watching*'. They must 'pledge' their 'identities' to the principle that every detail of their emotions, sensations, and actions, however intimate, is worth making manifest with all the style and form they can muster. And they must have the courage to do so in spite of the constant possibility that no one is watching, that they are playing in a silent, unresponsive void, 'stripped naked in the middle of nowhere . . . every gesture, every pose, vanishing into the thin, unpopulated air'. (The actor speaking these lines, too, has the opportunity to voice his own sense of nakedness and vulnerability in performance.) In return for their playing, however, they are afforded the hope of giving meaning to an existence in which meaning may not be inherent. Thus they have access to a special kind of magic, a creation of something out of nothing. As the Player puts it, in a statement that expresses the core of his credo, 'I extract significance from melodrama, a significance which it does not in fact contain; but occasionally, from out of this matter, there escapes a thin beam of light that, seen at the right angle, can crack the shell of mortality' [p. 60].

Finally, Guildenstern rejects what the Player has offered him, lashing out at all the Tragedians represent: 'Actors! The mechanics of cheap melodrama!'. In particular, he refuses to recognize the worth and validity of what they claim as their greatest talent: 'No, no, no . . . you've got it all wrong . . . you can't act death. The fact of it is nothing to do with seeing it happen – it's not gasps and blood and falling about – that isn't what makes it death. It's just a man failing to reappear, that's all – now you see him, now you don't, that's the only thing that's real: here one minute and gone the next and never coming back – an exit, unobtrusive and unannounced, a disappearance gathering weight as it goes on, until, finally, it is heavy with death' [p. 61]. He denies, then, that death can be acted, that it can be accommodated into play and so endowed with man-made significance. And in denying this, he denies the same of life, insisting upon the dumb, blank illegibility of all existence: 'now you see him, now you don't, that's the only thing that's real'.

But Guildenstern has failed to grasp what has just occurred in his presence, the Tragedians' second major stroke of stage magic. What began as their dress rehearsal of *The Murder of Gonzago* has metamorphosed in the playing to *The Life and Death of Rosencrantz and Guildenstern*. The action of the 'cheap melodrama' has, impossibly, outstripped the present tense of the *Hamlet* plot and become a prophetic mirroring of Rosencrantz's and Guildenstern's future: their deputation by Claudius to escort Hamlet to England, their sea voyage, and finally their deaths at the hands of the English king. Thus the very sort of magic that the Player describes has come to pass. He and his troupe have, by their playing, created 'a thin beam of light' and trained it on the fact of Rosencrantz's and Guildenstern's mortality, offering to 'crack the shell' of its mystery. Lodged in the corny rhetoric of the playlet's closing chorus – 'Traitors hoist by their own petard? – or victims of the gods?' – is a very real assertion of the significative possibilities of their deaths. 'Victims of the gods', after all, bespeaks a tragic death, one in which some version of self or purpose has been expressed, while the alternative epithet indicates an ironic death, without dignity or import. But Guildenstern, confronted with a dramatic vision of his own death in a context of potential significance, denies that such a vision, or such a death, can be. The implications of that denial will become crucially clear in the third act. Meanwhile, face to face with a unicorn, he insists that he sees only a horse with an arrow in its forehead.

Although Guildenstern rejects the substance of the Player's advice, he and Rosencrantz do not cease to play. Midway through Act Three, in fact, they play their most important game of all. Finding themselves on a boat to England and moving irreversibly into darkness, they experience an uneasiness about their approaching destination, an inability to picture England as anything but a blank. We, of course, know that their premonition is fully warranted, that for them England will be the undiscovered country from whose bourn no traveler returns, the ending of their life-script. In the face of their growing anxiety, they resort once again to play, this time a dramatic acting-out of their arrival in England. Significantly, they need no preparatory discussion or agreement on the rules, as they did in the first act. Through their repeated contacts with the Tragedians, their playing has grown to be a sponanteous and intuitive activity. As they ponder what to say upon arriving, Rosencrantz instinctively assumes the role of the English king, and the dialogue begins. Their improvised scene quickly gathers momentum, and before either of them realises what has happened, Rosencrantz, in the heat of his performance, has torn open and read aloud Claudius's order for Hamlet's death.

Thus, Rosencrantz and Guildenstern reach their point of crisis as protagonists. In effect, they have managed to duplicate the sort of magic the Player has spoken of and demonstrated. Through the energy and commitment of their play-acting, they have created 'a thin beam of light' that has momentarily illuminated the shadowy workings of the script containing them. Suddenly, miraculously, they have what they had despaired of having: choice and the capability to act. Perhaps they are not Prince Hamlets nor were meant to be; perhaps anything they do to turn aside the course of events will prove futile, and the boat will carry them to England and death in any case. Nevertheless, their playing has made available to them the opportunity to define significant versions of self through a concrete moral decision and a subsequent action, even if a useless action. If the script has predestined them to obscure deaths, better to perform those deaths as victims of the gods than as traitors hoist by their own petard.

Yet, once again, and this time irrevocably, Guildenstern refuses the option that play has offered him:

GUIL: We are little men, we don't know the ins and outs of the matter, there are wheels within wheels, et cetera – it would be presumptuous of us to interfere with the designs of fate or even of kings. All in all, I think we'd be well advised to leave well alone. Tie up the letter – there – neatly – like that. – They won't notice the broken seal, assuming you were in character.
ROS: But what's the point?
GUIL: Don't apply logic.
ROS: He's done nothing to us.
GUIL: Or justice.
ROS: It's awful.
GUIL: But it could have been worse.   [p. 80]

Guildenstern deliberately looks away from what the thin beam of light has shown him. He denies that he is capable of knowledge and the responsibility that goes with it. He insists on being a little man, without choice or significance. And Rosencrantz goes along with him; moments later, he declares that they 'don't know what's in the letter.' Thus both of them specifically opt for a mode of life without meaning, even if at the expense of someone else's illogical and unjust death. In a sense, all that follows is anticlimax where Rosencrantz and Guildenstern are concerned. They have passed their crucial moment and they have chosen to be traitors – much more to themselves than to Hamlet. They will play out their arrival in England once more, only to discover that in denying their significance as actors they have acceded to insignificant deaths. But prior to that, Rosencrantz realises that, dead or alive, they have willed their own nonbeing: 'If we stopped breathing we'd vanish'.

One more significant episode remains. If the action involving Rosencrantz and Guildenstern is effectively over, the ongoing dialectic between Guildenstern and the Player stands unresolved. And so, for a final time, Rosencrantz and Guildenstern encounter the Tragedians. After reading the letter that seals their deaths, Guildenstern once more protests their helplessness and bewilderment as little men: 'But why? Was it all for this? Who are we that so much should converge on our little deaths? (*In anguish to the Player:*) Who are *we?*' That question is meant to be rhetorical, but the Player will not let it go unanswered:

PLAYER: You are Rosencrantz and Guildenstern. That's enough.
GUIL: No – It is not enough. To be told so little – to such an end   and still, finally,
to be denied an explanation.
PLAYER: In our experience, most things end in death.
GUIL: (*fear, vengeance, scorn*): Your experience! – *Actors!*
He snatches a dagger from the Player's belt and holds the point at the Player's throat: the Player backs and Guil advances, speaking more quietly.
I'm talking about death – and you've never experienced *that*. And you cannot *act* it. You die a thousand casual deaths – with none of that intensity which squeezes out life . . . and no blood runs cold anywhere. Because even as you die you know that you will come back in a different hat. But no one gets up after *death* – there is no applause – there is only silence and some second-hand clothes, and that's – *death* –
And he pushes the blade in up to the hilt.   [p. 89]

Again, Guildenstern denies that death can be acted, can in any way be encompassed or rendered legible by human means. At this point he *must* deny such a possibility, having foregone the chance to act his own death into meaning. Now, however, he intends not only to prove the Player wrong but to set a terrible certainty on his proof by inflicting on the Player a death as meaningless as he anticipates his own will be.

Yet, far from putting a stop to all playing, Guildenstern has set the stage for the Player's best performance. He recoils '*with huge, terrible eyes*', falls to his knees and then to the floor, suffers his death agony and '*finally lies still*'. A silence passes, the Tragedians '*start to applaud with genuine admiration*', and suddenly the Player bounces up to receive the congratulations of his fellow actors. It is a trick, of course. The Player has not in fact died and come back to life; freely, he demonstrates the retracting knifeblade. But there is much more significance to this, the play's ultimate stroke of stage magic, than that it was done with mirrors. The character of the Player, and the actor playing that character, *have*, literally, acted death, and the meaning of this accomplishment lies to a considerable extent in its dimension as performance. 'There's nothing more unconvincing', the Player has earlier confided, 'than an unconvincing death', and he might had added that there is nothing more difficult than a convincing one. This, then, is the most crucial point in the onstage career of the Player. At least, I found it the most exacting single task of the role. The actor must give living form to all he knows of death: bewilderment, fear, waves of physical pain; the fading of speech, of consciousness, and finally of breath. He must tax to the full his own observations (and thus his most painful personal experiences), as well as his powers of imaginative projection.

If the moment makes supreme demands on the actor, it can also evoke a peak of response from the audience. We are not duped to the extent that Guildenstern is; we do not actually believe that a man is dying onstage. We do, however, assume that a character called the Player is dying and that the actor playing him is bending all his abilities toward portraying that death. If the performance is a successful one, we pay it the tribute of our most serious attention. When the Player jumps to his feet again, we are shocked – not so much by the unexpected as by the sudden affirmation of what we already know. Simultaneously, both performer and character focus our awareness on the same truth. Through play, each has encountered the reality of death and accommodated it into the realm of human experience – as far as is humanly possible – by rendering it subject to artistic form.

Stoppard does not provide a formal resolution to the debate of Guildenstern and the Player. At the end, their opposing views, and the opposite approaches to existence they represent, are recapitulated side by side. The Player disappears into the gathering darkness on a characteristic note: '(*Dying amid the dying – tragically; romantically.*) So there's an end to that – it's commonplace: light goes with life, and in the winter of your years the dark comes early . . .' As always, death brings out the poetry in him. it's commonplace, he says, but he expresses that commonplace lyrically. And the commonest fact of all, enacted 'tragically, romantically', becomes something rich and strange, a miracle of art. Guildenstern's reply is equally characteristic: 'No . . . no . . . not for *us*, not like that. Dying is not romantic, and death is not a game which will soon be over . . . Death is not anything . . . death is not . . . It's the absence of presence, nothing more . . . the endless time of never coming back . . . a gap you can't see, and when the wind blows through it, it makes no sound' [pp. 90–1]. Guildenstern, too, retains an eloquence at the end, as well as a sad, stubborn insistence on the truth as he sees it. Stoppard does not unduly weight the case against him. It is plain enough that if we side with the Player we follow much more in the way of faith than of reason – everything, as the Player himself has said, has to be taken on trust – whereas Guildenstern's despair is born of an uncompromising empiricism.

Yet it seems to me that the play's ending is suffused with an unmistakable, if unstated, sense of resolution. Ultimately, Guildenstern does die the death he has opted for. His repeated insistence on the meaninglessness of death (and thus of life) becomes a self-fulfilling prophecy. He is, in fact, echoing an earlier phrase of his when the light unceremoniously winks out on him: 'Now you see me, now you – (*and disappears*.)' In every sense, his own words are his epitaph. By contrast, the Player has shown us the possibility of a significant mastering of death and life through play. He has insisted that it is 'enough' to be Rosencrantz and Guildenstern; that one's given name, even if a choice between interchangeable and objectively meaningless names, is enough with which to create one's own meaning. Finally, the play option is vindicated not only by the words and actions of the Player but also by the accumulated experience of the play itself in performance. The actors playing Rosencrantz and Guildenstern, too, have acted death and life; and we ourselves, by our presence in the theatre and our assistance as audience, bear an active witness to the validity and centrality of play as an indispensable – perhaps *the* indispensable – human skill.

SOURCE: extract from essay, 'A Thin Beam of Light; The Purpose of Playing in *R. & G. are Dead*', [*Education*] *Theatre Journal*, 31 (1979), pp. 60–9.

NOTE

1. See Jill Levenson, 'Views from a Revolving Door: Tom Stoppard to Date', *Queen's Quarterly*, 78 (1971), pp. 436–7 [excerpted in Section 2 of Part One, above – Ed.]; and T. R. Whitaker, *Fields of Play in Modern Drama* (Princeton, N.J., 1977), pp. 14, 16–17.

Normand Berlin   'The Playwright as Critic of Drama'   (1973)

Tom Stoppard's *Rosencrantz and Guildenstern are Dead* entered the theatre world of 1966–67 with much fanfare, and in the ensuing years it has acquired a surprisingly high reputation as a modern classic. It is an important play, but its importance is of a very special kind up to now not acknowledged. The play has fed the modern critics' and audiences' hunger for 'philosophical' significances, and as absurdist drama it has been compared favorably and often misleadingly with Beckett's *Waiting for Godot.* However, its peculiar value as theatre of criticism has received no attention. . . .

. . . The play takes Shakespeare's Rosencrantz and Guildenstern – time-servers, who appear rather cool and calculating in Shakespeare, and whose names indicate the courtly decadence they may represent – and transforms them into garrulous, sometimes simple, often rather likeable chaps. Baffled, imprisoned in a play they did not write, Rosencrantz and Guildenstern must act out their prearranged dramatic destinies. Like Beckett's Vladimir and Estragon, they carry on vaudeville routines, engage in verbal battles and games, and discourse on the issues of life and death. However, whereas Beckett's play, like Shakespeare's, defies easy categories and explanations, and remains elusive in the best sense of the word, suggesting the mystery of life, Stoppard's play welcomes categories, prods for a clarity of explanation, and seems more interested in substance than shadow.

Stoppard's play is conspicuously intellectual; it 'thinks' a great deal, and consequently it lacks the 'feeling' or union of thought and emotion that we associate with *Waiting for Godot* and *Hamlet.* This must be considered a shortcoming in Stoppard's art, but a shortcoming that Stoppard shares with other dramatists and one that could be explained away if only his intellectual insights were less derivative, seemed less canned. To be sure, plays breed plays, and it would be unfair to find fault with Stoppard for going to other plays for inspiration and specific trappings. In fact, at times he uses Shakespeare and Beckett ingeniously and must be applauded for his execution. But when the ideas of an essentially intellectual play seem too easy, then the playwright must be criticised. Whenever Stoppard – his presence always felt although his characters do the talking – meditates on large philosophical issues, his play seems thin, shallow. His idiom is not rich enough to sustain a direct intellectual confrontation with Life and Death. . . .

But there are indirect ways to deal with life and death, and here Stoppard is highly successful. And here we arrive at the heart of the discussion of Stoppard's art. According to Stoppard himself, his play was 'not written as a response to anything about alienation in our times. . . . It would be fatal to set out to write primarily on an intellectual level. Instead, one writes about human beings under stress – whether it is about losing one's trousers or being nailed to

the cross.'[1] Stoppard's words run counter to our experience of the
play and indicate once again that writers are not the best judges of
their own writing. Like all writers of drama, Stoppard wishes to
present human beings under stress, but he does so in the most
intellectual way. In fact, there is only one level to the play, one kind
of stance, and that level is intellectual. The audience witnesses no
forceful sequence of narrative, since the story is known and therefore
already solidified in the audience's mind. One could say that the
audience is given not sequence but status-quo, and status-quo points
to a 'critical stance' a way of looking at the events of the play as a
critic would, that is, experiencing the play as structure, complete,
unmoving, unsequential.

In the act of seeing a stage play, which moves in time, we are in
a pre-critical state, fully and actively engaged in the play's events.
When the play is over, then we become critics, seeing the play as a
structural unity and, in fact, able to function as critics only because
the play has stopped moving. In the act of seeing *Rosencrantz and
Guildenstern are Dead*, however, our critical faculty is not subdued.
We are always *observing* the characters and are not ourselves
participating. We know the results of the action because we know
Hamlet, so that all our references are backward. Not witnessing a
movement in time, we are forced to contemplate the frozen state,
the status-quo, of the characters who carry their Shakespearean
fates with them. It is *during* Stoppard's play that we function as
critics, just as Stoppard, through his characters, functions as critic
within the play. It is precisely this critical stance of Stoppard, of his
characters, and of his audience that allows me to attach the label
'theatre of criticism' to the play, thereby specifying what I believe
to be Stoppard's distinctiveness as a modern dramatist.

We recognize and wonder at those points in Shakespeare's plays
where he uses the 'theatre' image to allow us to see, critically, the
play before us from a different angle, where, for example, we hear
of the future re-creations of Caesar's murder at the very point in
the play where it is re-created, or where we hear Cleopatra talk
about her greatness presented on stage 'i' th' posture of a whore' at
the moment when it is presented in that posture. At these moments
Shakespeare engages us on a cerebral level, forcing us to think,
stopping the action to cause us to consider the relationship between
theatre and life. These Shakespearean moments are expanded to
occupy much of Stoppard's play, just as Shakespeare's minor
characters are expanded to become Stoppard's titular non-heroes.

I have indicated Stoppard's shortcomings when he wishes to
express truths about Life and Death. However, as critic discussing

Hamlet and Elizabethan drama, he is astute, sometimes brilliant, and his language is effective because it need not confront head-on the large issues that only poetry, it seems, is successful in confronting directly. . . . [This] pinpoints what Stoppard does best: what he can do with Shakespeare's minor characters to help us realise 'how remarkable Shakespeare is'. That is, Stoppard helps us to see more clearly not 'human beings under stress' but Shakespeare . . . and as we thread our way through the play Stoppard must be praised for precisely that function. . . .

Stoppard, as critic, through stichomythic dialogue, presents his thoughts on that vexing problem of Hamlet's madness.

ROS: Hamlet is not himself, outside or in. We have to glean what afflicts him.
GUIL: He doesn't give much away.
PLAYER: Who does, nowadays?
GUIL: He's – melancholy.
PLAYER: Melancholy?
ROS: Mad.
PLAYER: How is he mad?
ROS: Ah. [*to GUIL.*] How is he mad?
GUIL: More morose than mad, perhaps.
PLAYER: Melancholy.
GUIL: Moody.
ROS: He has moods.
PLAYER: Of moroseness?
GUIL: Madness. And yet.
ROS: Quite.
GUIL: For instance.
ROS: He talks to himself, which might be madness.
GUIL: If he didn't talk sense, which he does.
ROS: Which suggests the opposite.
PLAYER: Of what?
Small pause.
GUIL: I think I have it. A man talking sense to himself is no madder than a man talking nonsense not to himself.
ROS: Or just as mad.
GUIL: Or just as mad.
ROS: And he does both.
GUIL: So there you are.
ROS: Stark raving sane.   [pp. 48–9]

Here we proceed to a conclusion about Hamlet's insanity-sanity through a maze of conundrums, interestingly imitating Hamlet's own procedure of finding directions out by indirections. And along the way we begin to observe, again as critics, a condition of modern life, in which people do not reveal much about themselves 'nowadays', 'times being what they are'. Stoppard forces us to question certain assumptions about a character in another dramatist's play and, by extension, about man in the play-writ-large called life.

Stoppard confronts another critical crux in *Hamlet* when he has the Player present this brief statement on the dumb show: 'Well, it's a device, really; it makes the action that follows more or less comprehensible; you understand, we are tied down to a language which makes up in obscurity what it lacks in style' [p. 56]. Again we find that an attempt to answer the kind of question a critic would ask leads to a larger statement about the inability of language to communicate.

Quotations as evidence of Stoppard's critical examination of *Hamlet* can be multiplied. His critical interest, however, is wide and takes in Elizabethan drama and theatrical art in general. I offer only one example, an interesting dialogue on tragedy:

GUIL: You're familiar with the tragedies of antiquity, are you? The great homicidal classics? Matri, patri, fratri, sorrori, uxori and it goes without saying –
ROS: Saucy –
GUIL: – Suicidal – hm? Maidens aspiring to godheads –
ROS: And vice versa –
GUIL: Your kind of thing, is it?
PLAYER: Well, no, I can't say it is, really. We're more of the blood, love and rhetoric school.
GUIL: Well, I'll leave the choice to you, if there is anything to choose between them.
PLAYER: They're hardly divisible, sir – well, I can do you blood and love without the rhetoric, and I can do you blood and rhetoric without the love, and I can do you all three concurrent or consecutive, but I can't do you love and rhetoric without the blood. Blood is compulsory – they're all blood, you see.
GUIL: Is that what people want?
PLAYER: It's what we do.   [p. 23]

Stoppard, a drama critic before turning playwright and in this play a playwright as drama critic, crisply pinpoints the characteristics of Greek and Elizabethan tragedy and, enlarging the range of his criticism, uses these tragic characteristics to indicate what 'we' – players and audience – do.

I am arguing that Stoppard is most successful when he functions as a critic of drama and when he allows his insights on the theatre to lead him to observations on life. He is weakest, most empty, when he attempts to confront life directly. Stoppard is at his artistic best when he follows the advice of Polonius: 'By indirections find directions out.' This is as it should be, I think, because Stoppard's philosophical stance depends so heavily on the 'play' idea, the mask, the game, the show. Not only is the entire *Rosencrantz and Guildenstern are Dead* a play within a play that Shakespeare has written, but throughout Stoppard uses the idea of play. Rosencrantz and Guildenstern, and of course the Player, are conscious of themselves as players, acting out their lives, and baffled, even anguished, by the possibility that no one is watching the performance. All the world is a stage for Stoppard, as for Shakespeare, but Shakespeare's art fuses world and stage, causing the barriers between what is real and what is acted to break down, while Stoppard's art separates the two, makes us observers and critics of the stage, and allows us to see the world through the stage, ever conscious that we are doing just that. The last is my crucial point: Stoppard forces us to be conscious observers of a play frozen before us in order that it may be examined critically. Consequently, what the play offers us, despite its seeming complexity and the virtuosity of Stoppard's technique, is clarity, intellectual substance, rather than the shadows and mystery that we find in *Hamlet* or the pressure of life's absurdity that we find in *Waiting for Godot*. Of course, we miss these important aspects of great drama, and some critics and reviewers have correctly alluded to the play's deficiencies in these respects, but we should not allow what is lacking to erase what is there – bright, witty, intellectual criticism and high theatricality.

I present one final example, taken from the end of the play, to demonstrate Stoppard's fine ability to make criticism and theatre serve as a commentary on man. In this incident – 'Incidents! All we get is incidents! Dear God, is it too much to expect a little sustained action?!' – Guildenstern, who all along has shown contempt for the players and for their cheap melodrama in presenting scenes of death, becomes so filled with vengeance and scorn that he snatches the dagger from the Player's belt and threatens the Player:

I'm talking about death – and you've never experienced *that*. And you cannot *act* it You die a thousand casual deaths – with none of that intensity which squeezes out life . . . and no blood runs cold anywhere. Because even as you die you know that you will come back in a different hat. But no one gets up after *death* – there is no applause – there is only silence and some second-hand clothes, and that's – *death* –

[p. 89]

He then stabs the Player, who 'with huge, terrible eyes, clutches at the wound as the blade withdraws: he makes small weeping sounds and falls to his knees, and then right down'. Hysterically, Guildenstern shouts: 'If we have a destiny, then so had he – and if this is ours, then that was his – and if there are no explanations for us, then let there be none for him –' At which point the other players on stage applaud the Player, who stands up, modestly accepts the admiration of his fellow tragedians, and proceeds to show Guildenstern how the blade of the play dagger is pushed into the handle.

Here we seem to witness, for the only time in the play, an *act* being performed, a *choice* being made, not dictated by the events of Shakespeare's play – only to discover that we have witnessed playing, theatre. Guildenstern and Rosencrantz are taken in by the performance of a false death, bearing out the Player's belief, stated earlier in the play, that audiences believe *only* false deaths, that when he once had an actor, condemned for stealing, really die on stage the death was botched and unbelievable. What we have in Guildenstern's 'killing' of the Player, therefore, is a theatrical re-enforcement of the earlier observations on audiences by the Player as critic. As we spectators watch the event – Rosencrantz had remarked earlier that he feels 'like a spectator' – we intellectually grasp the fact that we had no real action, that no choice was made, Stoppard thereby making his philosophical point indirectly and with fine effect. In Stoppard a condition of life is most clearly understood, it seems, only when reflected in a critical, theatrical mirror.

In *Rosencrantz and Guildenstern are Dead* we do not have the kind of theatre characterised by such phrases as direct involvement, emotional, pre-critical, theatre of the heart, but rather a theatre of criticism, intellectual, distanced, of the mind. In a very real sense, Stoppard is an artist-critic writing drama for audience-critics, a dramatist least effective when he points his finger directly at the existential dilemma – 'What does it all add up to?' – and most effective when he confronts the play *Hamlet* and Elizabethan drama and theatrical art, thereby going roundabout to get to the important issues. Stoppard's play, because it feeds on both an Elizabethan tragedy and a modern tragi-comedy, gives us the opportunity to consider the larger context of modern drama. . . . We can say that *Rosencrantz and Guildenstern are Dead* is art that studies art, and therefore serving as a document, dramatic criticism as play presenting ideas on *Hamlet*, on Elizabethan drama, on theatrical art, and by so doing commenting on the life that art reveals. That is, Stoppard's play is holding the mirror of art up to the art that holds the mirror up to nature.

This double image causes the modern audience to take the kind of stance often associated with satire. And yet, Stoppard's play cannot be called satirical, for it makes no attempt to encourage the audience into any kind of action, as do Brecht's plays, or to cause the audience to change the way things are. The play examines the way things are, or, more precisely stated, it intellectually confronts and theatricalises the condition of man the player and the world as theatre. By the pressure of its *critical* energy, the play awakens in the audience a recognition of man's condition, not in order to change that condition, but to see it clearly. In short, by presenting a theatrical, artistic document, Stoppard makes us think – the words 'document' and 'think' pointing to the modernity, the impoverishment, and the particular value of *Rosencrantz and Guildenstern are Dead*. The play presents not revelation but criticism, not passionate art – Hamlet in the graveyard – but cool, critical, intellectual art – Hamlet playing with the recorders. *Rosencrantz and Guildenstern are Dead*, in its successful moments, brilliantly displays the virtues of theatre of criticism, and perhaps shows the direction in which some modern drama will be going – 'times being what they are'.

SOURCE: extracts from essay, '*Rosencrantz and Guildenstern are Dead*: Theatre of Criticism', *Modern Drama*, XVI (Dec. 1973), excerpted from pp. 269–77.

NOTE

1. Tom Prideaux, 'Uncertainty Makes the Big Time', *Life*, 9 (Feb. 1968), p. 76.

PART THREE

Jumpers

1. STOPPARD'S COMMENTS

I INTERVIEW WITH RONALD HAYMAN

... Jumpers *seems to take its starting point from that moment in* Rosencrantz and Guildenstern *when Rosencrantz says, 'Shouldn't we be doing something constructive?' and Guildenstern asks him, 'What did you have in mind? A short blunt human pyramid?'*

I did begin with that image. Speaking as a playwright – which is a category that must have its own boundary marks, because a novelist couldn't say what I'm about to say – I thought: 'How marvellous to have a pyramid of people on a stage, and a rifle shot, and one member of the pyramid just being blown out of it and the others imploding on the hole as he leaves'. I really like theatrical events, and I was in a favourable position. Because of the success of *Rosencrantz* it was on the cards that the National Theatre would do what I wrote, if I didn't completely screw it up, and it has forty, fifty actors on the pay-roll. You can actually write a play for ten gymnasts. I was in a fairly good position to indulge myself with playing around with quite complex – not to say expensive – theatrical effects and images, and I was taken with this image of the pyramid of gymnasts.

It's perfectly true that having shot this man out of the pyramid, and having him lying on the floor, I didn't know who he was or who had shot him or why or what to do with the body. Absolutely not a clue. So one worked from a curiously anti-literary starting point. You've simply committed yourself to giving nine hundred people in a big room which we call a theatre a sort of moment – yes? At the same time there's more than one point of origin for a play, and the only useful metaphor I can think of for the way I think I write my plays is convergences of different threads. Perhaps carpet-making would suggest something similar.

One of the threads was the entirely visual image of the pyramid of acrobats, but while thinking of that pyramid I knew I wanted to write a play about a professor of moral philosophy, and it's the work of a moment to think that there was a metaphor at work in the play already between acrobatics, mental acrobatics and so on. Actually it's not a bad way of getting excited about a play. ...

SOURCE: extract from Ronald Hayman, *Tom Stoppard*, 4th edn (London, 1982), pp. 4–5.

II INTERVIEW WITH R. HUDSON, S. ITZIN, S. TRUSSLER

. . . *Jumpers* obviously isn't a political act, nor is it a play about politics, nor is it a play about ideology. There is an element in it which satirizes a joke-fascist outfit but you can safely ignore that too. On the other hand the play reflects my belief that all political acts have a moral basis to them and are meaningless without it.

Is that disputable?

Absolutely. For a start it goes against Marxist-Leninism in particular, and against all materialistic philosophy. I believe all political acts must be judged in moral terms, in terms of their consequences. Otherwise they are simply attempts to put the boot on some other foot. There is a sense in which contradictory political arguments are restatements of each other. For example, Leninism and Fascism are restatements of totalitarianism. . . .

SOURCE: extract from interview in R. Hudson, S. Itzin, S. Trussler, 'Ambushes for the Audience: Towards a High Comedy of Ideas', *Theatre Quarterly*, IV, 4 (May/July 1974), p. 12.

2. REVIEWS OF FIRST PRODUCTION

B. A. Young (1972)

'A farce for people who relish truly civilised wit'

. . . What gives the play its real distinction is the quality of the conversations that bubble and glitter continuously from start to finish. Philosophy is a subject very easy to extract fun from, and Mr Stoppard, who is clearly well up in it, invents philosophical discussions with astonishing fertility of ideas and humour of expression. . . .

I can't hope to do justice to the richness and sparkle of the evening's proceedings, as gay and original a farce as we have seen for years, but a farce for people who relish truly civilised wit. . . .

SOURCE: extract from review of the London première, at the National Theatre, *Financial Times* (3 Feb. 1972).

John Barber (1972)

'As erudite as it is dotty'

. . . It is . . . a comedy as erudite as it is dotty, with some dark philosophic meaning buried under the fantastications.

You could say it was stark raving sane. . . .

The surrealist central theme, however, is less engrossing than the intellectual jokes and the whirlwind set speeches, cascades of words soaring like . . . comets. . . .

SOURCE: extracts from review of first production, *Daily Telegraph* (3 Feb. 1972).

Jeremy Kingston   (1972)

'Stalking the truth with determined tortuousness'

Tom Stoppard's play *Jumpers* (National Theatre) is to do with men
who puzzle, philosophers troubled by words, and in particular one
especially troubled puzzler, George, who believes there is a God or
thinks there is or feels or whatever the philosophic term is, *declares*
there is a God and is tortuously endeavouring to develop an
argument in which the phrases he employs correspond with his
belief, thought or declaration. . . .

The play's progress may not always be easy to follow, the
concurrence of events may be like trick pictures in which the pattern
does not become clear until the placing of the final piece; portions
of the play are flawed; yet the quality, in Peter Wood's direction,
rises above shortcomings. . . .

That good can still be recognized in a nasty world – a world
epitomized in Graham Crowden's malevolent, even devilish Vice-
Chancellor – would seem to be the core of Stoppard's argument.
He stalks this truth with a determined tortuousness, tossing out
paradoxes, intelligent jokes and absurd parallels. Rhetorical periods
lead up to a pair of alternatives, one outlandish, one comically
mundane, the good New Guinea cannibal and the good bacon
sandwich. Stoppard is obsessed with the nice employment of words
and with the terror of names. I wish he had not extended his two
sequences of cross-purpose comedy so long and I regret the bare
minimum of help he gives us to understand Diana Rigg's disordered
wife. But Mr Hordern's George is a masterly performance, proceed-
ing from a donnish impatience with the jejune by way of impishness
and distress to cosmic anguish.

SOURCE: extracts from review of first production, *Punch* (9 Feb. 1972).

J. W. Lambert   (1972)

'Shortcomings and shining virtues'

. . . It may be as well to establish at once that *Jumpers* is a most

imperfect play, with a number of bits that don't come off and a
rather feeble ending; but its shortcomings, compared with its shining
virtues, are in Daisy Ashford's phrase, 'as piffle before the wind'. . . .

. . . Since I have heard many smart persons sneer at the superfici-
ality of Mr Stoppard's treatment of philosphy, let me quote expert
evidence to the contrary. Sir Alfred Ayer, Wykeham Professor of
Logic at the University of Oxford, is on record (in the *Sunday Times*)
as finding this a very fine portrait of the genus philosopher, and his
verbal gropings an equally fine parody which 'like all good parodies,
could quite often be mistaken for the original'. What is good enough
for A. J. Ayer is in this field good enough for me. Certainly it is to
this layman, in its tortured pursuit of the existence of God,
relative values and absolute standards, both mind-stretching and
enchantingly funny. The absent-minded professor is a standard
figure; Michael Hordern has long been something of a specialist in
men whose minds churn like steam-engines but who can't see beyond
the ends of their noses. Seldom can genre and skill have married so
fruitfully as in his playing of Mr Stoppard's professor. Dragging his
cardigan almost down to his knees as he plunges his hands into its
pockets, setting out on a whole voyage of speculation prompted by
the realization that he is wearing odd socks, mislaying his notes,
straining every cell of his brain to try to encompass the notion of a
god who would not only have created the world but maintained its
moral values, he is the very model of all our bewilderment; I only
wish he had been given a more direct confrontation with his Vice-
Chancellor, into whose unexpected mouth Mr Stoppard puts a very
fine speech, based on St Augustine by way of Beckett ('Do not
despair, one of the thieves was saved; do not presume, one of the
thieves was damned'), reminding us that frightful as the world is
'more eat than starve, more are fit than disabled'. Clearly Mr
Stoppard intends a bitter irony here; certainly he is not offering an
invitation to complacency; but it is refreshing to hear the point made
at all in a society which, as early Christianity made a virtue, now
makes other people's suffering into a benediction, and self-satisfied
guilt into a sign of grace. Well, Mr Stoppard's play is to be taken
seriously; but I must not make it sound solemn, for it is long since I
have experienced in one evening so many flashes of brilliant comic
illumination. No other new play of the quarter begins to approach
Jumpers in stature. . . .

SOURCE: extracts from review of first production, *Drama* (Summer 1972),
pp. 15, 16–17.

John Weightman   (1972)

'A bit scrappy and incoherent'.

. . . a delightfully Absurdist play, more successful in some respects
than *Rosencrantz and Guildenstern*, although still a bit too scrappy and
incoherent for my taste. I laughed almost continually and came out
of the theatre feeling cheered up; but quite a bit of the action did
not seem necessary and I have failed to understand a number of
points, even after reading the text. Why, for instance, has Dorothy
gone off sex with her husband, after the shock of the de-poeticisation
of the moon? She is still fond of him, and she is not totally traumatised
since she is having some sort of affair with the Vice-Chancellor. I
suspect that it is simply because Mr Stoppard wants to make a pun
about a consummate artist refusing consummation. And why is the
play weighted down at the end with the rather tedious coda? It
could have stopped five minutes before it does. Is it because Mr
Stoppard cannot quite control his flow of language and gimmicks?
To judge by the extremely silly programme interview, it is almost
as if he were afraid to think commonsensically, in case his demon
should be castrated. In my opinion, this is an error which has
weakened the work of some other Absurdists, such as Ionesco. But
then my contention is that the conquests of the irrational should
always be explicable eventually in terms of the rational, and that
one should feel them to be rational even before one can discover
why they are so. According to my antennae, quite a few bits of this
play have not been brought fully into intellectual or aesthetic focus.

SOURCE: extract from review-article, *Encounter*, 38 (April 1972), p. 45.

Stanley Kauffman   (1974)

'Stageworn and shallow'

The curtain rises, and the heart sinks. On stage is a huge mirror
reflecting the audience. Thus *Jumpers* begins, with a metaphor not
only superficial but stale – Harold Prince used it twice in the last
decade, in *Cabaret* and *The Visit*. (And Genet uses it all through *The*

Balcony.) Then we get a long splash of vaudeville. A master of
ceremonies comes out and introduces a woman who appears in
cabaret costume to sing and who muddles the words. (*'Achtung!'*
says our already wary mind. 'This is a dream.') Out comes a troupe
of acrobats, introduced as the 'Radical Liberal Jumpers.' (Ho *ho!*)
Then comes an 'iron-jaw' act, a girl hanging by her teeth from a
swinging trapeze, shedding her costume as she swings. Then more
muddled singing by the first woman, then the jumpers come back
and perform at length – so long that even their obvious function as
symbol disappears while we concentrate on their act as act. They
form a pyramid, a shot rings out, and the top man falls; the lights
fade and come up in the fancy boudoir of the singer, who is in fact
a professor's wife and who has indeed been dreaming all the above.
Except that – and here our metaphysics begins to strain at the
leash – the murdered jumper is in her boudoir.

Tom Stoppard, the Englishman who wrote this play, is the author
of *Rosencrantz and Guildenstern are Dead*, which was hailed for its
novelty and its existential explorations. The latter seemed to me
even more tenuous than its novelty: W. S. Gilbert wrote a *Rosencrantz
and Guildenstern* in 1891. Stoppard's *R&G* was only a bright undergraduate's one-act prank waffled out to three acts. Then we got a
bill of his one-act plays, *The Real Inspector Hound* and *After Magritte*,
which showed the undergraduate being less bright, merely facetious.
In 1972 we read about Stoppard's new play, *Jumpers*, produced at
the (British) National Theatre and hailed as a work of philosophical
richness and wit.

Sorry. *Jumpers*, in proof, is a work of copious philosophical *allusion*,
written in that rhetorically ornate style brandished by a dramatist
who has more wish than need to write and who takes the offensive
stylistically in order to cow us. (Latter-day Albee is another
example.) But Stoppard slides even further. He tries to fob off one
more example of a stage-worn shallow genre: the play in which the
author shows that he has cosmic itches and tries to scratch them
with a mixture of facile intellectual rotundities and self-conscious
theatre mystique. Examples: Philip Barry's *Here Come the Clowns*,
Thornton Wilder's *The Skin of Our Teeth*, Max Frisch's *The Chinese
Wall*.

Stoppard attempts a triple counterpoint between his vaudeville,
a murder-mystery farce, and an intellectual comedy. A professor of
moral philosophy . . . is in his study trying to dictate a lecture on
God's existence to his secretary, while his wife . . . in her boudoir
is frantically trying to get rid of a body while dallying with her
psychiatrist lover, who is also a philosophy don and her husband's

boss. The corpse is clothed in one of the tumbler costumes; the
husband's secretary is the 'iron-jaw' stripper, now clothed and
wigged. This braiding of vaudeville-farce-cogitations is supposed to
stun us into perception of the relation of one to the other: the
acrobats as visual equivalent of moral flip-flop, the murder-farce
and sexual innuendo as gloss on the professor's moral speculations
and vice versa. Not one shadow of a hair of such relation or supportive
resonance is established. The elements are merely juxtaposed, that
is all; and the mere juxtaposition is itself supposed to create weight –
more, to bully us into fear of doubting that weight. Some physical
connections (the corpse's tumbler costume, the stripper-secretary)
are made; but there is no thematic resonance whatsoever between
the scurrying antics in the boudoir and the intellectual meanderings
in the study. And those meanderings end with the usual bland cop-
out in this kind of purportedly probing work. It turns its back on
query after the appropriate two and a half hours, and accepts the
universe so that we can all go home. From the closing speech: 'Do
not despair – many are happy much of the time. . . . No laughter
is sad and many tears are joyful.'

I won't dwell on the triteness of the characters: the bumbling
pedantic older husband, the frustrated wife who used to be on the
stage, the smoothie lover, the comic detective, the humble houseman
who turns out to be a juggler of philosophic jargon himself. The last
is rather like the housemaid in Muriel Spark's comedy *Doctors of
Philosophy*, produced in London in 1962 – a play similar in tone to
Jumpers, though not in plot, with dialogue more wittily polished.

Stoppard's dialogue has some sheen and a degree of donnish wit,
but it is less amusing than Spark's and much less surgical than
Simon Gray's in *Butley*, another play about English faculty people.
While the professor is dictating, his wife, trying to get attention,
screams from the bedroom: 'Murder – Rape – Wolves!' He goes to
his study door and shouts: 'Dorothy, I will not have my work
interrupted by these gratuitous acts of lupine delinquency!' Then,
returning to his God lecture, he dictates: 'My method of inquiry
this evening into certain aspects of this hardy perennial may strike
some of you as overly engaging, but experience has taught me that
to attempt to sustain the attention of rival schools of academics by
argument alone is tantamount to constructing a Gothic arch out of
junket.' In content the line is Stoppard's coy comment on his own
method. In style the deliberate circumlocution, lolloping along to a
point of heavy comic contrast, is the fake mandarinese of decadent
Albee. If you throw in references to Bertrand Russell and such
freshman chestnuts as Zeno's paradox of motion, you reduce the

starved theatre audience to quivering cries of gratitude for such profundities, cries mixed with gasps of wonder at a mind that can play so lightly with such deep thoughts.

The play is fake, structurally and thematically. All through it some recent similar experience kept nagging at me, and at last I remembered: Lindsay Anderson's film *O Lucky Man!* The film is on a quite different subject, but it too was a vehicle, groaning with effects, which toppled to show that Anderson, like Stoppard here, had absolutely nothing inside. But at least Anderson is a master of his craft as such; Stoppard is not. He is just one more half-baked egoist anxious for a cosmic grab, who thinks that the size of his ambition will certify his seriousness, particularly if he is comic, most particularly if he is reflexively theatrical. . . .

SOURCE: extracts from review of first New York production of 1974, included in Kauffman's *Persons of the Drama* (New York, 1976), excerpted from pp. 239–42.

3. CRITICAL STUDIES

James Morwood 'Earnestness and Comedy' (1981)

. . . One of the major points of interest of *Jumpers* lies in the fact that the philosophy, however comically presented, comes across as the serious centre of the play while paradoxically 'the real world' that surrounds it appears crazily surreal in its bizarre and dreamlike progress. On closer scrutiny, however, this world is revealed, within its farcical framework, as a singularly bleak one. The Radical Liberal Party has come to power in what looks more like a *coup d'état* than a general election [p. 34]. It is overtly militaristic and the Police Force is soon to 'be thinned out to a ceremonial front for the peace-keeping activities of the Army' [p. 65]. Journalism has been muzzled [p. 37] and we are told that 'the academics can look forward to rather more radicalism than liberalism' [p. 36]. Religion too is under fire. The new Archbishop of Canterbury is the erstwhile spokesman for Agriculture, an agnostic who plans to rationalize the Church; and the chapel of the University where George Moore, the philosopher, works has been converted into a gymnasium. The most sensational illustration of the extinction of moral values in this era is the grimly comic travesty of the heroism of Captain Oates of the Scott expedition, 'out there in the Antarctic wastes, sacrificing his life to give his companions a slim chance of survival' [p. 80]. For now a latter-day Captain Scott has found himself on the moon's surface with an Astronaut Oates and with enough power in the rockets to get only one of them back to earth. Knocking Oates to the ground, Scott has left him on the moon, 'a tiny receding figure waving forlornly from the featureless wastes of the lunar landscape' [p. 22].

Unsurprisingly Stoppard revisits further the glimpses of the moon. George's wife Dorothy has had a blooming career as a musical-comedy actress whose ideas of romance are inextricably linked with the subject of her songs, 'that old-fashioned, silvery harvest moon, occasionally blue, jumped over by cows and coupled by Junes, invariably shining on the one I love' [p. 41]. When the first moon landing occurred and she saw 'those little grey men in goldfish bowls, clumping about in their lead boots on the television news', it 'certainly spoiled that Juney old moon' [p. 39]. The sentiment has gone out of the journey; romance has been banished from her life. Her career terminated abruptly. And, as George remarks of this consummate artist, 'she retired from consummation about the same time as she retired from artistry' [p. 58].

It is not only the spoony June Moon of popular song that Dotty bids goodbye to. In a passionate speech she laments the demise of the moon in poetry, citing Keats, Milton and Shelley [p. 41], and, being not just a musical-comedy artiste but a graduate with second class honours presumably in philosophy, she tearfully reflects that the moon landing has made the world seem little and local and has thus undermined the absolutes men previously took on trust. Earlier she has asked whether it is '*significant* that it's impossible to imagine anyone building a church on the moon' [p. 39], and now she is appalled by her vision of the moral anarchy that she believes will be unleashed [p. 75]. When she had come into George's life, he had thought of her as the hyacinth girl, a symbol of the hope of renewal in Eliot's *The Waste Land* [p. 33]. Now the realization that the moon is like the moon and that is all has driven her to despair. Dotty Moore has in fact gone dotty under the malign influence of the arid planet that modern technology has revealed.

To some extent, therefore, it is our technological age that has emptied the universe of its values and emotion. The moon landing has reduced that familiar pitted circle, Milton's spotty globe, to an expanse of featureless wastes. Stoppard develops this theme by exploiting the de-romanticizing effect of the close-up. Dotty's skin, for example, the gorgeous sensuality of which is celebrated with entertaining lushness by Archie [p. 70], ceases to be a pin up. losing its glamour when magnified by the dermatograph to huge dimensions on the screen that Stoppard hopes will form a backdrop to the whole stage. To emphasize this point, the playwright plants discreet references to skin blemishes at various points of the play. George squeezes a blackhead [p. 25], Dotty has presumably been shaving her legs with her husband's razor [p. 35], and Archie remarks that 'All kinds of disturbances under the skin show up on the surface' [p. 62]. Even the Jumpers of the play's title, '*although they pass muster at first glance*', are not, when viewed more closely, '*as universally youthful or athletic-looking as one might expect*' [p. 15].

Politics and technology and the apparent death of altruism that has accompanied them have conspired to make the world of *Jumpers* a decidedly sterile location, but Sir Archibald Jumper, the University's Vice-Chancellor and the most fully developed of the play's grotesque array of minor characters, offers a framework, a design for living to those who jump to his tune. The first act finale is in part an illustration of this, and one significance of the Jumpers of the play's title, 'a mixture of the more philosophical members of the university gymnastics team and the more gymnastic members of the Philosophy School' [p. 51], is their evocation of the mindless obedience and cowardly uniformity (their uniforms are yellow) that serve to bolster a totalitarian regime. For the Vice-Chancellor, through whose hoop they jump, is not merely a psychiatrist, a coroner, a philosopher and a gymnast: he appears to be the power behind the new Radical Liberal Government as well. He is, of course, within the farcical context, the villain of the piece. And yet this urbane pragmatist with his unruffled equanimity does at least hold out the promise of order in a world without apparent values. His final speech is chilling [p. 87], but it insists that there is some happiness in the world, that things could be a lot worse and that there is no need to despair. To those who accept his discipline he will give membership of his team, a place in the pyramid, security.

But he will brook no opposition. His followers must espouse his vision of an amoral world uncompromisingly. Belief in God is for him anathema. George, a Don Quixote championing the God of Goodness, is a harmless eccentric. 'Moore himself is not important', comments Archie dismissively, ' – he is our tame believer, pointed out to visitors in much the same spirit as we point out the magnificent stained glass in what is now the gymnasium' [p. 63]. But McFee, the Professor of Logic, has become a believer in God and the possibility of altruism, has repented of 'giving philosophical respectability to a new pragmatism in public life' [pp. 79–80], and is about to go into a monastery. His imminent defection poses a serious threat to Archie's order, for, as the latter remarks, 'McFee was the guardian and figurehead of philosophical orthodoxy, and if he threatened to start calling on his masters to return to the true path, then I'm afraid it would certainly have been an ice-pick in the back of the skull' [pp. 63–4]. Perhaps it is not Archie who eliminates him – it could equally well have been the work of the Secretary, McFee's girl whom he was about to leave, and in the stage directions at the end of the first act, there is a hint that she may in fact have acted in collaboration with Archie over the killing. However that may be, his murder is very much in the Vice-Chancellor's interests. Later, in the dream or nightmare sequence of the play's Coda which is set in the Chapel-gymnasium, McFee's death is mirrored by the killing of Clegthorpe, the Archbishop of Canterbury, who has shifted from the agnosticism which has got him the job and now sees the need to 'find room for man's beliefs' [p. 84]. Archie will not tolerate the intrusion of spiritual values into his bleak world order and, in a sardonic reminiscence of a scene from *Richard III*, he has the Archbishop shot.

This is, of course, by no means the only reference to Shakespeare in the play. Dotty in a room with the dead Duncan McFee, borrows the words of Macduff and Lady Macbeth over the death of Shakespeare's Duncan: 'Oh, horror, horror, horror! Confusion now hath made its masterpiece . . . most sacrilegious murder! – Woe, alas! What, in our house?' [p. 24]. And then George comically addresses his tortoise in a line of Hamlet's, 'Now might I do it, Pat' [p. 43]. *Hamlet* is in fact the source for two texts that underlie much of the play's debate. One of these – we shall come to the other somewhat later – occurs in a scene with Rosencrantz and Guildenstern when Hamlet offers the latter a recorder and asks him to play it. When Guildenstern says that he cannot, Hamlet exclaims that if he cannot play a small pipe, he will certainly not be able to unravel the infinite complexities of a human being. ' 'Sblood', he cries, 'do you think I am easier to be played on than a pipe?' [*Hamlet*, III ii]. When George tells Archie 'that there is more in me than meets the microscope' [p. 68] – a form of words that gains in expressiveness from the use of the idea of close-up elsewhere in *Jumpers* –, he is asserting his individuality with much the same pride and conviction as Hamlet.

Remote and ineffectual don he may be; he feels that he cuts 'a ludicrous figure in the academic world' [p. 72] and he is certainly a failure as a husband. But George's intellectual debate, with its gritty, back to the wall optimism, shines like a good deed in a naughty world. Confronted with a society symbolized by the pyramid of yellow-uniformed and not very competent gymnasts, he remains nobly and absurdly himself.

By making philosophical debate the main focus of his play, Stoppard seems to be suggesting that the freedom of man is equivalent to the freedom of his intellect. The whole of the universe is grist to the philosopher's mill and it is the free play of the philosophical mind that sets the seal upon human liberty. (This symbolic use of Philosophy in fact renders scarcely relevant the strictures on George's specific lines of thought offered by A. J. Ayer in a friendly analysis [*Sunday Times*, 9 April 1972].) Archie, the implacable enemy of the spirit of inquiry that threatens to take off in awkward directions, wishes to play God in his world without values. But he is only the Vice-Chancellor. Can it be that somewhere, invisible to the purely rational mind, there lurks a Chancellor, a superior power, God? A joke altogether typical of Stoppard makes Archie the name not only of the play's great dictator but also of the most humble of its dramatic personae, the goldfish. It is perhaps because the philosopher reminds the tyrant of the littleness and brevity of his authority that he is a figure to be feared.

The second utterance of Hamlet that is of importance in our play is philosophically rephased by Dotty on p. 41. Again in a scene with Rosencrantz and Guildenstern, the Prince remarks that 'there is nothing either good or bad, but thinking makes it so' [ii ii]. George would dissent, believing that the sound of trumpets in Mozart simply *is* better than that of a trumpet falling down a flight of stone stairs. His Chair of Moral Philosophy is held in very low esteem in Archie's University – 'Only the Chair of Divinity lies further below the salt' [p. 51] –, and it is entertainingly obvious that George's philosophy is anything but materialistic as, in a struggle as Herculean as it is vain, he strives to find an explanation of what is good and bad in the universe. But the absence of materialism does not empty his quest of importance. Far from it. If God exists, he appears to think, then the life-enhancing and irrational qualities that Archie has banished are validated, altruism is a possibility and life is worth living. This is why George, who feels that his 'work on moral philosophy has always been based on logical principles' [p. 73], is forever trying to prove the existence of God through logical reasoning. He fails; but he still believes. Half St George and half a joke vicar, he is the unflinching champion of God and moral values.

Of course he is ridiculous. The absent-minded professor of popular mythology, he wears unmatching socks, tries to drink from a tumbler full of pencils, and answers the front door, in a reminiscence of *After Magritte*, with '*a bow-and-arrow in one hand and a tortoise in the other, his face covered in shaving foam*' [p. 43]. His gimmicks to enliven the talk he is preparing misfire pathetically when, at the climax of a series of hunting, shooting, fishing (and beetle-crunching) jokes, he finds that he has shot his pet hare with an arrow and then crushes his tortoise underfoot. Even so, there is a touch of the hero about him. He disdains to 'jump along with the rest' [p. 51]. And Archie, who does not take him seriously on his own, seems to feel, when he speaks of McFee playing 'St Paul to Moore's Messiah' [p. 63], that he might prove dangerous if he found support. Consigned he may be to the dreamland debating society, but the ideas he puts forward are nevertheless an affirmation of the value of life, and his philosophy cannot be tolerated, save as an irrelevant curiosity, in a society where a ruthless and materialistic government insists on obedience and conformity. . . . The philosopher may seem a laughable inhabitant of Cloudcuckooland. In reality, however, he is a profoundly serious native of the world we live in.

Thus *Jumpers* is in its way a deeply earnest play. It is at the same time enormously funny. This essay has dwelt largely on the seriousness of the comedy – which makes it all the more important to conclude by insisting on the extraordinary resilience of its high spirits. In the hierarchy of Stoppard's major plays, *Jumpers* is surely his most fully and brilliantly realized serious farce. The earnestness is there – but so is the comedy. And it makes a difference. The society the playwright envisages is dehumanized and grim but it is constantly being irradiated by shafts of benign laughter. No world that makes our risible muscles operate so freely can be altogether bad.

SOURCE. *'Jumpers* revisited', *Agenda*, 18–19 (Winter/Spring, 1981), pp. 135–41.

Victor Cahn   'A Reaction against Modern Man's Denial of Values' (1979)

. . . Clearly, George falls in the tradition of Stoppard's protagonists, those figures befuddled by the world and seeking some manner of counteracting its absurdity. His most important predecessor in Stoppard's work is probably Mr Moon, who sought order through historical study and literary discipline. George attempts to formulate order out of chaos through philosophical inquiry.

Much of George's ruminating is effective parody of philosophical thinking. The contemporary British philosopher A. J. Ayer has commented that the author's characterization is exceedingly funny and even affectionate. He even adds, 'This is very fine parody, and like all the best paraodies could quite often be mistaken for the original'.[1] For example,

To ask 'Is God?' appears to presuppose a Being who perhaps isn't . . . and thus is open to the same objection as the question, 'Does God exist?' . . . but until the difficulty is pointed out it does not have the same propensity to confuse language with meaning and to conjure up a God who may have any number of predicates including omniscience, perfection and four-wheel-drive but not, as it happens, existence.   [p. 24]

When these characters such as Dotty, George and the Jumpers are considered together, they seem perfectly suited to a standard absurd play and, in particular, a play by Stoppard. And when we consider, in addition, the dramatic structure of *Jumpers*, that impression is reinforced. The play is largely without plot, exposition, development and denouement. Rather it is a synchronization of events that deal with a certain group of characters. To insist on a more detailed organization would be inaccurate. Thus *Jumpers* seems to have all the characteristics of absurd drama, with the special addition that Stoppard has concretized his absurd world in the form of a university philosophy department.

Furthermore, were George's philosophical passages no more than parody, meaningless clusters of words unable to rise above the level of nonsense, the play would fit even more nicely into the absurdist format, in which rationality and communication are impossible. George's attempts at understanding his world would leave him nowhere, or at least in no better a situation than at the beginning of the play.

But such is not the case. Stoppard here is moving beyond that absurdist void, and George's extended disquisitions are a positive step out of the disjointed world of playwrights such as Beckett and Ionesco. His philosophical speeches are not simple parody; they are to be taken seriously and not just in relation to the academic and philosophical worlds. These speeches must be examined as reflective of society at large and as part of man's own contribution to the state of absurdity within which he exists.

A. J. Ayer has described the play as one with a central argument:

The argument is between those who believe in absolute values, for which they seek a religious sanction, and those, more frequently to be found among contemporary philosophers, who are subjectivists or relativists in morals, utilitarians in politics, and atheists or at least agnostics.[2]

The specific philosophical problem at the basis of George's inquiry is whether moral judgements are absolute or relative, whether their truth lies in correspondence with the facts of the world or whether they are merely personal expressions of emotion. Spokesmen for the two primary schools of thought on this issue have been G. E. Moore and A. J. Ayer.

According to Moore, goodness is an actual property possessed by things in the world. Thus if we affirm that some object is good and if, in fact, the object possesses the property of goodness, then our judgement is actually true. If we affirm that some object is good and the object does not possess the property of goodness, then our judgement is actually false. How is it known whether an object possesses the property of goodness? According to Moore, often referred to as an 'ethical intuitionist', moral truths can be known to be true 'by intuition', which is to say that their goodness is self-evident. In his book *Principia Ethica* Moore writes:

Whenever he thinks of 'intrinsic value,' or 'intrinsic worth,' or says that a thing 'ought to exist,' he has before his mind the unique object – the unique property of things – which I mean by 'good'.[3]

The opposing viewpoint has been defended by Ayer, who has argued that ethical judgements are no more than expressions of emotion:

Thus if I say to someone, 'You acted wrongly in stealing that money,' I am not stating anything more than if I had simply said 'You stole that money.' In adding that this action is wrong I am not making any further statement about it. I am simply evincing my moral disapproval of it. It is as if I had said, 'You stole that money,' in a peculiar tone of horror, or written it with the addition of some special exclamation marks. The tone, or the exclamation marks, adds nothing to the literal meaning of the sentence. It merely serves to show that the expression of it is attended by certain feelings in the speaker.[4]

The crucial aspect to this viewpoint is that, contrary to Moore's position, ethical judgements do not correspond to any facts of the world; they cannot be false or true. They are merely expressions of feeling, indicating one's own personal reaction to things in the world.

Stoppard's George Moore clearly represents the position of the philosopher G. E. Moore. George even goes so far as to indicate his plans 'to set British moral philosophy back forty years, which is roughly when it went off the rails' [p. 46]. A. J. Ayer's *Language, Truth and Logic* was published in 1936, so George's target is obvious. Perhaps the most important statement of George's philosophical commitment takes place in Act Two:

But when we say that the Good Samaritan acted well, we are surely expressing more than a circular prejudice about behaviour. We mean that he acted kindly—selflessly—*well*. And what is our approval of kindness based on if not on the intuition that kindness is simply good in itself and cruelty is not.   [p. 66]

Several characters, on the other hand, support the ethical position defended by Ayer, that known as 'emotivism'. Dotty, for instance, remarks, quoting Archie Jumper, 'Things and actions, you understand, can have any number of real and verifiable properties. But good and bad, better and worse, these are not real properties of things, they are just expressions of our feelings about them' [p. 41].

But the opponent who occupies George's thoughts for most of the play is Professor of Logic Duncan McFee, George's opponent in the upcoming annual debate on the topic of 'Man – good, bad or indifferent'. McFee is the assassinated gymnast, one learns later, but his philosophical statements, which approximate the ideas of

Ayer, are the ones George works hardest to counteract.

The essential predicament which confronts George is made clear at the beginning of a dictation to his secretary, when, reflecting on the nature of God, he comments. 'There is presumably a calendar date – *a moment* – when the onus of proof passed from the atheist to the believer, when, quite suddenly, secretly, the noes had it' [p. 25]. With some desperation he consistently tries to affirm belief in God, but he always concludes by relying on the first-cause argument, which, as Ayer explains, 'is notoriously fallacious, since it starts from the assumption that everything must have a cause and ends with something that lacks one'.[5] By the end of the play George is still insisting, though he has been unable to formulate specific proof:

I don't claim to *know* that God exists, I only claim that he does without my knowing it, and while I claim as much I do not claim to know as much; indeed I cannot know and God knows I cannot.   [p. 71]

Again he must resort to 'intuition'. Something innate within him tells him God exists, and that is what he believes.

Ultimately all George's beliefs rest on a faith that cannot be proven. He relies on something indefinable within him that makes him human, that offers him values of ethical, religious and aesthetic order.

Despite the nobility of George's intentions, he is, like all of Stoppard's protagonists, from time to time a comic figure. He is described as the classic caricature of a professor: 'flannels and shabby smoking jacket, hair awry, his expression and manner signifying remonstrance' [p. 19]. But even his philosophical arguments are somewhat confused. Most apparent is his reliance on the dubious first-cause argument. In addition, he manages to confuse two of Zeno's paradoxes with a fable of Aesop. The first paradox is 'Achilles and the Tortoise':

Imagine that Achilles, the fleetest of Greek warriors, is to run a footrace against a tortoise. It is only fair to give the tortoise a headstart. Under these circumstances, Zeno argues, Achilles can never catch up with the tortoise no matter how fast he runs . . . whenever Achilles arrives at a point where the tortoise *was*, the tortoise moves a bit ahead.[6]

The other paradox is 'The Arrow':

In this paradox, Zeno argues that an arrow in flight is always at rest. At any given instant, he claims, the arrow is where it is, occupying a portion of space equal to itself. During the instant it cannot move, for that would require the instant to have parts, and an instant is by *definition* a minimal and indivisible element of time. If the arrow did move during the instant it would have to be in one place at one part of the instant and in a different place at another part of the instant.[7]

George confuses these two paradoxes with Aesop's fable about the tortoise racing the hare. He even acquires a bow and arrow and a tortoise and a hare to bring to the proposed debate, in order to demonstrate that, indeed, the hare would win the race and that the arrow would reach its target.

In Ayer's words, 'What finally happens to the hare and the tortoise is the most moving moment of the play.'[8] But the moment has been properly set up by the preceding action. For two acts we have seen George struggling with his own mind against impersonal philosophical and religious forces that constantly confound him. He has been deserted by his wife and hounded by Inspector Bones, who suspects him of murdering Duncan McFee. Violence has broken out on all sides. The world seems to be exploding. Throughout he has been searching for the hare, who has disappeared and to whom George has grown quite attached, bestowing on him the nickname 'Thumper'. And we remember that earlier in the play George fired his arrow into the air and that it disappeared over his closet.

Thus, toward the end of the play, still searching for Thumper, George notices a spot of blood on his secretary's coat and realizes it must have come from on top of the wardrobe. He reaches upward and finds Thumper impaled on the arrow. As he steps down off the chair, he crushes the pet turtle with his foot.

The impact of this moment is many-sided. The sensation is, at first, horrific at the shock of sudden death; tragic, in the light of the loss of two creatures with whom we had become so well acquainted; even comic, at George's clumsiness and helplessness as he attempts to bring order to his world. The audience scarcely knows whether to scream, cry or laugh.

The crisis George faces is captured in the last speech of the play, offered by Archie Jumper at the symposium we have anticipated throughout. The event is presented more in the form of a trial run by a dictatorial government than as a free and open debate, and George's pleas for order and rationality are thrown aside amid songs and irrelevant questions. Finally George shouts for attention, and everyone freezes, but as he tries to articulate the values that he believes the world should hold, Jumper interrupts to insist on the values that the world does hold:

Do not despair – many are happy much of the time; more eat than starve, more are healthy than sick, more curable than dying; not so many dying as dead; and one of the thieves was saved. . . . millions of children grow up without suffering deprivation, and millions while deprived, grow up without suffering cruelties, and millions, while deprived and cruelly treated, none the less grow up. . . . Wham, bam, thank you, Sam.   [pp. 88–9]

The key to the speech is the last word. 'Sam' refers to Samuel
Beckett, and the phrase about 'one of the thieves' refers . . . to a
well-known statement made by Beckett:

There is a wonderful sentence in Augustine. I wish I could remember the Latin. It
is even finer in Latin than English. 'Do not despair: one of the thieves was saved.
Do not presume: one of the thieves was damned.'

Archie's exhortation is at its core an acceptance of the state of
the world, a reconciliation with the state of absurdity that Beckett
had dramatized. Jumper urges us to see only the good in life, as
there is little use in dwelling on the negative. His speech is a poetic,
nonphilosophical version of the emotivist argument that George
has been opposing throughout the play. Dramatic absurdity and
philosophical argument are thus tied together, and the union
reinforces the most crucial theme of the play: that mankind is not
simply a passive victim in this world but can be an active participant.

On the one hand, we are presented with the philosophic thrust of
the emotivists, McFee and Jumper, the view that goodness, truth,
and beauty are but personal prejudices. Under such conditions man
is condemned to react to stimuli, to decide which are pleasant and
which are unpleasant, and to continue in the direction of the
pleasant. He can ignore death, destruction, immorality. Man is thus
without responsibility. He denies himself reason, sympathy, and
understanding, everything that makes him human.

Stoppard, through George, is protesting such a world vision. Just
as the critics's dilemma in *The Real Inspector Hound* should not be
limited to members of that profession, so George's arguments should
not be directed simply to members of philosophy departments, nor
even just to intellectuals. Rather the play is a reaction against
modern man's denial of all values and a reaffirmation of the belief
that something within us makes us human, something which makes
us believe in goodness and beauty. And that something must never
be dismissed or forgotten.

To be sure, despite this play's intellectual interest and its place
as a turning point in Stoppard's career, it is not wholly successful
as drama. . . . George's long monologues, amusing and stimulating
though they may be, are not dramatic. And the audience is forced
to spend too much time pondering strictly academic philosophical
subtleties.

Granted these limitations on the play, it nevertheless remains
fascinating and important. For in this work Stoppard deals with
intellectual issues, and reasoned argument is an integral component
of the play. Such strategy marks a total break with absurdist writing,
in which language, communication, and, consequently, rational

debate have been impossible. In what stands as his boldest step in moving beyond absurdity, Stoppard dispenses with this limitation of human activity, and he begins to confront world issues directly. The difficulty of life on earth is now accepted. What matters here and in the plays to follow is how to live under those conditions.

SOURCE: extract from *Beyond Absurdity* (Rutherford, N.J., 1979), excerpted from pp. 116–24.

NOTES

1. A. J. Ayer, 'Love Among the Logical Positivists', *Sunday Times* (9 April 1972), p. 16.
2. Ibid.
3. G. E. Moore, *Principia Ethica* (Cambridge 1903; reissued Cambridge, 1980), p. 17.
4. A. J. Ayer, *Language, Truth and Logic* (London, 1936; reissued London, and New York, 1946), p. 107.
5. Ayer, 'Love Among the Logical Positivists', p. 16.
6. Wesley C. Salmon (ed.), *Zeno's Paradoxes* (New York, 1970), pp. 8–9.
7. Ibid, pp. 10–11.
8. Ayer, 'Love Among the Logical Positivists', p. 16.

G. B. Crump　　'Dorothy's Plight'　(1979)

. . . Dorothy plays a special role in the murder investigation. Although at times she herself expresses a pragmatic philosophy of sorts – 'Here is my consistent proposition / Two and two make roughly four' [p. 86] – Dorothy is chiefly concerned with the consequences of the murder rather than its solution and therefore must be distinguished from the three philosopher-detectives. Moreover, she forms the centre of emotional interest for the men. For these reasons, Dorothy occupies a unique position in the play's structure. In one sense, she represents man's nature uncomplicated and unrefined by intellect, his emotions and appetites; she is an entertainer and spends most of the play in the bedroom, a place of sleep, sexual intercourse and luncheon trays. Dorothy has been psychologically traumatized by the triumph of rationalistic material-ism in the modern world, epitomized by the ascendancy of logical positivism in philosophy and radical-liberalism in politics and by technological achievements such as moon landings. A symptom of the trauma is her loss of the ability to croon romantic songs about the moon after man's lunar landing destroyed the planet's aura of poetry and romance. Her collapse into insanity signifies the persistence of emotional and spiritual needs which seem irrational viewed from a 'sane' and materialistic perspective. She longs for something incredible rather than the 'credible and all too bloody likely' acrobatics of the jumpers [p. 20]. She wants to believe in God, the soul, or right and wrong, absolutes incredible to the philosophically up-to-date jumpers, who accept as credible only what is verifiable.

Dorothy's plight, symbolized by her need to dispose of McFee's body, corresponds to that of modern man, caught with life and death on his hands and in need of a reason for continuing to function in a grim and chaotic world from which the spiritual consolations of the past have been withdrawn. The moments of most intense feeling in the play are those in which she pleads for the emotional support that might make life worth living. Her involvements with George, Bones and Archie betoken three types of personal relations from which one might extract such support and also three stages in the historical development of the relationship between man and woman. George offers traditional married love, involving physical and emotional connection and a fair amount of realism about one's partner. Bones's idealistic love is callow and romantic in the nineteenth-century style, while Archie offers a crassly physical relationship of the modern type. All the men fail Dorothy in varying degrees, both as lovers and as philosopher-detectives trying to give her a convincing and sustaining picture of reality.

Dorothy, along with the secretary, also forms part of the puzzling reality the men strive to interpret. Both women play scenes in the nude; a metaphor for the *ding an sich*, this physical exposure hides more than it reveals. Stoppard invests the women with an air of engima which, like the world, defies male ratiocination. The opening scene makes this point in a parable: all the party guests but Crouch are aware of the secretary's striptease, but each time he turns her way, she has just swung her trapeze into the darkness. Elsewhere in the play the secretary is stolid and *'poker-faced'* [p. 14], never speaking and registering little emotion. The conclusions of Bones and George that Dorothy is a murderess are never verified, and the play leaves unanswered questions about her relations with the three leading men. It is not clear, as George himself says, 'what on earth made *her* marry *him*' [p. 35], or whether Dorothy's charge of rape against Bones is true or concocted in order to blackmail him. Although the available evidence suggests the hypothesis that Dorothy is having an affair with Archie, the same evidence could conceivably support her explanation that Archie is her psychiatrist. As the anecdote about Wittgenstein's comment on the rotation of the earth shows [p. 75], a single observed fact may have more than one possible explanation, and the most obvious is not necessarily correct. Faced with such ambiguity, George asks the question the entire play poses: 'How the hell does one know what to believe?' [p. 71].

The answer Inspector Bones gives to that question represents that of the man on the street, for he embodies the intellectual processes of ordinary people while Dorothy expresses their emotional need . . .

SOURCE: extract from essay, 'The Universe as Murder Mystery: *Jumpers*', *Contemporary Literature* xx, iii (1979), pp. 359–61.

J. A. Bailey   'The Importance of McFee' (1979)

. . . The plot of *Jumpers* hinges on McFee, the Jumper who is killed at the beginning. It is only after he is dead that we learn about him, first from George and then from Crouch, who alone knew him well enough to understand the significance of his life. McFee as a pragmatist held a position within the spectrum of philosophical views currently acceptable and therefore open to a Jumper; indeed, Archie calls him [p. 63] the 'guardian and figurehead of philosophical orthodoxy'. Originally, therefore, he is parallel to Archie, at least a member of his team. But the doings on the moon affected him, Crouch says after his death, as deeply as they did Dotty; in this he is parallel to her. According to Crouch, he contrasted the selfish act of Scott with the altruistic behavior of Captain Oates who on an expedition to the South Pole led by another Scott in 1912 sacrificed his life to give his companions a chance of survival. (Note that the name of this man who died for others is the same as that of the man who has just been left to die an unwilling victim of – or sacrifice to – Scott's selfishness on the moon. The two men are not the same, but their deaths are variations on a single theme. So too the lunar Scott, who saves himself but only at the cost of morality, has the same name as the heroic leader of the 1912 expedition who perished.) McFee, struck by the contrast between the altruism of the past deed (for which his philosophy left no room) and the moral cowardice of the present one, suddenly threw over his position and decided to become a monk. Like Dotty he was haunted by the men on the moon, but unlike her he is able to take a positive step as a result, and so becomes parallel to George, though hardly fully so. For George's life, fired by philosophical passion in the defence of the existence of good but pretty much devoid of good in the sense of selfishness, is a far cry from that of a monk.

But – one of the many ironies in *Jumpers* – the last word as regards McFee is ironic. Hoping to live his life for others in a monastery, he lost it – senselessly? – at the hands of an unknown killer. Archie, before Crouch tells him of Archie's conversion and the reason for it, tells [p. 63] the inspector that had McFee done just what in fact he did do ('decided that he was St Paul to Moore's Messiah'), he himself in the cause of philosophical orthodoxy would have killed him. After the fact he turned out to have a reason for killing McFee such as Dotty never had. Yet he cannot have known this when McFee was killed, unless (which is conceivable) he already knew what Crouch told him – though there is no other indication in the play that he did so, and it is exceedingly unlikely. Was Archie nevertheless responsible? Did, in this case, the crime not follow the motive for it but rather produce in its wake the motive? Was the motive not cause but effect? This is the kind of surrealistic twist with which Stoppard's plays are laden, often (as also in the case of *The Real Inspector Hound*) in connection with a whodunit plot. (One is reminded of the work of Nabokov, Stoppard's fellow Eastern European. Stoppard, whose name originally was Straussler, was born in Czechoslovakia in 1937, left when he was two, lived in Singapore and India and arrived in England in 1946.) McFee, in dying, may have been a martyr, in which case he was parallel to the archbishop. . . .

Source: extract from essay, '*Jumpers*: The Ironist as Theistic Apologist', *Michigan Acadamician*, XI (1979), pp. 241–2.

Ronald Hayman   'Architectonic Virtuosity'   (1982)

. . . Only a passionate lover of wordplay would have written the two lines in *Rosencrantz and Guildenstern* which was to become the germ of *Jumpers*:

– Shouldn't we be doing something constructive?
– What did you have in mind? . . . A short, blunt human pyramid. . . ?   [p. 30]

Starting from a narrow base, Stoppard uses puns to cantilever
out into the metaphysical void. In becoming more intricate, his
architecture annexes more space. *Jumpers* is, by any standards, an
extremely big play. Wanting to write about a moral philosopher
and seeing the verbal connection between mental acrobatics and the
pyramid of acrobats – unless they are acrobats it will be too short
and blunt – Stoppard seems to have found that the multiple meanings
of the word *jump* helped him to evolve his blueprint.

The audience's first encounter with the word comes near the
beginning, when Archie's voice announces 'And now! – ladies and
gentlemen! – the INCREDIBLE – RADICAL! – LIBERAL!! – JUMPERS!!' and
four of them come on from either side of the stage, jumping, tumbling
and somersaulting. Already coupled with the name of a political
party, the word soon acquires an overtone of expediency. Dotty –
the counterpart of Penelope in *Another Moon Called Earth* – drunkenly
orders them to jump when she says jump; the one character in the
play who will not 'jump along with the rest' is George, who is
stubbornly, unfashionably, a deist in the materialistic university
which serves as a microcosm for the new society. He is temperamentally incapable of 'jumping through the Vice-Chancellor's hoop'. In
the second act we find out that the surname of Sir Archibald, the
Vice-Chancellor, is Jumper, and when he refuses to let George
succeed the murdered McFee into the Chair of Logic, he says he
needs 'someone with a bit of bounce'. By the end of the play we
have been persuaded to associate the word *jump* with Kierkegaard's
leap to faith. George says:

The fact that I cut a ludicrous figure in the academic world is largely due to my
aptitude for traducing a complex and logical thesis to a mysticism of staggering
banality. McFee never made that mistake, never put himself at risk by finding
mystery in the clockwork, never looked for trouble or over his shoulder, and I'm
sorry he's gone but what can be his complaint? McFee jumped, and left nothing
behind but a vacancy.   [p. 72]

All these proliferations of *jump* are new, but much of the basic
material is developed from *Lord Malquist and Mr Moon* and *Another
Moon Called Earth*, with some drawn from *Albert's Bridge* and some
from *After Magritte*. If it is not already clear that I approve of
Stoppard's self-plagiarism, let me make it clear now. The advantage
of returning to areas that have already been explored is that one
has learnt which routes lead most directly to the points of interest.
Even in territory which is not autobiographical, there is always an
excitement in exploring. Strongly self-disciplined though he is,
Stoppard is liable to become over-excited on his first expedition: the
idea is then over-elaborated. In the television play *Another Moon*

Called Earth, as in the novel *Lord Malquist and Mr Moon*, charades
are used as a camouflage by the wife who seems to be deceiving her
husband. The sequences are highly entertaining, but the charades
of *Jumpers* make their points more economically and more casually.
The argument between George and Dotty is not interrupted when
she takes the goldfish into the bathroom, returning with its empty
bowl over her head as she imitates the leaded-footed gait of a
moonwalker. Her pretence of picking up a small coin gives George
the clue he needs and he interpolates the answer – 'The Moon and
Sixpence' – into his monologue without even pausing.

Like the millionaire who put only coin telephones at the disposal
of his house guests, Stoppard's plays grow richer by economizing
and economize more as they grow richer. It is characteristic of him
not to waste the goldfish. An hour later, George returns from the
bathroom, full of righteous indignation, the fish dead in his hands:
'You murderous *bitch*! . . . You might have put some water in the
bath!' The phrase has two layers of meaning because it seems she
may have murdered Professor McFee, the empiricist who has been
shot out of the acrobatic pyramid. And if Stoppard refuses to
characterize Dotty consistently as a musical-comedy actress, one
reason is that it would be uneconomical not to arm her with the wit
she needs for intellectual combat with George.

DOTTY: Don't you dare splash me with your sentimental rhetoric! It's a bloody
   goldfish! Do you think every sole meunière comes to you untouched by suffering?
GEORGE: The monk who won't walk in the garden for fear of treading on an ant does
   not have to be a vegetarian . . . There is an irrational difference which has a
   rational value.
DOTTY: Brilliant! You must publish your findings in some suitable place like the *Good
   Food Guide*.
GEORGE: No doubt your rebuttal would look well in the *Meccano Magazine*.
DOTTY: You bloody humbug! – the last of the metaphysical egocentrics! You're
   probably still shaking from the four-hundred-year-old news that the sun doesn't
   go round *you*!
                                                                    [p. 74]

In developing his architectonic virtuosity Stoppard has refined
his capacity for accommodating both halves of a contradiction. Part
of the appeal that puns have for him may lie in the means they
provide of coupling the unrelated meanings of a single sound, but
few of his conceits remain merely verbal. There are puns in George's
monologues when he reminisces about the punctuality of his late
friend Bertrand Russell, and theology and ethics are described as
two subjects without an object. But the pun becomes more like a
jump-cut in a film, when George, having ignored Dotty's gambit

(modelled on Penelope's) of shouting, 'Murder – Rape – Wolves!' prematurely shoots the arrow from his bow when she shouts 'Fire!' There are also the visual puns of her charades: lying nude and apparently lifeless on the bed, she is *The Naked and the Dead*; a vertical view of her naked back later prompts the guess '*Lulu's* back! – in town'.

One of Stoppard's greatest talents is for profiting from experience. Each new play has been an exercise, both in the sense of testing how far he can go and in the sense of giving himself practice that develops his muscles for future performance. Coming after he had taught himself to write for radio, the achievement of *Dogg's Our Pet* gave him new insight into the possibilities of making words and actions mutually independent. To employ both in the same statement may be extravagant; the playwright may be able to economize not only by giving dialogue a double meaning but by saying something separate and perhaps contradictory with the accompanying action.

Not that Stoppard is ungenerous or incapable of extravagance when it serves a purpose. In contrast to the calculated monotony of the coin-tossing sequence at the beginning of *Rosencrantz and Guildenstern*, the opening of *Jumpers* is spectacularly spendthrift. Dotty is given an upbeat introduction as if she is about to sing, and there is the immediate anti-climax of her failure. There is the striptease performed by the poker-faced Secretary on a swing hanging from a chandelier. There is the vaudeville-type comedy of the porter's appearance with a tray of drinks, wandering innocently towards the point at which he will be knocked over. There is the circus-type performance of the Jumpers, tumbling and somersaulting. There is the first rumble of marital conflict when George protests at the noise, and the first indication that Dotty is on the verge of a mental breakdown – both implicitly promising dramatic tension. Then there is the murder. With the acrobats standing on each other's shoulders in three-two-one formation, a shot rings out. A man in the bottom row falls dead. Dotty walks through the gap in the pyramid. The dying man pulls himself up against her legs, shedding blood on her billowy white dress. The pyramid collapses. It is almost as if Stoppard were taking excessive precautions against the possibility that his play would be condemned as wordy and boring. . . .

Nothing is harder for the serious critic to forgive than jokiness, but Stoppard's jokiness should be viewed against the perspective provided by James Joyce, Samuel Beckett and Modernist painting. For Joyce the pun was sometimes a self-indulgence, sometimes a means of bridging between conscious and unconscious memories. In *Ulysses*, as in Beckett's earlier novels, the most serious philosophical and theological problems are broached with a fruitful mixture of self-conscious literariness, literary self-consciousness and exuberant flippancy. Joyce is reported to have said of *Ulysses*: 'On the honour of a gentleman there is not a serious line in it'. But no one today would argue that the incessant joking makes the book unimportant, though it could be objected (as it could with Stoppard's plays) that the ingenuity of the pattern-making claims an unfair share of the creative energy.

Stoppard could hardly be accused (as Joyce has been, by Harry Levin) of equating language with experience, but they are both open to attack from the argument that structural intricacy camouflages a philosophical void. One of the main filters through which Joyce's influence passes into Stoppard's work is Beckett's fiction, especially *Murphy*, his first full-length novel. Murphy's mind

pictured itself as a large hollow sphere hermetically closed to the universe without . . . He neither thought a kick because he felt one nor felt a kick because he thought one . . . Perhaps there was, outside space and time, a non-mental non-physical Kick from all eternity, dimly revealed to Murphy in its correlated modes of consciousness and extension, the kick *in intellectu* and the kick *in re*. But where then was the supreme Caress?

Stoppard's recurrent Moon character is 'more kicked against than kicking'.

Stephen's stream of consciousness in *Ulysses* ripples along with the same mixture of wry hopelessness and triumphant word-spinning erudition in the involuntary attempt to explain the inexplicable relationship between the individual consciousness and the constants of the cosmos and of human reproduction:

Wombed in sin darkness I was too, made not begotten. By them, the man with my voice and my eyes and a ghost-woman with ashes on her breath. They clasped and sundered, did the coupler's will. From before the ages He willed me and now may not will me away or ever. A *lex eterna* stays about him. Is that then the divine substance wherein Father and Son are consubstantial? Where is poor dear Arius to try conclusions? Warring his life long on the contransmagnificandjewbangstantiality. Illstarred heresiarch. In a Greek watercloset he breathed his last: euthanasia.

While Rosencrantz's and Guildenstern's comic attempts to solve the cosmic riddles may be more reminiscent of Vladimir's and Estragon's, George Moore's derive more directly from the Joycean voice of Stephen. Stoppard has succeeded magnificently in canalizing the stream of highly educated consciousness into hilarious theatricality:

To begin at the beginning: is God? (*Pause*) I prefer to put the question in this form because to ask, 'Does God exist?' appears to presuppose the existence of a God who may not, and I do not propose this late evening to follow my friend Russell, this

evening to follow my late friend Russell, to follow my good friend the late Lord
Russell, *(He ponders a moment)* To ask, 'Is God?' appears to presuppose a Being who
perhaps isn't . . . and thus is open to the same objection as the question, 'Does God
exist?' . . . but until the difficulty is pointed out it does not have the propensity to
confuse language with meaning and to conjure up a God who may have any number
of predicates including omniscience, perfection and four-wheel-drive but not, as it
happens, existence. This confusion, which indicates only that language is an
approximation of meaning and not a logical symbolism for it, began with Plato and
was not ended by Bertrand Russell's theory that existence could only be asserted of
descriptions and not of individuals, but I do not propose this evening to follow into
the Theory of Descriptions my very old friend – now dead, of course – ach! – to
follow into the Theory of Descriptions, the late Lord Russell –!
                    (He continues smoothly, improvising off-script)

if I may so refer to an old friend for whom punctuality was no less a predicate than
existence, and a good deal more so, he would have had us believe, though why we
should believe that existence could be asserted of the author of 'Principia Mathemat-
ica' but not of Bertrand Russell, he never had time, despite his punctuality, not to
mention his existence, to explain, very good, keep to the point, to begin at the
beginning: *is God?*
                    (To SECRETARY*)* Leave a space.   [pp. 24–5]

The puns are more functional than Joyce's because they contribute
more to the structure. They also buoy the performance of the speech
on waves of laughter.

George's interest in the Greek philosopher Zeno may derive from
Beckett's. Zeno used the example of a heap of millet to argue that
movements in space and time are discontinuous with reality, the
essence of reality being infinity. If you pour half a sack of millet into
a heap, and then add half of what's left in the sack, and then go on
adding half of what's left in the sack, you will never empty it,
because you are moving in space and time. In infinity, all the grains
would pass from the sack to the heap. In *Endgame* the implication
for Hamm is that however long you go on living, the minutes never
add up to a life because the end is always ahead of you. Zeno also
argued that an arrow in flight is always at rest since, at any given
moment, it is where it is. His ambition was to prove that there could
be no such thing as change: there are things but no changes.
The rival argument – championed by both Heraclitus and Henri
Bergson – is that there are changes but no things. The chapter on
Bergson in Bertrand Russell's *History of Western Philosophy* introduces
St Sebastian to illustrate the difference between the two attitudes.
According to the 'static' school he is killed by the arrow; according
to the 'dynamic' school by its flight. Stoppard lets George suggest
that the saint died of fright.

The confusion of the argument about Achilles and the tortoise
with the fable about the tortoise and the hare is quite fruitful.

Together with George's illustrative bow and arrow, a tortoise and a
hare are introduced into the action. Like most elements in a
Stoppardian structure, they are used in several ways: both become
prominent in the multi-layered theatrical jokes. It is the death of
the tortoise which provides one of the main comic climaxes.
Distressed at his long-delayed discovery that he has killed the hare
by shooting the arrow, George steps backwards onto the tortoise.
The disappearance of the hare, Thumper, has created a minor
mystery that has run through the plot, interwoven with the mystery
of McFee's murder by some fine comedy of misunderstanding.
When, in George's hearing, Archie praises the casserole he is sharing
with Dotty, she replies, 'It's not casseroled. It's jugged.' After the
affair of the goldfish there is only one conclusion George can draw,
and when the porter, Crouch, comes in, he is talking about McFee
while George is talking about Thumper:

GEORGE: Who killed him?
CROUCH: Well, I wouldn't like to say for certain . . . I mean, I heard a bang, and
    when I looked, there he was crawling on the floor. . .
    (GEORGE *winces*)
    . . . and there was Miss Moore . . . well –
GEORGE: Do you realize she's in there now, *eating* him?
CROUCH (*pause*): You mean – *raw*?
GEORGE (*crossly*): No, of course not! – *cooked* – with gravy and mashed potatoes.
CROUCH (*pause*): I thought she was on the mend, sir.
GEORGE: Do you think I'm being too sentimental about the whole thing?
CROUCH: (*firmly*): I do not, sir.   [pp. 76–7]

Apart from her premature retirement, Dotty gives no sign of
wanting to withdraw from contact with humanity, but her instability
is a continuation from that of characters in Stoppard's earlier plays.
In his most solipsistic moments, the Albert of *Albert's Bridge* was in
the habit of crooning to himself and muddling one lyric with another:

> 'cos there'll be pennies fall on Alabama
> and you'll drown in foggy London town
> the sun was shi-ning . . . on my Yiddisher Mama.

Dotty's confusions are more pointedly limited to moon songs, and,
like Penelope in *Another Moon Called Earth*, she lost her perspective
when the astronauts landed on the moon. Penelope retired to her
bed; Dotty retired.

They thought it was overwork or alcohol, but it was just those little grey men in
goldfish bowls, clumping about in their lead boots on the television news; it was very
interesting, but it certainly spoiled that Juney old moon; and much else besides.
                                                                              [p. 39]

Her main disorientation speech draws on Penelope's, but it is stronger and more resonant, partly because Dotty has been more fully characterized, and partly because her cosmic disenchantment is complementary to George's stubborn theism:

> Not only are we no longer the still centre of God's universe, we're not even uniquely graced by his footprint in man's image. . . Man is on the Moon, his feet on solid ground, and he has seen us whole, all in one go, *little – local* . . . and all our absolutes, the thou-shalts and the thou-shalt-nots that seemed to be the very condition of our existence, how did they look to two moonmen with a single neck to save between them? Like the local customs of another place. When that thought drips through to the bottom, people won't just carry on. There is going to be such . . . breakage, such gnashing of unclean meats, such coveting of neighbours' oxen and knowing of neighbours' wives, such dishonourings of mothers and fathers, and bowings and scrapings to images graven and incarnate, such killing of goldfish and maybe more – *(Looks up, tear-stained)* Because the truths that have been taken on trust, they've never had edges before, there was no vantage point to stand on and see where they stopped. *(And weeps.)* [p. 75]

After George has expounded McFee's philosophy that there is no absolute or metaphysical sense in which telling the truth is 'good' and casual murder is 'bad', we hear Dotty trying to put his murder into perspective: 'It's not as though the alternative were immortality.'

Meanwhile the old Stoppardian theme of the credulous husband is being given a new dimension of serious interest by the comic investigation of how it is possible for us to believe anything:

> How does one know what it is one believes when it's so difficult to know what it is one knows? I don't claim to *know* that God exists, I only claim that he does without my knowing it, and while I claim as much I do not claim to know as much; indeed I cannot know and God knows I cannot. [p. 71]

Later he says 'There are many things I know which are not verifiable but nobody can tell me I don't know them'.

Alongside this good-humoured philosophical sabotage, Stoppard is sharpening his parody of the thriller to the point where there almost seems to be a metaphysical resonance even in the characterization of a policeman as corruptible and seducible. If everyone can be persuaded to distort or overlook the facts about past events, do they still have any solid existence or any meaning? Inspector Bones is an autograph-collecting Dotty-fan with one foot in *After Magritte* and the other in *The Real Inspector Hound*. Her romantic reception of him is like an episode from the play-within-the-play:

> *In front of the Bedroom door, he briefly smooths his hair, brushes his lapels with his hands, brings out the gramaphone record (which has a picture of* DOTTY *on it), and knocks on the Bedroom door, a mere tap, and enters the Bedroom. The light is romantic: pink curtains have been drawn across the french window and there is a rosy hue to the lighting.* DOTTY, *gowned, coiffed, stunning,*

rises to face the Inspector. Music is heard . . . romantic Mozartian trumpets, triumphant. DOTTY
and BONES *face each other, frozen like lovers in a dream.* BONES *raises his head slightly, and the
trumpets are succeeded by a loud animal bray, a mating call.* DOTTY, *her arms out towards him,
breathes, 'Inspector. . .' like a verbal caress. From* BONES'S *lifeless fingers, the vase drops. There
is a noise such as would have been made had he dropped it down a long flight of stone stairs.*

[p. 52]

Just as words can be made to register separately from the accompanying actions, actions can be made to register separately from the
accompanying sound effects, creating a mystery which will be
resolved by a subsequent development. George has simultaneously
been rehearsing an illustration he has prepared for his lecture. The
tape-recording contrasts beautiful Mozartian trumpet music with
the trumpeting of an elephant and the noise made by a trumpet
falling downstairs. Stoppard's joke is essentially theatrical: its effect
depends on the progressive reaction of an audience. There is also
some self-indulgent pattern-making in the play, like the allusion to
After Magritte when Inspector Bones makes his first entrance: George
is holding a tortoise in one hand and his face is covered in shaving
foam. But most reprises of earlier themes are more rewarding for
the audience. The point Stoppard made about unicorns in *Rosencrantz
and Guildenstern* is developed into something much more interesting
during one of Dotty's speeches about astronauts;

When they first landed, it was as though I'd seen a unicorn on the television news
. . . It was very interesting, of course. But it certainly spoiled unicorns. *(Pause)* I
tried to explain it to the analyst . . . I should never have mentioned unicorns to a
Freudian.   [p. 38]

It would be a mistake to end this chapter without stressing the
pathos of the human situation in *Jumpers*. It is an oceanic play with
a glistening surface and chillingly profound undercurrents, but
bobbing stubbornly about, like survivors clinging to the driftwood
of a shipwrecked culture, are Dotty and George. Stoppard gives us
a lively and sympathetic impression of their personal needs. When
they reach out towards each other, they fail to make contact; when
they reach out elsewhere, they are pathetic, especially George, with
his old-fashioned scruples about ethics and language. Like a more
articulate and logical Lucky, he struggles for semantic clarity as he
tries to reason his way backwards towards a First Cause, but he is
deriving his values and his words from a system which is disintegrating. Traditional ethics cannot survive in a universe where quarrelsome jumpers can land on the moon, churches are converted
to gymnasiums, an agnostic agriculturalist is appointed by the
government as Archbishop of Canterbury and the police can be
persuaded to connive at murder.

SOURCE: extract from *Tom Stoppard*, 4th edn (London 1982), pp. 97–109.

Richard Corballis   'Scientism versus Faith in Intuition'   (1984)

. . . The action is divided into two acts and a coda, but it seems reasonable to regard the party scene at the beginning of Act One as a fourth part – a typically Stoppardian prelude. It contains the event from which the Bones subplot develops: the shooting of McFee. (In the National Theatre production George, posing as Spinoza, was seen to make the telephone call of complaint to the police which also assumes some importance in the subplot. This is not described in the published texts.) More important, the prelude features a series of tableaux that introduce in graphic terms the thematic antinomy which underlies the main action. First of all we get in juxtaposition a characteristically glib speech from Archie, acting for the moment as Master of Ceremonies at Dotty's party, and an equally characteristic snatch of incoherent song from Dotty. This contrast will turn out to be of crucial significance but at this stage the audience is unlikely to appreciate its importance if only because Archie is as yet unseen. It is the simpler and more spectacular encounter between Crouch and the Secretary that makes the first real assault upon our faculties. The poker-faced Secretary performs a strip-tease on a swing, which moves like a pendulum in and out of the spotlight. She seems to symbolize the austere logic, the 'mental acrobatics' . . . the 'clockwork' – notice the image of the pendulum – of Archie, the Jumpers and the Radical Liberal Party to which they all belong. She turns out in fact to be the mistress of McFee, one of the Jumpers. And the nod which she directs at Archie when he first appears may indicate that she is in cahoots with him. Poor bewildered Crouch, the porter-turned-waiter, strays into the path of the swing unwittingly and is knocked over. His bewilderment anticipates the confusion experienced by Dotty, as she strives to retain her instinctive sense of mystery and romance, and to a lesser extent by George, as he strives, like Anderson in *Professional Foul*, to justify his instinctive sense of moral rectitude. And the physical crash which finally befalls Crouch prefigures Dotty's mental breakdown, as well as the demise of Pat and Thumper.

The second tableau, which is again vividly theatrical, juxtaposes Dotty and the Jumpers. Though they are not especially talented – a qualification which suggests by analogy the shortcomings of Archie's rationalism – the Jumpers perform well enough to convince Dotty that she cannot, as she at first claimed, sing better than they can jump. In fact at this stage of the play they are even capable of defying gravity for a few seconds by keeping their human pyramid intact after the shooting of McFee, one of the three Jumpers at the base of the structure. Once again we are prepared analogically for the triumph of Archie's reason over Dotty's romance.

Once these tableaux have been completed, Acts One and Two proceed to depict events in the Moore household on the morning after the party. The significance of these events is best conveyed by successive analyses of the roles of the three principals. And although he is actually the last of the three to appear, we shall look first at Archie.

Sir Archibald Jumper, M.D., D.Phil., D.Litt., L.D., D.P.M., D.P.T. (Gym.) embodies the spirit of the Radical Liberal Party which has just come to power in a general election. The Party is dedicated to rationalism, or scientism as George calls it. This attitude is epitomized by their plan to rationalize the Church. Already the Radical Liberal spokesman for Agriculture has been made Archbishop of Canterbury and an unspecified building containing magnificent stained glass has been converted into a gymnasium. Archie himself, as his qualifications suggest, is something of a Renaissance Man; he has expertise in an impossibly wide range of fields that has been acquired by dedication to rational inquiry. This same dedication causes him and his colleagues to associate themselves with classical Greece and with 'the Athens of the North', Edinburgh. Archie's dedication to reason has led him, like A. J. Ayer, whom some regard as his real-life prototype, to embrace an extreme form of positivism, which Dotty defines thus:

> Things do not *seem*, on the one hand, they *are*; and on the other hand, bad is not what they can *be*. They can be green, or square, or Japanese, loud, fatal, waterproof or vanilla-flavoured; and the same for actions, which can be *disapproved of*, or comical, unexpected, saddening or good television, variously, depending on who frowns, laughs, jumps, weeps or wouldn't have missed it for the world. Things and actions, you understand, can have any number of real and verifiable properties. But good and bad, better and worse, these are not real properties of things, they are just expressions of our feelings about them.   [p. 41]

Archie is capable of defending his position in glib and plausible terms but the play is at pains to point out that, at best, his interpretation of things is only skin-deep, like the superficial posturings of the Jumpers, and that, at worst – and this is what makes him a more disturbing character than Lord Malquist – this lack of depth can lead to tyranny after the manner of Henry II and Richard III or Hitler, Stalin or Nero or sundry military dictators of recent times.

Archie's shallowness is indicated in all sorts of ways, for instance by the fact that he needs only two minutes to prepare a philosophical paper. But it is the introduction of the dermatograph which demonstrates most forcibly that his scientism is, quite literally, only skin-deep. The machine is trundled on to the stage at the end of the first act and set in operation at the end of the second. Archie describes its function early in Act Two:

It reads the skin, electronically; hence dermatograph. . . . All kinds of disturbances under the skin show up on the surface. . .

In the first (1972) edition of the play Stoppard insists that the dermatograph is still ambiguous, that there is a hint of erotic obsession as well as a genuine interest in medical research about Archie's close analysis of Dotty's skin. That this stage direction is cut from the second (1973) edition makes it all the more clear that Archie's eroticism, if it exists at all, is only skin-deep compared to George's. The knowledge to which George aspires includes 'knowing in the biblical sense of screwing', although he has been hampered latterly by the fact that, as he wistfully puts it, Dotty 'retired from consummation about the same time as she retired from artistry'. Archie is well aware that George's lusts are more earthy than his own:

. . . you think that when I run my hands over her back I am carried away by the delicate contours that flow like a sea-shore from shoulder to heel – oh yes, you think my mind turns to ripe pears as soon as I press –   [p. 70]

George's blood is stirred and he interrupts viciously at this point. However, Archie is undeterred and he completes his distinction by defining his own professional attitude:

But to us medical men, the human body is just an imperfect machine. As it is to most of us philosophers. And to us gymnasts, of course.

The contrast between Archie's 'clockwork' aloofness and George's full-blooded sensuality is reflected on a more abstract plane in the contrast between Archie's scientism and George's faith in intuition, which leads him to insist that 'there is more in me than meets the microscope'. Like Professor Anderson in *Professional Foul*, with whom he also shares an interest in sport, a respect for instincts, and a conviction that rights are different from rules, George is better at criticizing the principles of his antagonists than at proving his own case. He establishes easily that 'if rationality were the criterion for things being allowed to exist, the world would be one gigantic field of soya beans', and again that Archie's positivism makes 'one man's idea of good . . . no more meaningful than another man's whether he be St Francis or. . .' – and it is Archie himself who completes the statement – 'Hitler or Stalin or Nero'. But when it comes to establishing the existence of God or the validity of the proposition that 'Good and evil are metaphysical absolutes', George runs into all sorts of difficulties, both in theory (witness his ridiculous attempts to dictate a lecture on these topics at the beginning of Act One) and in practice (witness the apparent failure of providence which allows George unwittingly to kill his hare and his tortoise in the course of the play).

George's bewilderment is very like that of Rosencrantz and Guildenstern, and Moon in *Lord Malquist and Mr Moon*. Moon was always at his most confused when confronted by a mirror, and George has the same experience; he stares into a mirror while dictating his hopelessly bungled lecture. This mirror is an imaginary one so that when George looks into it he is actually looking straight at the audience. This establishes a bond between George and the audience that is reminiscent of the link between the audience and protagonists both in *Rosencrantz and Guildenstern are Dead* and in *The Real Inspector Hound*.

But in the last analysis George is a much more positive character than Moon or Rosencrantz or Guildenstern. Rosencrantz hardly tries to control or understand his world; Moon makes a few desultory attempts but finally opts despairingly to make 'a great big bang that snuffs it out'; Guildenstern rises to what Helen Keyssar-Franke calls 'the full tragic perception' of his predicament but still fails to do anything about it. George, however, finally manages to turn his back on the mirror and put together a coherent and powerful justification of his faith in God and goodness.

Towards the close of Act One George dictates to the secretary a three-page chunk of argument which, apart from three retractions of potentially slanderous material, is a coherent whole, quite devoid of the tangles and confusions that marred his earlier pronouncements. He begins with a discussion of aesthetic judgements, which involves the three sound-effects (Mozartian trumpets, the trumpeting of an elephant and 'the sound made by a trumpet falling down a flight of stone stairs') of which, as we have seen, punning use is made in the sub-plot. His aim is to ridicule the positivists' contention that 'it could not be said that . . . any one set of noises was in any way superior to either of the other two' – to ridicule it, but not absolutely to refute it, since he cuts short his argument with the concession

that the positivists' conclusion 'may, of course, be the case'. And
now he moves on to the all-important field of ethics. George
cavalierly concedes the positivists' point that 'the word "good" has
. . . meant different things to different people at different times'; he
maintains, in fact, that this 'is not a statement which anyone
would dispute'. He then woos his audience with some hilarious
juxtapositions of different moral values before summoning all his
energy for the knock-out punch:

> What is surely . . . surprising is that notions such as honour should manifest
> themselves at all. For what *is* honour? What are pride, shame, fellow-feeling,
> generosity and love? . . . Whence comes this sense of some actions being better than
> others? – not more useful, or more convenient, or more popular, but simply pointlessly
> *better*? What, in short, is so good about *good*?   [p. 55]

Professional philosophers, including Bennett, Henning Jensen and
even Ayer, have not been very impressed by George's arguments,
though Ayer admires *Jumpers* as a play and respects Stoppard. But
there can be no doubting the excellence of George's rhetoric, and in
the theatre this more than compensates for the inadequacy of his
metaphysics. And the speech we have been examining is not just
powerful in itself; it is also powerfully placed, constituting as it does
the closing statement, the verbal climax, so to speak, of Act One.
No doubt it was this passage in particular that Stoppard had in
mind when he claimed in 'Ambushes for the Audience' that *Jumpers*
was the first play in which he 'set out to ask a question and try to
answer it, or at any rate put the counter-question'. George's
intuitionism, as defined here, provides a most effective counter to
Archie's scientism.

    Unfortunately, George is not always so coherent or so eloquent.
As we have seen, his earlier attempts to expound his views are
vitiated by a series of gross linguistic blunders. And in Act Two,
although he manages a few telling points and evocative images, as
when he likens his belief in God to being 'ambushed by some quite
trivial moment – say the exchange of signals between two long-
distance lorry-drivers in the black sleet of a god awful night on the
old A1', he never really gets back into top gear. And for a man bent
on justifying the notion of providence George suffers an inordinate
number of personal disasters in Act Two. He loses his hare, his
tortoise and his goldfish, and looks to be well on the way to losing
his wife as well.

    George is a complex and intriguing character. Bigsby notes that
there is a curious paradox in his predicament – a paradox which –

. . . resides in the fact that while he elaborates his defence of values . . . the world outside is renouncing all interest in the matter. Engaged only on a theoretical level, he implicitly compounds the forces which he deplores. Just as life inevitably evades his attempt to pin it down with words, his elaborate arguments sliding off into anecdote and parenthetical by-ways, so his grasp on the real world is seen to be tenuous at best.[1]

George fails where Professor (George) Anderson and (George) Guthrie will later succeed; he cannot effect a marriage between theory and practice. He can praise the Good Samaritan while failing to emulate him by rescuing Dotty from her predicament. His extreme impracticality is manifested by his failure to see the body of the dead Jumper in Dotty's bedroom during Act Two. As an academic he is, as he admits himself, at one remove from the centre of events. In this respect he is exactly like McKendrick in *Professional Foul*; both men have the right sort of ideas but they are, like the philosopher George Edward Moore, *naifs* who are better at expounding ideas than at putting them into practice. Both lack the sort of flexibility or pragmatism that enables Professor Anderson to combine principle and practice. But George Moore does give voice to the kind of principles on which right action might be based, and to that extent he represents a real advance on Rosencrantz, Guildenstern and Moon, all of whom were paralysed mentally as well as physically.

In *Jumpers* it is Dotty who appears to be paralysed. She is caught between the new 'clockwork' (represented by Archie) and the old 'mystery' (represented by George), and the tension has driven her 'dotty'. In the introductory tableau where she and the Jumpers are juxtaposed she demonstrates her inability to sustain the romantic celebrations of the moon which made her a much-loved star of the musical stage. Whenever she attempts to sing she finds herself unable to distinguish between one moon-song and another and her efforts peter out in confusion. In the middle of the first act she explains her predicament to George:

It'll be just you and me under that old-fashioned, silvery harvest moon, occasionally blue, jumped over by cows and coupleted by Junes, invariably shining on the one I love; well-known in Carolina, much loved in Allegheny, familiar in Vermont; [*the screw turning in her*] Keats's bloody moon! – for what has made the sage or poet write but the fair paradise of nature's light – And *Milton's* bloody moon! rising in clouded majesty, at length apparent queen, unveiled her peerless light and o'er the dark her silver mantle threw – And Shelley's sodding maiden, with white fire laden, whom mortals call the – [*weeping*] *Oh yes, things were in place then*!   [p. 41]

For the difference between this disordered 'then' and the chaotic 'now' we are offered a quite specific explanation, lifted and elaborated from Stoppard's earlier radio play, *Another Moon Called Earth*. After the introductory tableaux the very first action that we see is the television coverage of the first British landing on the moon. This turns a romantic image into something matter-of-fact and it is this which kills Dotty's old aptitude for moon songs. It also kindles an unwonted sadism in her: in Act II it is revealed that she has sacrificed the family goldfish in order to imitate the moonmen. This in turn is a symptom of a thorough-going revision of values that the moon-landing has wrought in her; now that 'Man is on the moon, his feet on solid ground',

> . . . he has seen us whole, all in one go, *little – local* . . . and all our absolutes, the thou-shalts and the thou-shalt-nots that seemed to be the very condition of our existence, how did *they* look to two moonmen with a single neck to save between them? Like the local customs of another place . . .   [p. 75]

As this quotation suggests, the implications of the landing itself are graved deeper for Dotty by the circumstances in which it takes place. The space-ship is damaged so only one of the two astronauts can be lifted off the moon. The two men, Captain Scott and Astronaut Oates, struggle until Oates is knocked to the ground. This fracas makes the moon an even less romantic place. At the same time it destroys one of the great myths of English decency: the story of 'the first Captain Oates, out there in the Antarctic wastes, sacrificing his life to give his companions a slim chance of survival. . .'

Dotty follows the progress of the moon-landing on the television set in her bedroom. From time to time she changes channels and gets coverage of a procession to celebrate the election victory of Archie's Rad-Lib Party. The television screen on which the images appear is another of Stoppard's distorting mirrors, and the alternating images define the tension between 'mystery' and 'clockwork' in Dotty's distorted mind. This tension is established by other means as well. When Dotty calls out 'Darling!', George and Archie both respond instinctively; indeed Dotty does show genuine affection for both of them, though in very different ways. With George she is sincere, confiding and emotional, while with Archie she is gay and composed. By the end of Act Two, however, Archie's influence seems to have prevailed; Dotty is trying to 'Forget Yesterday', and one of the last images we have of her is the close-up of her skin projected on the television screen by the dermatograph. (This image closes the act in the first published edition but in the second it is moved back a few pages.) We see her, as it were, through Archie's eyes, and what we see closely resembles the unromantic close-up of the moon which helped to bring on her dottiness in the first place.

Act Two therefore ends very dismally. Dotty has been reduced to Archie's level, while George has, for the moment at least, been reduced to Dotty's, his cry of 'Help! Murder!' echoing her earlier appeals for attention, and his destruction of Pat and Thumper recalling her murder of the goldfish – and perhaps of McFee. And in the sub-plot Bones has had to abandon his quest for McFee's murderer after Archie has discovered him in a compromising situation with Dotty.

At the same time, however, a more optimistic note has been introduced by Crouch, who has been pressed into service as a sort of *deus ex machina* or catastatic character to provide a modicum of approval for George's ideas and to reveal more fully the circumstances surrounding McFee's death, which turn out to be rather damaging for Archie. Crouch confides that McFee . . . had been going through a crisis and had intended entering a monastery (like a number of Stoppard's earlier heroes). The causes of this crisis were twofold. Firstly, at an abstract level, the astronauts fighting on the moon had led him to question the implications of the pragmatism or scientism to which he had been helping Archie to lend philosophical respectability. Secondly, at a personal level, he had begun to crack under the strain of a clandestine affair with George's secretary. This sounds very like a case of 'mystery in the clockwork', and if we assume, as I think we may, that the Secretary is somehow in league with Archie, then McFee's liaison becomes a double betrayal of his Vice-Chancellor, both in principle and in practice, so to speak. Archie certainly seems to suspect such a thing, to judge by these remarks to Bones:

With the possible exception of McFee's fellow gymnasts, anybody could have fired the shot, and anybody could have had a reason for doing so, including, incidentally, myself. . . . McFee was the guardian and figurehead of philosophical orthodoxy, and if he threatened to start calling on his masters to return to the true path, then I'm afraid it would certainly have been an ice-pick in the back of the skull.
[pp. 63–4]

Crouch himself is a curiously ambiguous figure. His support for George's argument goes only so far: 'I grant you he's answered Russell's first point . . . – the smallest proper fraction is zero – *but* . . . the original problem remains in identifying the *second* term of the series . . .' And in his capacity as porter he threatens, unnecessarily as it turns out, to remove two of the key props to George's argument, his hare and his tortoise: 'No pets allowed in the flats'. Moreover, Crouch's very name suggests that he is a potential 'jumper' and supporter of Archie. But then it has been observed (by Zeifman) that George too is a kind of 'jumper', since his proof of the existence of God involves a Kierkegaardian leap of faith. So the name betokens no definite allegiance.

The net result of Crouch's intervention late in Act Two is to warn the audience that Archie's triumph may not be as absolute as it seems. At the same time we may begin to see that George's collapse is less than total. Very early in the play George insures himself against the debilitating effect of his chronic linguistic ineptitude by insisting that there is a great difference between language and meaning and that confusion in the former does not necessarily signify confusion in the latter. The unfortunate deaths of his pets do not scupper George's religious instincts either, since he makes it clear that the God he acknowledges is not the naively providential God of religious observance. Moreover, long before he steps on Pat (the tortoise) George has contemplated the case of a man who accidentally crushes a beetle and has succeeded in extracting moral significance from the event. And the killing of Thumper (the hare), while it is distressing, does have a positive aspect: it demonstrates the point, which is an integral part of George's proof of the existence of God, that arrows do reach their targets, so that Saint Sebastian need not have died of fright.

And so as the Coda begins, the tension between Archie's scientism and George's intuitionism has still to be finally resolved. Technically this scene is a dream sequence devised by George's fevered imagination, and the depiction of events is certainly somewhat bizarre. But despite this dislocation in the mode of presentation there is no real discontinuity in either the themes or the characterization. It is particularly remarkable that there is no change in the portrayal of George; although the George of the Coda is his own projection of himself he remains the same old impractical figure, who refuses to intervene to save Clegthorpe from death. As far as the ideas are concerned, the Coda may be considered as a direct continuation of the preceding two acts.

For the most part the Coda is quite flippant in tone – too flippant perhaps to serve the purpose for which it seems to have been designed: to recommend George's views and discredit Archie's. The discrediting of Archie is effected by a number of factors, for example by Archie's own nonsense-speech in defence of scientism, by the way in which he manipulates Captain Scott's defence of his conduct on the moon (in the first edition only), and by Clegthorpe's betrayal of Archie, which re-enacts McFee's betrayal, as it was described by Crouch in Act Two. The killing of Clegthorpe, with its echoes of Richard III's murder of Hastings and Henry II's disposal of Thomas à Beckett, brings out Archie's tyrannical propensities, while the fact that the pyramid of Jumpers disintegrates as soon as Clegthorpe is shot out of it, instead of staying intact for a time as it did under similar conditions at the beginning of the play, seems to indicate that the morale of the Rad-Lib party is weakening. Dotty's song, which follows, is still fairly dotty, but we note that she is now longing for the happy days when she could hold a tune instead of persisting in her attempts to 'Forget Yesterday'. And indeed she *does* hold a tune for five verses; and the tune in question is 'Sentimental Journey', whose very title, coupled with the fact that Crouch sings it early in the play, suggests that there are still feelings lurking beneath her skin. Moreover, her line 'Two and two make roughly four' is a slogan for individual freedom, derived ultimately from Orwell's *1984*. In short, to quote Weldon B. Durham, Dotty seems to experience 'reintegration' in the Coda. When Dotty finishes, George takes over, and at last he manages to put together a defence of intuitionism which is as powerful and coherent as his big speech at the end of Act One. Even logical positivists, he contends,

> . . . *know* that life is better than death, that love is better than hate, and that the light shining through the east window of their bloody gymnasium is more beautiful than a rotting corpse.   [p. 87]

But the last word goes to Archie. His curtain-speech is nothing if not ambiguous. The Bible rubs shoulders with Beckett. . . .

Still, even if Archie's final stance remains a shade obscure, it seems reasonable to conclude that the play comes down on the side of George and the angels. Morally, if not in fact, 'mystery' has triumphed over 'clockwork' once again.

SOURCE: extract from *Stoppard: The Mystery and the Clockwork* (Oxford, 1984), pp. 61–76

NOTE

1. C. W. E. Bigsby, *Tom Stoppard* (London 1976) p. 21.

PART FOUR

Travesties

1. STOPPARD'S COMMENTS

I INTERVIEW WITH NANCY SHIELDS HARDIN

. . . *Q*. Would it be accurate to say that you frequently seem to deal with what it is to be an artist?

A. Yes, I have been preoccupied with that. In *Travesties* I found that various voices of my own which were on a collision course made up whole scenes of *Travesties* for me, if you like. Henry Carr's scepticism about the valuation which artists put on themselves is very much my own scepticism. But then Joyce's defence of art is mine, too. I mean, one doesn't think, as it were, with one mind on these matters. One has two or three minds battling with each other. And even in the case of Tristan Tszara [sic. Ed.] in that play, who had to put the case for his particular form of anti-art, I went into that having as I thought to create his arguments from nothing since I had no sympathy with them to start with. He wasn't speaking for me at all. But in the event I found some of the things Tszara had to say quite persuasive.

Q. Speaking for him were parts of yourself, maybe . . .

A. Exactly so! Exactly so. If I had to make an ultimate statement about where I think true value lies, I don't think that I'd give much house room to anti-art and anarchic art. But I found what Tszara had to say quite interesting in some curious way. . . .

Q. Would you like to direct?

A. No, not particularly, no. Certainly not the first time a play is done. I think the plays have gained a lot from things that I can't bring to them, especially in music. Peter Wood has done *Jumpers, Travesties* and *Night and Day*. In all three cases, the production has had a dimension which wasn't really on paper – more theatricality. Obviously I see the thing much more as a verbal event. To some extent I count on certain theatrical effects, but Peter Wood has a way of drawing them out and making more of them. I remember Tristan Tszara entering in *Travesties* to this great noise of an orchestra playing 'Louise' which became one of my favorite tunes. I can't take any credit for it . . .

SOURCE: extracts from Nancy Shields Hardin, 'An Interview with Tom Stoppard', *Contemporary Literature*, XXII (1981), pp. 156, 160.

II PROGRAMME NOTE

Travesties is a work of fiction which makes use, and misuse, of history. Scenes which are self-evidently documentary mingle with others which are just as evidently fantastical. People who were hardly aware of each other's existence are made to collide; real people and imaginary people are brought together without ceremony; and events which took place months, and even years, apart are presented as synchronous. For the luxury of such liberties I am indebted to writers who allowed themselves none. I have leaned most heavily on – and occasionally quoted from – the following books, to which I would like to make grateful acknowledgement:

Lenin by Michael C. Morgan; *Lenin* by Robert Payne; *Lenin and the Bolsheviks* by Adam B. Ulam; *To The Finland Station* by Edmund Wilson; *Days With Lenin* by Maxim Gorky; *Memories of Lenin* by Nadezhda Krupskaya; Lenin's Collected Writing; *The First World War, an Illustrated History* by A. J. P. Taylor; *James Joyce* by Richard Ellmann; *Joyce* by John Gross; *Dada, Art and Anti-Art* by Hans Richter; and *The Dada Painters and Poets* edited by Robert Motherwell. I am also indebted to Mr James Klugmann for material relating to Lenin in Switzerland, particularly for a typescript translation of part of Fritz Platten's book, *Lenin's Journey through Germany in the Sealed Train*. The responsibility for the use to which this and all other material is put is my own.

It can be safely inferred from the above list that history rather than imagination places Lenin, Joyce and the Dadaist Tristan Tzara in Zurich at one and the same time. History, too, offers us one short conversation between Lenin and a Dadaist, recounted in the Motherwell book, and also the possibility of a meeting between Lenin and Joyce (though it is hard to imagine what they would have had to say to each other). But for the most part *Travesties* is presented through the fevered imagination of its principal character; which brings us to Henry Carr.

Carr existed. I have been able to discover nothing about his life after 1919, and his name would be lost to posterity but for an event of such engaging absurdity that it might be thought to be the play's chief invention. In fact, it is one of the play's chief holds on historical truth. 'The Zurich years (runs an abridged quotation from Gross's short book) were also notable for Joyce's prolonged wrangle with the British Consulate General, a grotesque storm in a teacup which had its origins in a quarrel over the cost of a pair of trousers worn in a local production of *The Importance of Being Earnest*.'

SOURCE: Tom Stoppard's Note in the programme of the original Royal Shakespeare Company production of 1974.

III   INTERVIEW WITH R. HUDSON, S. ITZIN, S. TRUSSLER

... You said that in Travesties *you asked the question whether the terms artist and revolutionary were capable of being synonymous – did you come to any sort of conclusion?*

The play puts the question in a more extreme form. It asks whether an artist has to justify himself in political terms *at all*. For example, if Joyce were alive today, he would say, juntas may come and juntas may go but Homer goes on for ever. And when he was alive he *did* say that the history of Ireland, troubles and all, was justified because it produced *him* and *he* produced *Ulysses*. Okay. So clearly one now has to posit a political prisoner taking comfort from the thought that at least he is in the country of Joyce, or of Homer, and to ask oneself whether Joyce, in moral terms, was myopic or had better vision than lesser men. And my answer to that question is liable to depend on the moment at which you run out of tape. Of course one feels uneasy in trying to work out questions that involve *oneself*, in terms of authentic geniuses, but it helps to clarify the issue. How do you measure the legacy of a genius who believed in art for art's sake? ...

SOURCE: extract from interview in R. Hudson, S. Itzin and S. Trussler, 'Ambushes for the Audience: Towards a High Comedy of Ideas', *Theatre Quarterly*, IV, 14 (May/July 1974), p. 16.

2. REVIEWS OF FIRST PRODUCTION

Milton Shulman (1974)

'Paradox, pastiche and puns'

. . . Mingling fact and fiction with scant respect for both, Stoppard has set out to show, amongst other irrelevant things, that between a revolutionary and an artist no twain will ever meet.

If the theme sounds serious, the method of telling is intellectual slapstick.

All Stoppard's passion for paradox, pastiche and puns are here, displayed with little regard for the educational limitations of his audience.

If you are familiar with the subtleties of Joyce's *Ulysses*, the background of the Dadaist movement, the story of Lenin's return to Russia, your amusement is likely to be much greater than that of the bewildered many who will be able to enjoy these antics only on their simplest level.

But, as Stoppard himself has said, he is not out to please everybody like so much breakfast food.

I can only be grateful that he pleases me. It is a long time since my dramatic bowl has contained such crunchy, crackling wit. . . .

SOURCE: extract from review of the London première by the RSC, *Evening Standard* (11 June 1974).

Irving Wardle (1974)

'A structural flaw'

. . . One of the great pleasures of the evening is Stoppard's skill in moving in and out of Wilde's dialogue, and rewriting it for his own purposes ('Are they Bolsheviks?' 'They dine with us; or come in the evening at any rate').

No one can accuse him of irreverence, as the action takes place in the memory of his old hero – first seen shuffling on in carpet slippers to bash out old favourites on an upright piano and reminisce about his great days in the war. His opening speech is one of Stoppard's star turns: marvellously organised under its rambling surface, getting the basic facts across and contrasting the official romantic view with private animosities, in order finally to imply the futility of any hope for an objective account of the past. . . .

The weakness of the scheme is its complete failure to absorb Lenin: quotes from Krupskaya's bland memoirs, interwoven with Lenin's own implacable statements, offer a chilly Soviet equivalent of *Mrs Wilson's Diary*, but one still has the feeling that the main play has come to a stop. Otherwise Peter Wood's production, with its manifold time changes and action recaps (prompted by a peremptory cuckoo clock), its limerick and musical comedy dialogue, and its use of simultaneous events, works with a beautifully controlled fluency and vigour.

Source: extract from review of first production, *The Times* (11 June 1974).

Benedict Nightingale   (1974)

'Carried away in his own mental helter-skelter'

. . . Stoppard's great gift is to treat solemn subjects with a gaiety that enlightens without trivialising. So it was with *Jumpers*, which was about the discomfort of inhabiting a world left bereft of all moral certainties; and so, to a lesser extent, it is here. Perhaps I expected too much. Perhaps we've grown accustomed to his amusement-arcade style. Whatever the reason, I couldn't respond as wholeheartedly as I'd wished to the puns and Wildean *mots*, the long, sparkling monologues, the limericks and songs, the disguises and misunderstandings, all packing the action like pinball machines in a debating chamber. Stoppard's wit isn't in question, nor his intelligence, nor his audacity – who else would import Cecily from *The Importance*, and have her start a striptease on a library counter to the accompaniment of a speech about socialism? What troubles me is his propensity to get carried away in his own mental helter-skelter. Joyce, when first mentioned, is mistaken for a woman, then called Doris, then Janice, then Phyllis, then Deirdre – get Stoppard stuck into a joke, and you have to prise him out with a crowbar. Indeed Johnson's notorious words about Shakespeare apply more aptly to him: a quibble is 'the gilded apple for which he will always turn aside from his career, or stoop from his elevation'. There's so much chasing of ideas that we never get around to evaluating them, so much fun with characters that we cannot finally tell what, why, how or even who they are. . . .

SOURCE: extract from review of first production, *New Statesman* (17 June 1974), p. 859.

Clive James   (1975)

'Plurality of contexts'

. . .   Before John Wood was half-way through his opening speech I already knew that in Stoppard I had encountered a writer of my generation whom I could admire without reserve. It is a common reaction to *Travesties* to say that seeing it is like drinking champagne. But not only did I find that the play tasted like champagne – I found that in drinking it I felt like a jockey. Jockeys drink champagne as an everyday tipple, since it goes to the head without thickening the waist. *Travesties* to me seemed not an exotic indulgence, but the stuff of life. Its high speed was not a challenge but a courtesy; its structural intricacy not a dazzling pattern but a perspicuous design; its fleeting touch not of a feather but of a fine needle. For me *Travesties* was a personal revelation. . . . It is the plurality of contexts that concerns Stoppard: ambiguities are just places where contexts join. And although Stoppard's transitions and transformations of context might be thought of, either pejoratively or with approval, as games, the games are, it seems to me, at least as serious as Wittgenstein's language games – although finally, I think, the appropriate analogies to Stoppard's vision lie just as much in modern physics as in modern philosophy.

Even among those who profess to admire his skill, it is often supposed that there is something coldly calculated about Stoppard's technique. By mentioning his work in the same breath with modern physics one risks abetting that opinion. But there is no good reason to concede that modern physics is cold, or even that to be calculating precludes creativity. Guildenstern is not necessarily right when he tells Rosencrantz (in *Rosencrantz and Guildenstern are Dead*) that all would be lost if their spontaneity turned out to be part of another order – one of the play's themes is that Chance, while looking deterministic if seen from far enough away, is random enough from close to. Both views are real, just as the two different views of the Plough are real. It could even be assumed that each viewpoint is fixed. That would be a Newtonian picture of Stoppard's universe, and like the Newtonian picture of the real universe could go a long way towards explaining everything in it.

But physics, to the small extent that I understand it, ceased being Newtonian and started being modern when Einstein found himself obliged to rule out the possibility of a viewpoint at rest. Nobody could now believe that Einstein did this in order to be less precise – he did it in order to be precise over a greater range of events than Newtonian mechanics could accurately account for. *Mutatis mutandis*, Stoppard abandons fixed viewpoints for something like the same reason. The analogy is worth pursuing because it leads us to consider the possibility that Stoppard's increasingly apparent intention to create a dramatic universe of perpetual transformations might also spring from the impulse to clarify.

It is perhaps because there is little recognisably *mystical* about him – scarcely a hint of the easy claim to impenetrability – that people are inclined to call Stoppard cold. It might have been a comfort to them if Stoppard had rested content with merely saying: listen, what looks odd when you stand over There is perfectly reasonable if you stand over Here, whereupon the place you left begins looking odd in its turn. That would have been relativity of a manageable Newtonian kind, which anyone patient enough could have hoped to follow. But Stoppard added: and now that you're Here, you ought to know that Here is on its way to somewhere else, just as There is, and always was. That was Einstein's kind of relativity – a prospect much less easily grasped. In fact grasping doesn't come into it. There is not much point in the layman trying to grasp that the relative speed of two objects rushing away from each other at the speed of light is still the speed of light. What he needs to realise is that no other explanation fits the facts. Similarly with Stoppard's dramatic equivalent of the space-time continuum: it exists to be ungraspable, its creator having discovered that no readily appreciable conceptual scheme can possibly be adequate to the complexity of experience. The chill which some spectators feel at a Stoppard play is arriving from infinity.

Critical talk about 'levels of reality' in a play commonly assumes that one of the posited levels is *really* real. By the same token, it would be reasonable to assume that although everything in a Stoppard play is moving, the play itself is a system at rest. But in Stoppard's universe no entity, not even a work of art, is exempt from travel. *The Importance of Being Earnest* is moving through *Travesties* like one stream of particles through another, the points of collision lighting up as pastiche. The same kind of interpenetration was already at work in *Rosencrantz and Guildenstern are Dead*, through which the play *Hamlet* made a stately transit like a planet encountering a meteor shower, and with the same pyrotechnic consequences.

'Every exit', the Player tells Rosencrantz, 'is an entrance somewhere else.' The idea holds true for both space and time. In *The Real Inspector Hound* Felicity repeatedly enters at the same moment to instigate different versions of the action. In *Travesties* Tristan Tzara enters up-stage to begin a scene and later exits stage-right uttering the same initial line, so that the exit becomes an entrance in a play (the *other* play) speeding away from us into the off-prompt wing. It isn't helpful to call such effects dazzling, since they are not meant to dazzle nor be effects – they are glimpses into the kaleidoscope of possibilities, devices by which you see further. They are Stoppard's own and growing artistic realisation of the hero's view from on high in the radio play *Albert's Bridge*, whose text is perhaps the most easily approachable example of Stoppard's fascination with the long straight lines – curves of infinite radius – leading up to and away from here and now. . . .

Here and now in Stoppard is a time and place defined by an infinite number of converging vectors each heading towards it at the speed of light and steadily slowing down to nothing before passing through it and speeding up again. Ignoring for the moment that the still point is itself moving, here and now is what things tend towards, with a tantalising slowness as they swell into proximity. In this resides much of the significance of Stoppard's fascination with Zeno's paradox – the asymptotic frustration by which the hare never quite catches up with the tortoise. In *Jumpers*, George Moore the philosopher (the *other* George Moore the philosopher) concludes that since the arrow could not have quite reached Saint Sebastian he must have died of fright. It is a fabulous joke but there is fear in it – the awe of watching a slow approach down long perspectives.

Guildenstern says that the more witnesses who attest to the remarkable the thinner it gets and the more reasonable it becomes until it is thin as reality. Here and now is Zero – a word which rings like a gnomic tocsin in Beckett's *Endgame* and arrives in Stoppard's plays as a developed vision. . . .

In fact the weaknessess of *Travesties*, such as they are, seem to me to crop up in those places where Stoppard atavistically makes concessions to the standard theatrical conception of human warmth. This, I think, is the real problem with the Lenin role, which is recognised by everyone – including the author – to be a small but troublesome spanner in the play's glistening works. It is generally supposed that there is not much in the part for an actor to bite on. My own view is the opposite: I think there is too much. As it happened, the part was wrongly cast in both runs of the production. In the first run Lenin was too sympathetic and in the second he was too diffident. (It is a measure of the play's robustness, incidentally, that it could survive weak casting even among the principal roles. In the second run James Joyce could neither sing nor dance and threw away his key speech on the first night.)

But even if Lenin had been played up to the full power inherent in the role he would still have stood revealed as a personality conceived in terms of show-biz meatiness, with a built-in conflict to suggest complexity. In *Travesties* Lenin is polarised rather too easily between ruthlessness and an appreciation of creative achievement, the latter quality having apparently been extrapolated from his well-known contention that the *Appassionata* moved him to tears. But the real-life Lenin was not divided along so elementary a line. Stoppard emphasises Lenin's self-contradictions at the expense of playing down his monolithic purposefulness – a purposefulness which we can scarcely begin to contemplate without raising the question of Evil. There is less to the *complexity*, and more to the *force*, of Lenin's personality than Stoppard allows. Lenin's historical significance doesn't even begin to be reconciled within a scheme that adduces Tristan Tzara and James Joyce as revolutionary exemplars, and by suggesting that it does, Stoppard starts a hare which really never *can* catch the tortoise.

This is not to say that Stoppard is disqualified from treating tough subjects. Quite the reverse. In my admittedly limited experience it has usually been the playwrights already famous for treating them who are disqualified, and in the long run it is more likely to be Stoppard who says what counts on the subject of, say, the Final Solution – even if he never approaches it more than tangentially. But Stoppard's is an aesthetic which demands an unfalteringly sensitive apprehension of the real world. A moment's coarseness and the game is lost: astrophysics becomes Construct-O-Straws. . . .

SOURCE: extracts from review-article on the 1974 and 1975 productions, *Encounter*, 45 (Nov. 1975), excerpted from pp. 68–76.

3. CRITICAL STUDIES

Joan F. Dean   'Four Distinct Views on Art'
(1981)

. . . *Travesties* is well named for several specific reasons. Its fictional-ization of historical characters is a travesty of the individual, but that travesty is inevitably and necessarily committed whenever historical personages appear on stage. Its debates about art and artistic responsibility reduce delicate aesthetic theories to the level of name-calling, brawling invective. ('By God, you supercilious streak of Irish puke! You four-eyed, bog-ignorant potatoe-eating ponce!' [p. 62] is Tzara's way of addressing the most influential, adulated novelist of the twentieth century.) The play's action is, quite literally, the travesty of human existence, the reductio ad absurdum that found dramatic life in, among others, the plays of Oscar Wilde. Finally, its plot is a travesty, however laudatory and respectful, of Wilde's *The Importance of Being Earnest*. Stoppard's own devotion to Wilde dates back at least to when he was reviewing in Bristol. In *Travesties*, both Joyce and Carr show great respect for Wilde and for his belief that art need not be politically or socially oriented.

The principal cause of these travesties is that most of the play, with the possible exception of the first section of Act Two, is governed by the recollections of Henry Carr, who supposes himself to have been the British Consul in Zurich in 1918. Like Ros and Guil, the historic Carr (actually a minor official at the British Consulate) played a nearly insignificant role in this momentous political situation, although he did play the pivotal role of Algernon in a production of *The Importance of Being Earnest* arranged by Joyce in Zurich. He has twice been immortalized in literature: first by Joyce who portrayed him as the loathsome Private Carr of the Circe episode of *Ulysses*; and second by Stoppard's play. *Travesties* shows us Carr both as a dapper civil servant (Young Carr) and as a broken old man trying to live down the humiliation of Joyce's treatment by telling his story in his memoirs. But Carr's memory is hardly accurate; as Stoppard tells us in a stage direction:

The [first] scene (and most of the play) is under the erratic control of Old Carr's memory, which is not notably reliable, and also of his various prejudices and

delusions. One result is that the story (like a toy train perhaps) occasionally jumps
the rails and has to be restarted at the point where it goes wild.   [p. 27]

Travesties presents four distinct views on art through its four male
principals: Lenin professes a belief in art as an instrument of the
Marxist revolution; Tzara represents Dadaist anti-art; Joyce is the
spokesman of art for art's sake; and Carr holds a relatively innocuous
bourgeois view of art. Lenin's Marxist aesthetic is also voiced by
his disciples, Cecily (his secretary and librarian), and Nadya (his
wife). Interestingly, Carr echoes a number of Joyce's statements
about art (and especially about Wilde) by rephrasing them in his
confrontation with Cecily in Act Two.

Tzara's and Carr's respective notions about art are the obstacles
to their romances with Cecily and Gwen. Whereas Tzara is at least
willing to sidestep a confrontation with Gwen about the quality of
Joyce's manuscript (he tells her that he is not Tzara that Dadaist,
but his brother, Jack Tzara), Carr is uncompromising in his
condemnation of both the politics and aesthetics of Lenin. Hence,
the love interest is complicated not by the insistence upon the name
Ernest, but by the demand for compatible aesthetic theories.

Of the four perspectives set forth by Lenin, Carr, Joyce and Tzara,
three are presented with considerable care and perhaps even
sympathy. Tzara's Dadaism is treated fairly, but with little credibility
in *Travesties*. It is, in fact, the most easily dismissed of the four
theories of art presented. Tzara's attack on Joyce, for instance, does
not deny the genius of Joyce's work but instead argues that the
twentieth century can no longer accommodate art for art's sake:

You've turned literature into a religion and it's as dead as all the rest, it's an overripe
corpse and you're cutting fancy figures at the wake. It's too late for geniuses! Now
we need vandals and desecrators, simple-minded demolition men to smash centuries
of baroque subtlety, to bring down the temple, and thus finally, to reconcile the
shame and the necessity of being an artist!   [p. 62]

Strangely, Tzara's Dadaism functions as Lenin would have art
function – as social criticism.

John Simon assumes that Stoppard presents Lenin in a more
favorable light than the other characters:

But the second act, where Lenin preponderates, things get serious, in fact, downright
ponderous. All London is trying to figure out why. Did Stoppard consider Lenin's
humorless zeal, transposed to the stage, funny enough *objet trouvé* as is? Or is he too
much of a Marxist to dare poke fun at Lenin? Or are some of his best friends, whom
he wants to keep, Marxists?[1]

Simon is mistaken on at least two counts: the very notion that the audience or Stoppard finds Lenin's speeches funny is itself ludicrous; at least tacitly it implies that everything in a comedy should be humorous. Moreover, the notion that Stoppard himself is a Marxist using this play to protect and defend his own beliefs is patently ridiculous. Nothing could, in fact, be further from Stoppard's own beliefs and his dramatic techniques. Clearly, however, the structure, characterization and dialogue of the first section of the second act – especially as they regard Lenin – are radical departures from those of the first act.

The demonstration of the failure of the Marxist aesthetic, in truth, is the principal point of the play's second act. Critically, the second act was poorly received and became something of a scapegoat for the play's shortcomings (its lengthy set speeches, its inclusion of Lenin and Nadya, and its digressiveness). Stoppard would have had little difficulty in portraying Lenin as a comically exaggerated character along the lines of Tzara or Joyce. That he chose, instead, to depict Lenin considerably more realistically than either Tzara or Joyce suggests that the particular travesty connected with Lenin lies outside of his portrayal – lies instead in his contradictory aesthetic statements and his eventual rejection of art. Moreover, Lenin's portrayal anticipates Stoppard's overt protest of the communist repression in *Every Good Boy Deserves Favor, Professional Foul*, and *Cahoot's Macbeth.*

The failure of Lenin's aesthetic theories is evident on two grounds: first, they are self-contradictory, and, second, they are contradicted by his own visceral response to art. On the first count, Lenin argues that only the communist political state can free the artist from his capitalistic shackles and thereby offer him true independence. Simultaneously he asserts that only one style of art, which came to be known as socialist realism, is acceptable or even tolerable. For the Marxist, art can have only one function; as Cecily says in voicing the Marxist line in her confrontation with Carr, 'the sole duty and justification for art is social criticism' [p. 74]. Lenin, in historically accurate dialogue,[2] addresses this paradox directly but fails to appreciate the implicit contradiction:

We want to establish and we shall establish a free press, free not simply from the police, but also from capital, from careerism, and what is more, *free from bourgeois anarchist individualism*! These last words may seem paradoxical or an affront to my audience. Calm yourselves, ladies and gentlemen! Everyone is free to write and say whatever he likes, without any restrictions. But every voluntary association, including the party, is also free to expel members who use the name of the party to advocate anti-party views.   [p. 85]

Surely, Lenin places the party before art, and the reason for this grows out of his personal response to art, which is not as predictable as his politics and which is the second cause of the failure of his aesthetic suggested by Stoppard's play.

In Act Two, Stoppard juxtaposes Lenin's readings from letters to various party officials with Nadya's recollections of his o 6ςΙ ˙eaction to plays, concerts and novels. Lenin preferred Pushkin to Mayakovski and changed his mind only after being told that Pushkin was bourgeois. He favored Chekhov's *Uncle Vanya* over Gorki's *The Lower Depths* even though he recognised Gorki's politics as acceptable and Chekhov's as inappropriate. But that he is genuinely moved by Beethoven's 'Appassionata' evinces the second contradiction in Lenin's aesthetic; because art kindles in him a sense of human dignity and worth, he must restrain himself from its enjoyment. As he says:

I don't know of anything greater than the Appassionata. Amazing, superhuman music. It always makes me feel, perhaps naively, it makes me feel proud of the miracles that human beings can perform. But I can't listen to music often. It affects my nerves, makes me want to say nice stupid things and pat the heads of those people who while living in this vile hell can create such beauty. Nowadays we can't pat heads or we'll get our hands bitten off. We've got to *hit* heads, hit them without mercy, though ideally we're against doing violence to people . . . Hm, one's duty is infernally hard.   [p. 89]

These, Lenin's final words in *Travesties*, indicate the paradoxical nature of the Marxist philosophy of art. Even without touching upon the question of the repression and the persecution of artists who do not conform to the party line, issues that will resurface as immediate concerns in Stoppard's subsequent work, the failure of Lenin's aesthetic is self-evident – literally evident from his own response to art. Marx said that religion is the opiate of the people; Lenin seems to realize that art is dangerous for similar reasons.

The aesthetic position represented by Joyce is essentially a belief in art for art's sake. As Stoppard notes in the stage directions, the James Joyce who appears to perform magic tricks and to speak in limericks 'is obviously an Irish nonsense' [p. 33]. In Act One, Joyce squares off against Tzara's Dadaism, but he is never pitted against the Marxist position or Carr's eclectic views of art. Most of the confrontation between Tzara and Joyce is little more than exposition concerning the Dadaist's perspective; Joyce's own view on art is, in fact, limited to one speech in which he describes the artist as 'the magician put among men to gratify – capriciously – their urge for immortality' [p. 62]. In direct antithesis to Lenin's art-as-social-criticism aesthetic, Joyce cites the Trojan War as an example in which great art was derived from suffering and death that otherwise have been relegated to widely unknown ancient history.

Joyceans were generally tolerant if not enthusiastic of the travesty of their master. Myron Schwartzman in *James Joyce Quarterly* writes: 'The portrait is light, funny, and finally complimentary. Joyce through Carr's memory comes away no worse than Bloom in the eye of the "Cyclops" narrator.'[3] Others, however, assume that Joyce fares no better than Tzara or Lenin. Craig Werner argues that Joyce's position is undercut because Carr, who typifies the modern reader to whom literature must appeal, 'actively rejects both Lenin (on patriotic grounds) and Joyce (for personal reasons)'.[4] But Joyce's aesthetic, even his very presence, stimulates Young Carr and agitates Old Carr. The antipathy between them centres on a financial squabble over twenty-five francs for tickets to *Earnest* and the purchase of a pair of trousers. Carr, even as an old man, infamously humiliated in *Ulysses*, begrudgingly respects Joyce. Although Carr initially prefers Gilbert and Sullivan to Wilde (whom they satirised), the dispute between Carr and Joyce is primarily of a legal rather than an artistic nature.

After Joyce's key speech near the end of Act One, the curtain speech for that act is a long monologue in which Old Carr bitterly recalls the litigation between him and Joyce that grew out of the production of *Earnest*. It ends with Carr's recollection of a frustrating and troublesome dream:

I dreamed about him, dreamed I had him in the witness box, a masterly cross-examination, case practically won, admitted it all, the whole thing, the trousers, everything, and I flung at him – 'And what did you do in the Great War?' 'I wrote *Ulysses*', he said. 'What did you do?'
Bloody nerve.   [p. 65]

Importantly, this is Old Carr's nightmare; Joyce never actually said this – even Old Carr's erratic memory cannot recall him saying it. But his dream is the denial of both his lawsuit and his fondest self-aggrandizements; thus, it haunts Carr.

Carr, in fact, emulates Joyce as demonstrated by two parallel encounters. In the first, Joyce offers Carr the part of Algernon; in so doing he quotes Jack Worthing's famous line: 'I may occasionally be a little overdressed but I make up for it by being immensely overeducated' [p. 52]. Carr paraphrases this statement when, in Act Two, discussing the function of art he tells Cecily: 'Wilde was indifferent to politics. He may occasionally have been a little overdressed but he made up for it by being immensely uncommited' [p. 74]. The importance of the parallel lies not so much in Stoppard's or Carr's witty play on Wilde, but in the fact that Carr praises Wilde (and Joyce indirectly) by describing them as politically uncommitted. For both of them, politics has little place in their art. Joyce specifically states this when he says, 'As an artist, naturally I attach no importance to the swings and roundabout of political history' [p. 50]. Carr thereby models not only his sentence construction but also his apolitical view of art on borrowings from Wilde and Joyce.

Stoppard's dramatic technique often calls for him to diffuse the most significant statements with a vigorous stroke of physical comedy. In *Jumpers*, this ploy is illustrated by the rare succinctness and lucidity of George's statement that 'if rationality were the criterion for things being allowed to exist, the world would be one gigantic field of soya beans' [p 40] followed by a rhetorical question addressed to a pet. In *Travesties*, the technique is used after Joyce's catechistic interrogation of Tzara that addresses the function of art in society and its importance as a means to immortality. The speech culminates with Joyce bidding Tzara 'Top o' the morning' [p. 63] and then pulling a rabbit out of his hat. The delight in seeing this bit of prestidigitation, coupled with the unlikeliness of Joyce's valediction, overshadows and undercuts what Joyce has just said.

Travesties, like *Jumpers*, does indeed take up serious themes although they are submerged beneath a highly wrought dramatic structure, dazzling dialogue, and historical or quasi-historical interludes. The examination of the question of God's existence in *Jumpers* and art's function in *Travesties* culminates Stoppard's attempt to bring about the perfect union of the comedy of ideas and farce. The satisfaction that comes, however, at the end of these plays rests principally in the legerdemain that Stoppard affects: the design is completed, the loose ends drawn together, the couples harmoniously paired off. Like Joyce, Stoppard stands as the magician of the piece.

However convincing Joyce's statements that art need not be political, Stoppard himself pursues distinctly more political themes in his subsequent work. There is no radical shift in his dramaturgy or convictions about art because whatever didacticism emerges in the most recent works again undercuts the legacy of Lenin by attacking the treatment of artists, intellectuals, and dissidents in communist countries. . . .

SOURCE: extract from *Tom Stoppard: Comedy as a Moral Matrix* (Columbia, Mo., 1981), pp. 76–83.

NOTES

1. John Simon, 'London Diary v: Éclat,' *New York Times* (26 Aug. 1974), p. 67.
2. Like many of Lenin's speeches in *Travesties*, this speech is taken from Lenin's own writings.
3. Myron Schwartzman, 'Wilde about Joyce? Da! But My Heart Belongs to Dada', *James Joyce Quarterly*, 13 (1975), p. 123.
4. Craig Werner, 'Stoppard's Critical Travesty, or Who Vindicates Whom', *Arizona Quarterly*, 35 (1979), p. 235.

David K. Rod   'The Importance of Carr' (1983)

Most critical treatments of Tom Stoppard's *Travesties* have character-ized the play as a debate about the proper relationship between art and politics.[1] Critics have recognized that the three major historical figures in the play – James Joyce, Lenin and Tristan Tzara – represent contrasting views on the issue, views that Stoppard juxtaposes with one another within the comic framework of the play. For the most part, critics have focused on the conflict between Joyce's and Lenin's positions; Tzara is generally acknowledged as a third party in the debate but not considered to be a serious contender.[2]

The aesthetic-political views of Henry Carr, the protagonist of *Travesties*, are frequently ignored altogether.[3] Yet the debate occurs, as the critics point out, within Carr's memory, and the play makes it clear that the events presented are highly colored by Carr's remembering them. Indeed, Carr's introductions of each of the other three participants in the debate emphasize their status as products of his memory: 'James Joyce As I Knew Him' [p. 22], 'Lenin As I Knew Him' [p. 23], '*Memories of Dada by a Consular Friend of the Famous in Old Zurich: A Sketch*' [p. 25]. Furthermore, Carr takes his own position on the aesthetic-political issue, a position which he defends against the opposing views of Tzara, Joyce and Lenin (as he remembers them). By contrast, Joyce and Lenin never argue directly with each other in the play. Given the controlling perspective provided by Carr and his active participation in the debate embodied in *Travesties*, the widespread critical inattention to his views seems unjustified.[4] A careful examination of the scenes in which Carr's views conflict with those of Tzara, Joyce and Lenin will reveal both Carr's centrality to the aesthetic-political debate and a clearer picture of the position he espouses.

In Act One, Carr's views are contrasted with those of Tzara and
Joyce. The contrast appears first, in caricatured form, in the scene
where Tzara and Joyce behave in nonsensically exaggerated fashion
and the dialogue takes the form of a series of limericks. This scene
establishes the basic position that each of the three characters will
develop later. Tzara protests against the artistic tradition represented
by Joyce; he is scornful of '[c]ulture and [r]eason' [p. 34] and rejects
'[t]he classics – tradition' [p. 35]. Joyce asserts the value of his own
work – he calls himself '[a] fine writer who writes caviar/for the
general, hence poor' [p. 33] – and he asks for money. Carr takes
the middle ground. He accepts neither Joyce's valuation of traditional
art for its own sake nor Tzara's outright rejection of traditional art;
instead, Carr comments that 'H.M.G, is considered pro-Art' [p. 34]
and considers the possibility of scoring diplomatic points against
the Germans by means of the play that Joyce proposes to produce.
On the whole, Carr's approach might be characterized as practical,
even if his selection of Gilbert and Sullivan's *Iolanthe* as the prime
representative of British culture reveals the limits of his vision. Of
course, the manic nature of the scene will predominate, at the
expense of any careful examination of the issues. Still, the scene sets
forth the basic positions that will be explored later.

The more careful examination begins in the following scene, which
parodies the conversation between Jack and Algernon in Act One
of *The Importance of Being Earnest*. The very fact that Carr and Tzara
assume the major roles here should suggest that their views will
weigh heavily in the aesthetic-political debate. Joyce and Lenin, to
the extent that they can be identified with characters in Wilde's
play at all, assume subordinate roles. Furthermore, the interchange
between Carr and Tzara constitutes the first extensive discussion of
aesthetic and political issues in *Travesties*.

Tzara's argument is that the war has made a mockery of the
values and the schemes of logic and causality which have served as
the basis for traditional art. Without logic, art must be nonsense,
and Tzara rejects all attempts to present art as anything other than
nonsense:

TZARA: I am sick of cleverness. The clever people try to impose a design on the world
and when it goes calamitously wrong they call it fate. In point of fact, everything
is Chance, including design.
CARR: That sounds awfully clever. What does it mean? Not that it has to mean
anything, of course.
TZARA: It means, my dear Henry, that the causes we know everything about depend
on causes we know very little about, which depend on causes we know absolutely
nothing about. And it is the duty of the artist to jeer and howl and belch at the
delusion that infinite generations of real effects can be inferred from the gross

expression of apparent cause.   [p. 37]

Tzara wants to redefine art: 'Nowadays, an artist is someone who
makes art mean the things he does' [p. 38]. By means of this
redefinition, Tzara apparently hopes that art can regain the importance it once had as an improver of the human condition:

> When the strongest began to fight for the tribe, and the fastest to hunt, it was the
> artist who became the priest-guardian of the magic that conjured the intelligence
> out of the appetites. Without him, man would be a coffee-mill. Eat – grind – shit.
> Hunt – *eat* – fight – *grind* – saw the logs – *shit*. The difference between being a man
> and being a coffee-mill is art.   [p. 47]

Thus, in spite of his rejection of traditional art forms, Tzara sees
art itself as a superior kind of activity. In this regard, he chides
Carr, who has escaped the war by coming to Switzerland, for
spending his time as a diplomat rather than as an artist [p. 38].

Carr's position develops out of the interchange with Tzara. In
the first place, Carr disagrees with Tzara's account of the demise of
traditional values and of logic and causality. He claims vehemently
to have gone to war out of a sense of duty, for the sake of patriotism
and love of freedom, and he dismisses Tzara's more cynical
interpretation – that war is 'capitalism with the gloves off' – as being
mere phrasemaking [pp. 39–40]. Furthermore, Carr's view of the
war gains credence from his actually having served in the trenches.
While he admits to having forgotten what the causes of the war
were, still he maintains that the war had causes and therefore cannot
be pointed to as proof of the inapplicability of causality to human
affairs [p. 36]. Also, he undercuts Tzara's rejection of cleverness by
pointing out that the rejection itself is cleverly phrased [p. 37].

Secondly, Carr refuses to accept Tzara's redefinition of art. As
before, he insists that Tzara's reassigning of labels cannot change
the reality of the things labelled; just as to call a pedestrian activity
'flying' does not lift one off the ground, so to call a nonartistic
activity 'art' does not make that activity artistic [pp. 38–9]. Carr
himself defines art in a more traditional way: 'An artist is someone
who is gifted in some way that enables him to do something more
or less well which can only be done badly or not at all by someone
who is not thus gifted' [p. 38]. Like much of Carr's thinking, this
definition lacks brilliance but possesses a certain aura of practicality
or common sense.

Finally, Carr assigns to art a much lower valuation than Tzara
does. To be an artist, according to Carr, is to abandon more serious
concerns, such as those of the political realm: 'to be an artist *at all*
is like living in Switzerland during a world war' [p. 38]. The business

of the artist is 'to beautify existence' [p. 37], and while this purpose
has some importance, it does not have the overwhelming importance
that has been assigned to it by artists:

CARR: Art is absurdly overrated by artists, which is understandable, but what is
strange is that it is absurdly overrated by everyone else.
TZARA: Because man cannot live by bread alone.
CARR: Yes, he can. It's *art* he can't live on. . . . What is an artist? For every thousand
people there's nine hundred doing the work, ninety doing well, nine doing good,
and one lucky bastard who's the artist. . . . The idea of the artist as a special kind
of human being is art's greatest achievement, and it's a fake!   [pp. 46–7]

In sum, Carr seems to consider art a form of clever nonsense,
capable of providing amusement and even beauty to human life,
but not deserving the kind of esteem that has been bestowed on it
either for its contribution to the improvement of the human situation,
as Tzara would have it, or for its own sake, as Joyce will argue.

The discussion between Carr and Tzara ends inconclusively, and
Joyce enters with Gwendolen. The remainder of Act One deals
primarily with Joyce's views and the reactions of Tzara and Carr to
them. Joyce's arguments with Tzara serve to establish Joyce's status
as defender of the traditional approach to art. At the same time, he
shares Tzara's evaluation of art as an activity of great importance.

For the most part, the interaction between Carr and Joyce in Act
One focuses on Joyce's proposal to mount a production of *The
Importance of Being Earnest* and his invitation to Carr to take part in
the production. Little overt discussion of contrasting views of art
and politics takes place between Carr and Joyce, but a criticism of
Joyce's position is implicit in the version of their interaction which
is supplied by Carr's memory. In the first place, Carr cannot
remember Joyce's name; he calls the Irishman Doris, then Janice,
then Phyllis [pp. 49, 51, 53]. Of course, this misnaming serves in
part to point up the limits of Carr's intelligence. Carr pretends to
knowledge but does not, in fact, even know who the Prime Minister
of England is [p. 50]. Still, the device of misnaming must also
suggest that the one whose name cannot be remembered is, to some
extent, insignificant, lacking an important or memorable identity.[5]

In the second place, there is clear indication in this scene, as in the
earlier limerick scene, that Joyce's artistic efforts require monetary
support from just such ordinary people as Carr. If art, in Joyce's
view, is valuable for its own sake, it still cannot pay its own way.
Joyce even offers to rewrite Wilde's play in order to accommodate
Carr's penchant for fashionable costume, all presumably for the
sake of the two pounds that Joyce hopes to borrow [pp. 52–3].

Hence, in Carr's memory, Joyce's idealistic views on art are tainted by a mercenary motive, so that artistic integrity becomes the servant of financial gain.

To be sure, the picture of Carr that emerges from this interchange with Joyce is not especially admirable either. As before, Carr asserts his preference for the dramatic entertainments of Gilbert and Sullivan, and he seems to object to *The Importance of Being Earnest* primarily because of the moral reputation of its author [p. 51]. Joyce persuades him to take part in the production by appealing to Carr's vanity in matters of dress [pp. 51–3]. In sum, Carr appears to be silly, prudish and vainglorious, especially if he is judged by a standard which assumes the intrinsic artistic value of Wilde's play. But it should be remembered that Carr makes no such assumption. Given his low valuation of art as expressed in the previous scene with Tzara, Carr might be expected to treat the production of *Earnest* as a matter of little consequence; by doing so, he merely confirms the consistency of his aesthetic position.

In Act Two, a disguised Carr seeks out Cecily in the library and argues with her about Lenin's views on the relationship between art and politics. Cecily maintains that art is not valuable except for the sake of the political ends it might serve: 'The sole duty and justification for art is social criticism' [p. 74]. Furthermore, she relegates to the realm of decadence all nonpolitical art, including both Joyce's traditional and Tzara's revolutionary forms. A few scenes later, Lenin expresses the same opinions in his speech to the Russian crowd:

Today, literature must become party literature. Down with non-partisan literature! Down with literary supermen! Literature must become a part of the common cause of the proletariat, a cog in the Social Democratic mechanism. . . .   [p. 85]

Given the close correspondence between Lenin's views and Cecily's, Carr's argument with Cecily can be taken as a confrontation between his aesthetic position and that of Lenin; Cecily serves as Lenin's spokesperson.

Although Carr shares Lenin's low estimation of the intrinsic value of art, he does not agree with the complete subordination of art to political ends. Lenin's position, like Joyce's and Tzara's, constitutes an idealistic extreme, and Carr again chooses a more practical, middle position. He points out to Cecily that her assertion about social criticism being the sole duty of art contradicts practical experience; in fact, much of what is called art has no socially critical function [p. 74]. While Cecily purports to be *describing* the purpose of art, she is actually attempting, Carr notes, to *redefine* art, and her proposed redefinition suffers from the same shortcomings as Tzara's.

What Carr demands is that any definition of art correspond, not to the ideological goals of the definer, but to the phenomenon of art as it has been experienced historically. He rejects Cecily's definition because of the existence of Victorian high comedy and, especially, of Gilbert and Sullivan [p. 74].

At this point, particularly in his defence of Victorian high comedy, Carr seems to have come around in support of Joyce's aesthetic position, for Victorian high comedy (i.e., *Earnest*) has been associated in the play with Joyce, and Carr has not previously seemed much in favor of it. Still, Carr makes no great claims for the worth of Victorian high comedy or of any other form of art; he contends only that they deserve to be called art and not artistic decadence. He does suggest, for the first time, that art satisfies a basic human need: ' . . . in some way it gratifies a hunger that is common to princes and peasants' [p. 74]. He had not admitted even this much to Tzara. Nevertheless, this is far from an affirmation of the intrinsic value of art, all the more so because Carr apparently believes that Gilbert and Sullivan gratify the artistic hunger more effectively than does anyone else.

In the conversation with Cecily, Carr makes clear his rejection of Lenin's aesthetic position. Later, he further undercuts Lenin's insistence on the social utility of art by reminding himself that Lenin's personal tastes in art did not coincide with his public pronoucements about art. The Lenin that Carr remembers liked Chekhov's *Uncle Vanya* and Beethoven's *Appassionata* [pp. 88–9], neither of which functions as social criticism. As a whole, then, Act Two focuses on pointing up the contrast between Carr's view and Lenin's, just as Act One set up oppositions between Carr and Tzara and between Carr and Joyce.

In the final analysis, Carr supports none of the views represented by the three major historical figures. Instead, he presents an independent position of his own, a position which rejects the various idealisms of Tzara, Joyce and Lenin in favor of a practical consideration of what art has been and what it has accomplished. In this respect, Carr's position is as worthy of consideration in its own right as any of the others that the play presents.

Of course, Carr does not win the debate. Stoppard creates a balance among the four opposing aesthetic viewpoints presented in the play, a balance that does not tip in Carr's favor even though his memory controls most of the events in the play. First, there is Carr's relatively minor status as a historical figure by comparison to his better-known opponents, and Stoppard's comic treatment of him as excessively vain about his personal appearance and inordinately

fond of Gilbert and Sullivan. Second, none of the other participants
ever acknowledges the validity of Carr's ideas; the various arguments
inevitably end as standoffs. Third, even in his own version of the
events, Carr must acknowledge that he has been neither as artistically
successful as Joyce nor as politically effective as Lenin. Finally, the
play closes with Old Cecily reminding Carr and the audience
that, however convincing Carr's arguments may have seemed, the
situations that stimulated them never really occurred.

SOURCE: essay on 'Carr's View of Art and Politics in *Travesties*', *Modern
Drama*, XXVI (1983), pp. 536–42.

NOTES

1. A recent exception is John William Cooke, who acknowledges the existence of
the debate but considers it unimportant to an understanding of the play: 'This level
of argument, though it energizes the play, fails to touch its soul. On this point one
may momentarily, I think, rely on intuition: these grandiose pronouncements about
duty and patriotism, art and artist, history and life emanate from a stage world that
is nothing if not chaotic. . . . To understand *Travesties* we have to look at the chaos'
('The Optical Allusion: Perception and Form in Stoppard's *Travesties*', *Modern Drama*,
24 [Dec. 1981], p. 527). Cooke argues that the play is actually about the way meaning
is created out of diverse acts of perception, and his discussion focuses on the numerous
verbal and visual devices in the play that support this claim.
   Nonetheless, most critics have followed the lead suggested by Stoppard himself,
who asserted that the play 'asks whether the words "revolutionary" and "artist" are
capable of being synonymous, or whether they are mutually exclusive, or something
in between' ('Ambushes for the Audience: Towards a High Comedy of Ideas', *Theatre
Quarterly*, 4 [May–July 1974], p. 11). Craig Werner provides a review of early critical
reactions to *Travesties* in 'Stoppard's Critical Travesty, Or, Who Vindicates Whom
and Why', *Arizona Quarterly*, 35 (Autumn 1979), pp. 228–30.
   2. Werner asserts that 'the critics have interpreted the play as either a rejection
of Lenin or as a vindication of Joyce (views which amount to much the same thing
since no critic has stepped forth to declare Tzara the victor or even to give him
serious philosophical consideration)' (p. 228).
   3. For example, Gabriele Scott Robinson identifies Joyce, Tzara and Lenin as
presenting opposing viewpoints in the play and relegates Carr to the role of spectator
('Plays Without Plot: The Theatre of Tom Stoppard'. *Educational Theatre Journal*,
29 [March 1977], p. 42). Similarly, Philip Roberts argues that the central question
of the play 'is stated dogmatically in three forms.' i.e., by Joyce, Tzara and Lenin
('Tom Stoppard: Serious Artist or Siren?', *Critical Quarterly*, 20 [Autumn 1978], p.
90). Joan Fitzpatrick Dean pays some attention to Carr, identifying four distinct
views on art in the play and describing Carr's as 'a relatively innocuous bourgeois
view'. Later, though, she concludes that Carr supports Joyce's position rather than
representing an independent position of his own (*Tom Stoppard: Comedy as a Moral
Matrix* [Columbia, Mo., 1981], pp. 77, 82). [Excerpted above – Ed.]
   4. Werner acknowledges the importance of Carr's perspective to the interpretation
of the play: 'Carr . . . stands firmly at the centre of *Travesties*' thematic structure. . . .
By installing Carr, in many ways a flawed, petty man, as the central stage presence,

Stoppard indicates that the nature of his mind and values is at least as much at issue
as those of the three obviously important intellectual characters' (p. 230). Yet in the
remainder of his article, Werner ignores the implications of this observation, choosing
instead to refute the idea that the play vindicates Joyce and to argue for an increased
importance for Tzara.

    5. Stoppard makes similar use of the misnaming technique to suggest the
insignificance of the title characters in *Rosencrantz and Guildenstern are Dead*.

Margaret Gold   'A New Chapter in the History of the Comedy of Ideas'   (1978)

. . . *Travesties*. . . . mediates upon its own dramatic origins and at
the same time dramatizes questions concerning the proper relation
of politics to art. The stylistic and thematic ventures proceed in
tandem, as Stoppard harks back to the plays of Oscar Wilde and
George Bernard Shaw. He defines his most serious concerns against
theirs and raids their arsenal of techniques and characters. Glittering
in borrowed finery, he creates a distorted likeness of their plays
called travesty. And in so doing he writes a new chapter in the
history of the comedy of ideas.

    Initially a small germ of fact allows Stoppard to bring together
bourgeois and revolutionary, political leader and artist for one
evening on a single stage. James Joyce, Lenin and the Dadaist
Tristan Tzara were all in Zurich at the time of the First World War.
Fact even conspired to give Stoppard his bourgeois hero, one Henry
Carr, a minor official at the British Consulate in Zurich at that
time. Carr, it seems, acted the role of Algernon in a production of
Oscar Wilde's play *The Importance of Being Earnest* staged by James
Joyce.

    Stoppard claims that Carr appealed to him as a means for using
the actor he wanted the play to be for, John Wood. Stoppard's
account is that:

Originally, *Travesties* was a play about Lenin and Tristan Tzara. I knew what Lenin
looked like, so John had to be Tzara. Then I discovered that Tzara was a small
dapper man so I had to find another way. When I discovered that James Joyce was
also in Zurich, John was Joyce for a while. I hadn't written a word. Then I was
reading Richard Ellmann's biography of Joyce and I came across this Carr figure.
He's tall! So I wrote a play about Carr. Gods being gods, I said, if he was tall, John
could play him. As it turned out Mrs Carr is still alive, and she sent me a photo of
her late husband who I thought I invented. He did actually look like John.[1]

It must, however, be at least as true that in Carr Stoppard discovered

the slightly pathetic and immediate focal point recognizable in his
plays from the George Riley of *Enter a Free Man* (1968) to the George
Moore of *Jumpers* (1972). As Stoppard told an interviewer when he
was still writing *Travesties:* 'I write out of my experience as a middle-
class bourgeois who prefers to read a book to doing anything else.'[2]

In addition to seizing upon Carr when he found him in Ellmann's
biography of Joyce, Stoppard picked up the idea of using the Oscar
Wilde play Carr appeared in as a skeleton for his own play, doubtless
in line with T. S. Eliot's observation that while immature poets may
borrow, mature poets steal. It was also, of course, a technique that
had already worked very well for Stoppard (in a more straightforward
way) in *Rosencrantz and Guildenstern are Dead* (1967). What the plot of
The Importance of Being Earnest initially supplied to Stoppard's play
was its two young lady characters, Gwendolen and Cecily. Between
them they manage to create plot links, plausible enough at least in
the context of farce, to draw the disparate crew of characters
together. The young ladies cement the chummy relationship of Carr
and Tzara, since Tzara is in love with Gwendolen, who is Carr's
sister. Carr, meanwhile, is in love with Cecily, who is Tzara's friend.
Gwendolen, Carr's sister, is employed as a secretary to Joyce, while
Cecily searches out volumes in the economics section of the Zurich
library for Lenin, whom she passionately admires.

Given a device like manuscripts in identical folders which become
confused, the characters inevitably meet, aided in this case by the
additional time-tried mechanism of the play within a play. If all this
sounds frivolous, an audience still ought not to lose sight of the fact
that as Wilde pointed out, 'burlesque and farcical comedy, the two
most popular forms [of theatre], are distinct forms of art'.[3]

Stoppard's vaudeville is only a bare-bones skeleton, a travesty of
Wilde's exquisite comedy; the likeness is grotesque. But there is a
more subtle relationship between the two plays. Oscar Wilde in
Earnest wrote a play as deliberately emptied of content – politically,
emotionally, and philosophically – as can be imagined, and while
he was engaged in making light of most of the sacraments and
almost every bourgeois notion of seriousness, he called his play *The
Importance of Being Earnest*. Stoppard, on the other hand, has written
a play called *Travesties* and filled it with serious matter. Wilde also
comes into *Travesties* as a character. Henry Carr is very much like
Wilde, the dandy, when he dwells lovingly on his involvement in
the First World War entirely in terms of the styles of the trousers he
wore and ruined in each battle. In his imaginary role as British
Consul, Carr takes on Wilde's aristocratic stance. But the stance is
a travesty. The real Carr, survivor of the trenches and minor

functionary, is *au fond* a bourgeois, Wilde's favorite target.

There is a real sympathy, however, between Stoppard and Wilde, the aesthete, on issues involving the status of art. Wilde foresaw in 1891 that there could be no regular partnership between the arts and the state. He almost seems to have known what the masterpieces of Soviet Realism would look like. In 'The Soul of Man Under Socialism', Wilde wrote that 'whenever a community or a powerful section of a community, or a government of any kind, attempts to dictate to the artist what he is to do, Art either entirely vanishes, or becomes stereotyped, or degenerates into a low and ignoble form of craft. *A work of art is the unique result of a unique temperament. Its beauty comes from the fact that the author is what he is It has nothing to do with the fact that other people want what they want.*' [4] Stoppard has the benefit of hindsight. That is why Lenin's monologue in Act Two of *Travesties* refers so often to Gorki and Mayakovsky. Carr has learned the lesson well enough to tell Tzara, who has called for 'the right to urinate in different colors' [p. 61], that 'multi-colored micturition is no trick to those boys, they'll have you pissing blood' [p. 83].

George Bernard Shaw is the second of the dadas in *Travesties*. The political debates in *Travesties* have an unmistakably Shavian crackle. The clash, for example, of Carr and Tzara over the justice of fighting the First World War is very much like the clash between the Devil and Don Juan in Shaw's *Man and Superman* over man's essential nature. Shaw's devil believes that man is merely intent upon destruction: 'The tiger and crocodile were too easily satiated and not cruel enough: something more constantly, more ruthlessly, more ingeniously destructive was needed: and that something was Man, the inventor of the rack, the stake, the gallows, the electric chair: of sword and gun and poison gas: above all, of justice, duty, patriotism and all the other isms by which even those who are clever enough to be humanely disposed are persuaded to become the most destructive of all destroyers.' Don Juan's response is essentially that men always win when they are fighting for an idea and the hope is that eventually men will be persuaded to win on behalf of the best ideas.

In Stoppard's play, Tristan Tzara is concerned to show, in a more limited and specific way than Shaw's Mephistopheles, that the war is prompted by greed. '*Patriotism, duty, love, freedom* ...' says Tzara, 'all the traditional sophistries for waging wars of expansion and self-interest, presented to the people in the guise of rational argument set to patriotic hymns.' [p. 39]. Carr, like Don Juan, can answer Tzara only by continuing to insist that he himself fought for '*love of freedom.*' [p. 40]. Whereas Shaw's dialectics has an easy awareness of ironies and a more broadly metaphysical context. Stoppard's in *Travesties* is more passionately personal, as in the *ad hominem* strains of Carr's reply to Tzara: 'My God, you little Rumanian wog – you bloody dago – you jumped-up phrase-making smart-alecy arty-intellectual Balkan turd!!!' [p. 40].

Shaw has supplied his complement of characters to *Travesties* as well. Bennet, the butler, who patiently explains the political situation to his employer, Carr, the diplomat, raises echoes of the delightful 'enry Straker, the chauffeur mechanic in *Man and Superman*, who with his polytechnic education is so much better informed than his employer, Tanner, the Oxford educated Romantic socialist. James Joyce as a character here is sometimes reminiscent of Shaw's artist-as-superman Louis Dubedat, the painter in *The Doctor's Dilemma*, whose loyalty to his art is so perfect that he does not need to bother at all about common morality, just as Joyce can afford to play at being Mr Dooley and ignore the war. And if Carr, the play's major character, is a travesty of Oscar Wilde, aristocrat and dandy, then Tristan Tzara, Carr's foil and opposite, is a travesty of Bernard Shaw, artist and socialist. Shaw as gadfly of the bourgeoisie triumphantly united the roles of playwright and Fabian reformer. Tzara, who attempts the pose in *Travesties*, is defeated. He loses as artist in Act One to Joyce, who points out that Tzara has no talent, and he loses as socialist in Act Two to Lenin, who gives every sign of being able to crush more artists than merely Tzara.

As was the case with Wilde, where Stoppard finally meets Shaw is within the realm of ideas. *Travesties* seems to pick up where Shaw's *Heartbreak House* leaves off. Shaw lays the blame for the First World War on the political irresponsibility of the upper middle class in his preface to *Heartbreak House*. Stoppard seems to wonder in *Travesties* whether in fact they could have done anything.

Shaw defined Heartbreak House as cultured, leisured Europe before the war, and Carr is Heartbreak House, unchanged, a couple of years later. Shaw said that Heartbreak House 'hated politics', and he accused them of 'taking the only part of our society in which there was leisure for high culture and making it an economic, political and as far as practicable a moral vacuum'. Carr apologises for the fact that his work leaves him no time for politics. Shaw's indictment of Heartbreak House is that 'they refused the drudgery of politics and would have made a very poor job of it if they had changed their minds'. Like them, Carr as imaginary consul makes a hash of blocking Lenin's return to Russia. By the time he figures out that a Kerensky government is going to be a whole lot easier to live with, Lenin's train has already pulled out of the Zurich station.

But Stoppard carries the whole problem a step closer to the abyss
that yawns between ordinary men and Supermen. Men like Joyce
and Lenin who are the children of Genius and Destiny elude the
chains of common reasoning, and the rest of us never know when
the whole situation is going to be radically altered by the appearance
of such a character. As poor Old Carr says, 'To those of us who
knew him Lenin's greatness was never in doubt. (*He gives up again*).
So why didn't you put a pound on him, you'd be a millionaire' [p.
24]. And this may be the heart of the pathos that always surrounds
the bourgeois in Stoppard's plays. He does not make anything
happen, and he exists on a different plane from those who do.

Carr is nevertheless the play's most complex character, and
through all his shifting gallery of poses, from aesthete to bitter old
man, from horrified soldier to make-believe consul, he preserves a
very appealing and tenacious intelligence. It is visible in the political
debates where he more than holds his own against Tzara and Cecily,
and in the verbal facility and especially the self-irony of the
monologues of Old Carr. There are moments when he breaks
through the poses to become real, when a short circuit in his brain
flings his mind and body into a spasm and catapults him back to
the trenches. This horror is real, and so is Carr's love for Cecily,
who survives as Old Cecily into the present when the rest of the
phantasmagoria disappears.

It seems to me that the great achievement of the play is the
amazing freedom with which such a hero as Carr is made to move
among so many different stylistic levels. The play is arranged so
that the whole is conceived as the fantasy of Old Carr, who like
Samuel Beckett's Krapp, replays the spool that contains his past.
There is a nice tension that arises at the opening of the play between
Old Carr's monologue – which keeps foundering in its attempt to
find a memoir style that will resuscitate Zurich-during-the-war –
and the final bursting of the imagined play out of the limiting
monologic chrysalis as a dramatic butterfly. In addition to the
primary Wildean farce and Shavian debate, still further stylistic
possibilities are thrown into the *mélange* by Joyce and Lenin.

Joyce contributes the limerick and his rendition of Mr Dooley, as
well as the interrogation of Tzara in what Joyce called the 'constabu-
lar' style of the Eumaeus episode in *Ulysses*. Even more important
for *Travesties* may be, via *Finnegan's Wake*, the pun. Lenin in Act Two
brings in overtones of the agit-prop drama which can be Brechtian
at its best whereas at its worst it has the flavor of amateur history
pageants. In its most impoverished form, the narrator speaks all the
parts, as Nadya does in *Travesties*, while the main character speaks

his own lines, transcribed directly from the memoirs. While informative, it can be very flat, unless one understands some subtle irony by which the very form intended to educate us to the tenets of Marxism educates us here to its dangers.

As characters the supermen, Joyce and Lenin, appear as caricatures, music-hall versions of themselves, Joyce spouting limericks and songs, and Lenin seeming a kind of escapee from Edmund Wilson's book *To the Finland Station*, plotting his return to Russia disguised as a Swedish deaf mute with a wig. But in terms of the argument of the play, which might be phrased in one sense as a debater's proposition that goes 'Art or Politics; Both or Neither?', these two hold down the extreme and limiting conditions of the debate. Joyce weighs in for the supreme value of art, and Lenin for politics as an absolute. Carr and Tzara exist in a situation where they attempt to mediate between those extremes, with Tzara standing for both art and politics, perhaps, and Carr standing for neither.

The way in which *Travesties* encounters its dadas is through travesty, a likeness that is grotesque; it is also pastiche, a cut and paste job like the one Tzara performs on Shakespeare's sonnet number 18, 'Shall I compare thee to a summer's day?' When Tzara cuts up the sonnet into individual words and then draws the words out of his hat to make a new and infinitely more vulgar poem, the lovely original is none the less discernible beneath its surface, and the function of both original and travesty is the same, the wooing of a lady. As such Tzara's pastiche is a metaphor for Stoppard's methods. His combination of multiple travestied styles allows him to focus a dazzling multiplicity of perspectives all played off against the pathos of his hero. It allows him too to pick his way lightly among thorny matters and to put forward views of real seriousness while distancing them in a healing way through laughter.

SOURCE: essay on 'Who are the Dadas in *Travesties?*', *Modern Drama*, XXI (1978), pp. 59–65.

NOTES

1. Mel Gussow, 'Playwright, Star provide a Little Curtain Raiser', *New York Times*, (31 Oct. 1975), p. 21.
2. 'Ambushes for the Audience: Towards a High Comedy of Ideas,' interview with Tom Stoppard, *Theatre Quarterly*, 4 (May-July 1974), p. 14.
3. Oscar Wilde. 'The Soul of Man Under Socialism', in *The Artist as Critic: Critical Writings of Oscar Wilde*, ed. Richard Ellmann (New York, 1969),p. 272.
4. Wilde, p. 270.

Allan Rodway   'A Thematic
Network'   (1976)

. . . *Travesties* is Stoppard's greatest and most superficial play – as
Wilde's *Importance of Being Earnest* is his. There is more, however, to
Travesties' travesty of Wilde than there is to Wilde's travesty of
Scribean melodrama. Like Wilde, it is everywhere paradoxical, but
its paradoxes far more often open up the nature of reality. Though
blatantly artificial it resembles reality by being ambiguous and
multi-layered. In fact, Stoppard's latest play is an onion; superficial
at every level; *profoundly* superficial. Like the world of appearances
it is heartless; no inner truth or more real reality is to be found by
stripping off layers of appearance. An idea anticipated by the
striptease that opens *Jumpers*. . . . In *Travesties* the idea is given an
extra twist when Cecily strips . . . while incongruously purveying
at length the Marxist 'truth' about the economic nature of reality.

If some truths, as distinct from mere facts, involve values then
such values, not being given, must be constructed (as Joyce put it)
'upon the incertitude of the void'. Or so it would seem. To say so
definitely would not only be undramatic but also unStoppard-
ian.   . . .

Fundamentally, all three of his plays deal with the problem of
knowledge (how do we know we really *know* what we think we
know?); and all three are travesties: of *Hamlet*, Agatha Christie
and Wilde (the last being scrambled formally, and appropriately
considering its setting, with the expressionist techniques of Joan
Littlewood's *Oh! What a Lovely War*). Moreover, something of each
is to be found in all. In *Jumpers* philosophical debate, not quite
travestied, but satirical in so far as it concerns Archie, dandy leader
of the scientific rationalists, humorous in connection with George
Moore, outgunned but undefeated metaphysician. *Rosencrantz and
Guildenstern,* texturally, often travesties philosophical debates on
reality and illusion while structurally calling in question the nature
of reality through its triple perspective: of the worlds of *Hamlet*, the
Players, and Rosencrantz and Guildenstern. And *Travesties* travesties
not only Wilde (and Joyce) but also Shakespeare:

GWEN: Truly I wish the gods had made thee poetical.
TZARA: I do not know what poetical is. Is it honest in word and deed? Is it a true
    thing?
GWEN: Sure he that made us with such large discourse, looking before and after,
    gave us not *that* capability *and* godlike reason to fust in us unused.   [p. 54]

(Which, incidentally, is the true Tzara? The anti-poet or the man who knows his Shakespeare so well?)

All three plays, by evoking literature as often as life, merge questions of art with those of nature and reality – and also, almost inevitably (as in this passage) raise questions of identity. Is 'the truest poetry the most feigning' as Shakespeare said? Is the truest person the most posing, as Wilde maintained? After all, characters are not being 'themselves' when travestying some other author (or even travestying the travesty, as when Gwendolen and Cecily change from Wildean elegance to doggerel or to the music-hall dialogue of 'Mr Gallagher and Mr Shean'). This particular aspect of the problem of knowledge, of course, crops up more evidently in, say, the rapidity with which Rosencrantz and Guildenstern cease to be sure who is which when they are removed from their normal environment, in Archie's variedly ambiguous status, in Joyce's becoming 'Doris', 'Elsie', and 'Bridget', Rumania 'Bulgaria' for Carr, or in Lenin's dual personality as lover of Beethoven wanting to pat heads and as politician wanting to hit them 'without mercy'.

So one could go on, enumerating common concerns, common techniques. All are remarkable comedies combining brilliant surfaces with deep themes. The difference is that in *Travesties* Stoppard has so mastered his medium that with deceptive ease he provides more of everything, as if it were nothing.

So much more, that this play requires a new concept. Where most, including *Rosencrantz and Guildenstern* and *Jumpers*, have a theme or themes, *Travesties* is constructed as a thematic network: some twenty interrelated aspects of the problem of knowledge, areas of uncertainty, working in varied permutation. All, of course, are dramatised either in the Library, repository of fiction and faction (mirrored in the characters of Joyce and Lenin), of illusions and truths, or they are set in the Room, where Carr's often unreliable memories are cultivated.

That life is layered is most obviously, but by no means only, suggested by the underlying Wilde play and the fact that *Travesties* is a play about doing a play, in the middle of a war. The problem of layered personal identity is constantly posed by Carr (not to mention Wilde's Jack and Algernon, especially when both are playing Ernest, and thus acting actors). Properly then, at the end of the play as performed (though it is not in the stage-directions) Carr casts off the drab grey dressing-gown of the old man to reveal – another drab grey dressing-gown. Wilde said men speak the truth only through a mask (a thematic concern that first crops up on p. 28 of *Travesties*), become real only by adopting a pose. So was the real

Henry Carr the debonair clothes-conscious youth we see as an
embodied memory, or was he always really a grey sloven? (Though
who's to say, anyway, the play implies, that what a man is in his
imagination is less real than what others see him as?). Well, we
learn at the end that he was not really the Consul and hardly knew
Lenin, and that his main relationship with Joyce consisted in a
dispute over tickets and trousers. But he *did* play Algernon –
simply for the aesthetic sake of the costume-changes, yet with such
dedication that he let Lenin escape to Russia ('But he wasn't *Lenin*
then!'). Was this art imitating his real nature, as Wilde said art did?
And if he was *really* an Algernon, in youth, though only when he
could dress up on stage, is there still a bright butterfly under the
second grey dressing-gown in age? After all, he has just created, as
much as recreated, the youthful Joyce, Tzara, and Lenin (a fact,
again, underlined in production by the maestro-manner of his
beckoning them from the wings at the final curtain). And are *they*
thus nearer to what they *really* were, if we can judge by their art,
than what they actually were? On the other hand, perhaps Carr is
now just a travesty of what he was, and has produced a mere –
rather than a graphic – travesty of what they really were? Or, again,
is he a travesty of what he should have been, had he really worked
at his pose to create a truly tuppence-coloured being?

Such questions inevitably shimmer subliminally as the warp and
weft of a thematic network shuttles from Art and Reality in the
opening scenes to truth and Illusion and Youth and Age [p. 27],
Masks and Truth [p. 28], Truth and Relativity [p. 29] and so on in
various combinations through matters of fact, theory, language,
experience, memory, deception, pose, rhetoric, feeling, chance,
sincerity and travesty, in so far as they constitute aspects of the
central problem stated forcibly on p. 37:

TZARA: I am sick of cleverness. The clever people try to impose a design on the
world and when it goes calamitously wrong they call it fate. In point of fact,
everything is Chance, including design.
CARR: That sounds awfully clever. What does it mean? Not that it has to mean
anything, of course.
TZARA: It means, my dear Henry, that the causes we know everything about depend
on causes we know very little about, which depend on causes we know absolutely
nothing about. And it is the duty of the artist to jeer and howl and belch at the
delusion that infinite generations of real effects can be inferred from the gross
expression of apparent cause.

Design and Chance, Appearance and Reality, Art and Delusion, all
touched on here, are reflected throughout in innumerable touches,

for the thematic network is built up, insinuated almost, by a verbal *pointillisme*. In that way contextual density is triumphantly married with textural lightness, gravity with levity.

The general flippancy over the great and bloody issues of the First World War and the Russian Revolution, too, avoids censure by being always relevant to such highly abstract concerns. (This is a play of ideas, not characters; that is why the characters have no characteristic diction.) Joyce's rejoinder to Carr is a miniscule example: '"And what did you do in the Great War?" "I wrote *Ulysses*," he said. "What did you do?".' In retrospect, which *was* the better thing to do? Carr's mistaking the nature of the revolution in Russia, too, instances a flippancy that is directly relevant to an aspect of the problem of knowledge: is interpretation always a matter of relativity? (Compare the passage where the communist Tzara thinks Lenin's writing worthless when he believes it to be Joyce's, while Carr, the aesthete, thinks Joyce's writing rubbish when he believes it to be by Lenin):

CARR: ... I don't wish to appear wise after the event, but anyone with half an acquaintance with Russian society could see that the day was not far off before the exploited class, disillusioned by the falling value of the rouble, and above all goaded beyond endurance by the insolent rapacity of its servants, should turn upon those butlers, footmen, cooks, valets ...   [p. 29]

In the latter, more political part of the play the touch is possibly a trifle less light, the serious implications a shade more obvious. Witness the plain use of paradox as self-deception and political rhetoric (i.e. public deception):

LENIN: ... Publishing and distributing centres, bookshops and reading-rooms, libraries and similar establishments must all be under party control. We want to establish and we shall establish a free press, free not simply from the police, but also from capital, from careerism, and what is more, *free from bourgeois anarchist individualism*. ...   [p. 85]

In brief, the mode of *Travesties* is metaphoric, parodic, and semi-factual – constantly, therefore raising the question: What is literal truth? What is authentic? What is fact? The mood, appropriately paradoxical, is hilarious and nostalgic: gradually Carr's youth is revealed as the youth of our world and of modernism in art (and this hints – no more – that these, like Carr himself, may have turned to seediness and disillusion now). The form is almost a contradiction in terms – again appropriately, for we are not to be allowed to settle into assumptions of certainty. Wild Wilde, it mingles the well-made play and its elegance of dialogue with the dislocations of Brechtian expressionism and its shock tactics (imagine *Wilde's* Gwendolen musing: 'Gomorrahist . . . Silly bugger!) The texture is shotsilk, always shifting and shining – and, like life, paradoxical. Patches of rhyme and dance demonstrably turn life into art and, some might argue (depending on their views of modernist art), *vice versa*.

Travesties travesties both the literature and the lives it is based on, in the cause of something other than 'the facts'. Concerned *with* the problem of knowledge, however, it is unconcerned *about* it; like most of the best comedies it encourages us to enjoy what we must endure.

SOURCE: essay, 'Stripping Off', *London Magazine*, 16 (1976), excerpted from pp. 66–72.

Thomas R. Whitaker   'The Prism of Travesty' (1983)

Jumpers invites of us, as actors and witnesses, an attentive ethical concern that we can observe nowhere within the ominously absurd world we are playing. *Travesties* proposes a yet trickier game. It asks us to refract both the content and the style of our playing through an ironic prism that illuminates several large questions: How do we make art? Or revolution? Or history? Or, indeed, any kind of meaning?

Suppose we are at the Aldwych Theatre on a June evening in 1974, when *Travesties* was first being performed by the Royal Shakespeare Company under Peter Wood's direction. The lights come up on what seems a section of the Zurich Public Library, though at downstage right we also see a dimly lit piano and an old man (played by John Wood) whom we infer to be Henry Carr. At the library tables, busy with their books and papers, are Tristan Tzara (played by John Hurt), James Joyce (Tom Bell), and Lenin (Frank Windsor). With Joyce is a young woman (Maria Aitken) who must be Gwendolen. During the next few minutes we watch a bizarre series of disturbances in the library.

Tzara first reads out (in a Rumanian accent) an English poem that he has just composed, according to his Dada recipe, by cutting up what he has written and shaking the words out of a hat. If we pay close attention to its incoherent lines, we may discover that we are hearing intelligible French. 'Ill raced alas whispers kill later nut east', for example, sounds rather like 'Il reste à la Suisse parce qu'il est un artiste'. But who has made coherent meaning from those fragments – Tzara, Stoppard, or we ourselves? ('Ssssssss!' says the librarian Cecily, played by Beth Morris, as she enters and crosses the stage.) Joyce then dictates to Gwendolen some obscure invocations: 'Deshill holles eamus', 'Send us bright one, light one, Horhorn, quickening and wombfruit', and 'Hoopsa, boyaboy, hoopsa!' If we have read *Ulysses*, we may recognise bits from the Oxen of the Sun episode, which, as it recounts the birth of a baby, recapitulates in pastiche and parody the history of English prose. ('Sssssh!' says Cecily again.) After an accidental swapping of two folders, which leaves Cecily with Joyce's manuscript when she thinks she has Lenin's, and Gwendolen with Lenin's when she thinks she has Joyce's, Lenin begins to speak in Russian with his wife Nadya (Barbara Leigh-Hunt), who has just entered. If we understand that language, we know that Nadya is reporting a revolution in St Petersburg and a rumour of the Tzar's imminent abdication. Meanwhile Joyce is now walking about, searching in his pockets for scraps of paper that contain phrases he may want to use in *Ulysses*, and reading them out. Retrieving another scrap from the floor, he reads: 'GEC (USA) 250 million marks, 28,000 workers . . . profit 254,000,000 marks'. But that scrap has been dropped by Lenin, who now engages Joyce with quadrilingual courtesy: 'Pardon! . . . Entschuldigung! . . . Scusi! . . . Excuse me!' Finally Joyce exits, declaiming a limerick about a 'librarianness of Zurisssh' (which Cecily, entering, fortuitously completes with another 'Ssssssh!') and singing 'Galway Bay' – a tune that Carr now picks up on the piano as the set changes from the Library to his room. As he begins to speak, we realise that this scrappy and imperfectly intelligible counterpoint of languages, arts, and revolutions has been a Prologue to the old man's retrospective meditation, itself a thing of shreds and patches. And we will soon find that it also serves as a Joycean overture to a play that repeatedly asks us to collaborate in transforming other people's fragments into fresh meaning.

As the main character on his own historical stage, 'Carr of the Consulate' begins by recalling how he had known Joyce when he was writing *Ulysses*, had shaken Lenin's hand before he was known to the world as Lenin, had lived through the early days of Dada, and had even taken part in a play produced by Joyce, achieving a 'personal triumph in the demanding role of Ernest, not Ernest, the other one, in at the top, have we got the cucumber sandwiches for

Lady Bracknell' – all in that Switzerland of 1917 which was for artists and other refugees 'the still centre of the wheel of war'. Though Carr's bits of narrative and semi-soliloquy seem a travesty of both 'history' and 'art', we may doubt (after the Prologue) that greater minds have been much less egocentric and scrappy. Nevertheless, because the Prologue had also prepared us for something more sharply ironic than Carr's self-indulgent aestheticism seems likely to provide, we expect some parodic variations on his account. We do not have to wait long. His fatuous rhetoric has already absurdly applied the same formulas to Joyce, Lenin and Dada. And when, removing hat and dressing-gown and letting the crustiness of age disappear from his voice, John Wood suddenly becomes the young Carr of 1917, we find that yet bolder patterns of repetition give ironic shape to the ensuing flashbacks.

A manservant enters with a tray of tea things and sandwiches, almost as if he were Lane in Wilde's *The Importance of Being Earnest.* It is Bennett, played by John Bott. With more than a little help from Stoppard, Carr is already imagining his early life as something out of that 'theatrical event of the first water' in which he had played not Ernest but 'the other one', Algernon Moncrieff. He has cast himself as a British Consul rather like the aesthete Algernon, with a sartorial obsession that will assume for us a thematic importance. More than once this play will remind us of Carlyle's *Sartor Resartus* (or 'the tailor retailored'), in which history is reconstituted from scaps of paper and a 'clothes philosophy' explains the changing world of appearance. As Carr now re-imagines what led up to his meetings with Tzara, Joyce and Lenin, he goes through five variations on Algy's opening conversation with Lane, each introduced by a 'time-slip' and Bennett's repeated line: 'I have put the newspapers and telegrams on the sideboard, sir'. But who *was* this 'manservant' Bennett? At the end of the play old Cecily will make old Carr confess that Bennett, and not Carr, had been the British Consul in Zurich.

When Bennett-Lane announces Tzara, the pastiche of Wilde's play continues without a hitch: 'How are you, my dear Tristan?' says Carr-Algy. 'What brings you here?' And quite as if he were John (alias Ernest) Worthing transformed into a Rumanian nonsense, Tzara answers: 'Plaizure, plaizure! What else? Eating ez usual, I see 'Enri?!' The arrival of Tzara here leads directly to that of Gwendolen (Carr's sister, cast in his memory as Wilde's Gwendolen) and Joyce (an Irish nonsense, cast as Lady Bracknell), and then into a manic explosion of shared limericks. But the scene between Carr-Algy and Tzara-Jack will be twice repeated at greater

length as *Travesties* edges toward a fuller engagement with Wilde's
script and with its own themes of art, revolution, and history.

'I don't know how radical you are', Lenin once said to a Rumanian
Dadaist in Zurich, 'or how radical I am. I am certainly not radical
enough; that is, one must be always as radical as reality itself.' But
how radical would that be? What is the 'reality' to which our so-
called 'radicals' are always inadequate? *Travesties* plays with that
question through its dialectic of flashbacks. . . . But in *Travesties*
the flashbacks are quite different – and not just because Henry Carr
was in fact a consular employee who played in Joyce's production
of *The Importance of Being Earnest*, quarrelled with him, and was then
travestied by Joyce in the Circe episode of *Ulysses* as a drunken
soldier. The mode of *Travesties* itself results from a fusion of Wildean
farce, Joycean fiction, Dadaist spontaneous negation, epic theatre,
and Shavian dialectic. Balancing an array of radical principles and
egocentric procedures, *Travesties* suggests that our 'reality' is at best
a shared construction from fragmentary data.

Auden once called *The Importance of Being Earnest* 'perhaps the only
purely verbal opera in English'. Wilde's solution there, he said, 'was
to subordinate every other element to dialogue for its own sake and
create a verbal universe in which the characters are determined by
the kinds of things they say, and the plot is nothing but a succession
of opportunities to say them'. Stoppard fastens with delight upon
that solution, enriches it with Joycean pastiche, parody, and
wordplay, and turns it into a medium for a Shavian dialectic that
wittily explores the claims of rival principles. (Shaw, we may
remember, also insisted on the operatic form of his debates.) In Act
One of *Travesties* this dialectic is nearly derailed by the effervescent
Tzara, whose serious spoofing infects the play's own style. In Act
Two the play swerves in a different direction as Cecily, Nadya, and
Lenin nearly turn it into an epic 'teaching play' in the socialist style
of Erwin Piscator. The precariously balanced result manages to
extend Wilde's achievement, pay tribute to Joyce's artistic faith,
acknowledge the power that resides in both Tzara's levity and
Lenin's gravity, and offer a more iridescent display of multiple roles
and visions than occurs even in Shaw's *Man and Superman* and
Heartbreak House.

According to Peter Wood, Stoppard had thought of calling
this play *Prism* because, through Carr's memory, it views history
'prismatically'. But surely the appeal of that working title was
manifold. *Travesties* refracts our approach to history, art, and
revolution through the triangular prism of Joyce-Tzara-and-Lenin,
refracts it again through Carr's memory, and again through Stop-

pard's own multifaceted parody. It therefore becomes a model of
the indirections by which we must move toward the white light of a
truth beyond our full perception or expression. Tzara has his own
version of this rainbow effect, the Dada demand for the 'right to
urinate in different colours'. 'Each person in different colours at
different times, or different people in each colour all the time?' asks
Joyce. 'Or everybody multi-coloured every time?' But *Travesties* also
bears a whimsically indirect relation to another Prism, the elderly
governess in *The Importance of Being Earnest*, who, twenty-eight years
before the action of that play, had accidentally switched the baby
'Ernest' and the manuscript of her triple-decker sentimental novel.
In *Travesties* that Prism does not appear as a single character.
Her baby-and-manuscript switching is echoed by the manuscript-
swapping in the Prologue and the dénouement; her role as Cecily's
teacher is assumed by the seemingly untravestied Lenin; her fatuous
moralising reappears in old Carr's reminiscences; and her name is
everywhere an implicit metaphor in a play that has transmuted
Wilde's own *Earnest* into a triple-decker didactic farce. A full
appreciation of the prismatic shimmer of this role-switching and
role-splitting verbal opera requires our shared presence in the
theatre. But some spectroscopic analysis may be useful – beginning
with the band of light emitted by the ironic travesty of Wilde's play
on earnestness.

Act One of *Travesties* recapitulates Act One of *The Importance of Being
Earnest* with varied repetitions that reduce Wilde's high farce to
broad absurdity, load it with ironically qualified didacticism, and
employ its epigrammatic style for witty assessments of artistic and
political doctrine. After Carr-Algy's conversations with Bennett-
Lane, Tzara-Jack's first entrance has led to a manic scene of shared
limericks that, like the Prologue, declares the characters to be no
more than fragments of a collaborative meaning. When Tzara enters
for the second time, however, he too is one of Wilde's sophisticated
dandies. In this guise he offers a rather persuasive defence of Dada,
provokes Carr into a yet more persuasive attack upon Dada, and
then abandons all style as he pursues Carr into an absurdly heated
argument. Entering for the third time, Tzara comes yet closer to
Wilde's plot and dialogue. Speaking of Cecily and Joyce, he
establishes the Library as the equivalent of Jack Worthing's house
in the country: 'Well, my name is Tristan in the Meierei Bar and
Jack in the library, and the ticket was issued in the library'.
('Tristan', we gather, will be this play's coded name for 'Ernest'.)
Then, after defining his political agreement and artistic disagreement

with Lenin, Tzara erupts once more in a raving defence of anti-art.
At this point Gwendolen and Joyce make their second entrance.
After Tzara defines his artistic position against that of Joyce, and
Joyce defines his political position against that of Tzara and Lenin,
Joyce invites Carr to take Algernon's part in the very play that we
have, in effect, been watching for some time. When the two retire
to discuss the matter, even as Algy and Lady Bracknell retire to
discuss the music for her reception, *Travesties* is at last ready for
Wilde's scene between Jack and Gwendolen.

Tzara will offer as a tribute to his Gwendolen his own kind of
poem, Shakespeare's eighteenth sonnet reshuffled by the hand of
chance. Thanks to Stoppard's farcical magic, however, the preliminary conversation between Tzara and Gwendolen is already composed of tags from *Julius Caesar, Hamlet, As You Like It, Much Ado
About Nothing, Henry V, Henry IV (Part One), Othello, The Merry Wives
of Windsor,* and the thirty-second sonnet. We are therefore prepared
to see a collaborative meaning emerge once more from random bits
and pieces. When Gwendolen draws the words of 'Shall I compare
thee to a summer's day . . .' from Tzara's hat, they have become a
free-verse poem of unmistakably phallic excitement. She is prettily
flustered; but after the poem's temperature has dropped, she gives
Tzara the folder containing what she supposes to be Joyce's
manuscript – for this Gwendolen insists on loving not an 'Ernest'
or even a 'Tristan' but an admirer of Joyce. As they embrace, Joyce
himself returns, now fully identified with the role of 'Lady Bracknell':
'Rise, sir, from that semi-recumbent posture!' But he is also now
fully himself: his interrogation of Tzara proceeds in the catechistic
style of the Ithaca episode in *Ulysses.* Indeed, he now becomes a
more astonishing conjurer than Tzara as he takes handkerchiefs and
flags from his own hat, reduces Tzara to histrionic violence, lectures
him on the nature of the artist, and, reaching once more into his
hat, pulls out a rabbit.

Carr ends this first act with a warning that he will now tell us
how he met Lenin 'and could have changed the course of history
etcetera'. And indeed, Act Two begins in a totally different style
with Cecily's lecture on Marx and Lenin. That lecture, however,
substitutes for the pedagogical scene between Cecily and Prism that
opens Act Two of *The Importance of Being Earnest.* And though the
rest of *Travesties* often seems dominated by such didactic material, it
also contains an accelerated recapitulation of the second and third
acts of Wilde's play. Just as we earlier watched three versions of
Tzara-Jack's entrance, so we now watch three versions of Carr-
Algy's arrival at the library as 'Tristan Tzara' in pursuit of Cecily.

During the first version, he offers his own view of art – a defence of
'Victorian high comedy' against Cecily's charges of bourgeois
decadence. During the second, she gives him the folder containing
what she supposes to be Lenin's manuscript, and seduces him with
her increasingly frenetic defence of revolution – finally appearing to
him, and so to us, as a haranguing stripper. During the third
version, which echoes the second of Wilde's scenes between Algy
and Cecily, the action moves swiftly to a Wildean capitulation
('Ever since Jack told me he had a younger brother who was a
decadent nihilist it has been my girlish dream to reform you and
love you') and an unWildean dive behind the librarian's desk for
an embrace. The prickly meeting of the two 'brothers' – Tzara-Jack
and Carr-Algy – then comes to us in counterpoint with Nadya's
account of Lenin's plan to return to Russia. And after a narrative
bridge spoken by old Carr, that counterpoint continues through the
narrative and demonstration of Lenin's political and aesthetic
views. Soon, however, the strains of Beethoven's 'Appassionata',
which have accompanied Nadya's poignant memory of her
separation from Lenin during his imprisonment, degenerate
absurdly into the mechanical tune of a patter song, 'Mr Gallagher
and Mr Shean', and the stage is taken over by socially conscious
art of a different kind: a music-hall version of Wilde's upper-class
tiff between Cecily and Gwendolen. With heightened artifice and
lowered social tone, Stoppard's young ladies translate the
elaborately pseudo-polite insults of Wilde's dialogue into neatly
rhymed stanzas.

   In its closing moments, *Travesties* briskly alludes to Act Three of
The Importance of Being Earnest. Like their counterparts at the
beginning of that act, Stoppard's Cecily and Gwendolen have 'just
one question' to put to their young men; but this question is about
the manuscripts they have given Tzara and Carr to read, and it
leads directly into the dénouement. The left-wing Tzara rejects
Lenin's manuscript (which he thinks to be Joyce's) as 'unreadable';
the aesthete Carr rejects Joyce's (which he thinks to be Lenin's) as
the work of a 'madman'. Their verdicts, though demonstrating to
us their political and aesthetic incompetence, pose for the couples
an 'insuperable barrier' of 'intellectual differences'. But with Joyce's
arrival all is resolved. In Wilde's play, Lady Bracknell thunders:
'Prism, where is that baby?' In Stoppard's, Joyce thunders: 'Miss
Carr, where is the missing chapter?' And he alludes, of course, to a
chapter of *Ulysses* that does in fact recount through parody and
pastiche the birth of a baby. Now, in accord with the Scribean
conventions already burlesqued by Wilde, the lovers swiftly untie

the knots of misunderstanding, swap folders, embrace, and tie the knots of love with a brief dance.

In the coda old Carr returns to admit, at Cecily's insistence, his most flagrant distortions of history, and to leave us with a rather futile moral:

> I learned three things in Zurich during the war. I wrote them down. Firstly, you're either a revolutionary or you're not, and if you're not, you might as well be an artist as anything else. Secondly, if you can't be an artist, you might as well be a revolutionary.
> I forget the third thing.   [pp. 98–9]

Though his speech is partly cribbed from the end of *Dogg's Our Pet*, its circle of antitheses and forgotten 'third thing' aptly sum up a play that is yet more elaborately and ironically symmetrical than *The Importance of Being Earnest*. For Stoppard as for Wilde, the foundation of style is a paradoxical antithesis. And as Gwendolen says in *The Importance of Being Earnest*, 'In matters of grave importance, style, not sincerity, is the vital thing'. Though Gwendolen's stylishness is absurdly pretentious, both Wilde and Stoppard would agree with her remark. Both know that style permits a critique of the self-deceptions enjoyed by those who think themselves either sincere or stylish. Both also know that a counterpoint of eccentric styles can illuminate what is central. What Wilde called his 'trivial play for serious people' therefore sparkles with epigrammatic exposures of our folly. And *Travesties*, more brazenly trivial and more insistently serious, uses its symmetries not only to speed up the farce but also to engage at length the antithetical doctrines that have shaped modern art and politics. Carr's forgotten 'third thing' ought ideally to be some synthesis of those doctrines, more genuinely radical than they because more adequate to our scrappy reality. If you cannot be a revolutionary like Lenin, or an artist like Joyce, or a revolutionary anti-artist like Tzara, and if you do not want to be a philistine aesthete like Carr, might you not find such a synthesis of genuine importance? But no doubt that is why Stoppard has allowed it to remain the implicit dialectical burden of this prismatic play.

SOURCE: chapter 6, 'The Prism of Travesty', in *Tom Stoppard* (London and Basingstoke, 1983), pp. 108–19.

Tim Brassell   'Concern with the Concepts of Art and Revolution'   (1985)

. . . The play breaks with Stoppard's previous custom by treating historical figures in an historical setting. Set in Zurich, it contrives to bring together a number of distinguished exiles who were in the city in the later years of the Great War: Lenin, on the verge of revolutionary success in Russia; James Joyce, engaged in creating the revolutionary prose edifice of *Ulysses*; and the artist Tristan Tzara, who, with his fellow Dadaists, revolted against practically all established notions of art and culture. These three revolutionary figures – two in the arts, one in the fiercer world of politics – provide the play with its main themes and its central characters. But in general Stoppard does not treat them historically and their individual lives and achievements serve chiefly as the pretext for a playfully disrespectful comedy which, as its title suggests, makes 'travesties' of the characters which it presents.

For at the hub of the drama is a fourth 'real' character, Henry Carr, who also chanced to be in Zurich in 1917, based at the British Consulate in Zurich while recovering from a serious wound sustained in action in France. There is no evidence to suggest that Carr ever met Tzara or Lenin, but it is by dramatising his humorous, bigoted and largely fictitious recollections of the great men living alongside him in the city that the travesties are perpetrated. And since Carr provides the frame for the entire action, it appears to be he, rather than Stoppard, who is their source. His one genuine connection is with Joyce and this is well-documented. They met when Carr was enlisted to play the role of Algernon Moncrieff in a production of *The Importance of Being Earnest* given in the city with Joyce as business manager (and an English actor named Claude Sykes as producer) and their relationship, never amicable, blew up into a storm after the production when they commenced legal proceedings against each other – Carr seeking reimbursement for clothes he had bought specifically for his performance and Joyce, by way of riposte, demanding money for the tickets that Carr had sold. As a result Carr assumes sufficient importance to figure in Richard Ellmann's biography of Joyce, and Stoppard liberally expands upon the minimal information offered therein:

From these meagre facts about Henry Carr – and being able to discover no others – I conjured up an elderly gentleman still living in Zurich, married to a girl he met in the Library during the Lenin years, and recollecting, perhaps not with entire accuracy, his encounters with Joyce and the Dadaist Tzara. [p. 12]

The character thereby created is, of course, just as much of a travesty as those which Carr himself perpetrates – a fact obscured by the real Carr's relative unimportance in historical terms, but wryly underlined when Mrs Noel Carr, his widow, wrote to Stoppard after the play's reviews had appeared!

Carr's role, then, is roughly that of the pseudo-biographer and Stoppard employs a series of devices to warn us of the unreliability of his hazy recollections. He presents the character in two distinct guises: in the present time, as a rambling old man fancifully recalling his past, and as his imagined younger self, reliving that past in 1917. Both Carrs are played by the same actor, moving from the theatre fore-stage of Old Carr's drawing room where the play begins and ends and to which, intermittently, it briefly returns – to the scene, behind it, of his imaginary former glories, the elegant drawing room of the British Consulate in Zurich (though this is swiftly transformed for a number of scenes into the city's Public Library). Here, as Old Carr invests himself with an importance very much greater than that which history actually afforded him,[1] we meet Young Carr the British Consul, intimately mingling with the great artists and revolutionaries exiled in the city. Stoppard thus brings to life a Zurich landscape that exists only inside Carr's head, where fact, fiction and jumbled reminiscence whirl around in glorious abandon. The time-scale, for instance, is obviously implausible; the characters were never all in Zurich at *exactly* the same time and by the opening of *The Importance of Being Earnest* in April 1918, Lenin had been back in Russia for almost a year. Old Carr himself eventually concedes at the end of the first act that he may not have got all the details quite right as his memory travels back over sixty years, mixing wile with forgetfulness:

Incidentally, you may or may not have noticed that I got my wires crossed a bit here and there, you know how it is when the old think box gets stuck in a groove and before you know where you are you've jumped the points. [p. 64]

Right from the start, though, Stoppard demonstrates his concern to emphasise that his character's hit-or-miss recollections are based much less on first-hand memory than on what he has subsequently read or heard about the great men in question by deflating the pompous literary tone of Old Carr's first explanatory soliloquy. An enormously long monologue, crowded with contradictions, puns, inaccurate quotations and humorous wordplay, it provides a mischievously telling parody of the august tone adopted by so many biographers and autobiographers, while at the same time enabling

Stoppard to lay much of the groundwork for what follows, not only in respect of the suspect basis of Carr's memoirs but by sketching the characters whom we subsequently encounter in scenes which, because they reflect the confusion in Carr's thinking, can be equally confusing for the audience.

These main 'dramatised' sections of the play are often rapid, chaotic and contradictory, but one strand provides a constant point of reference: the role of Algy which Carr played in *The Importance of Being Earnest* and which is his sole authentic link with his subjects. As his 'wires' cross and re-cross, he frequently attributes to those around him lines and structures borrowed from the play in which he performed (apparently with considerable distinction) in Zurich and although these are often employed in fairly unlikely contexts, they produce a quite remarkable effect. For Stoppard so engineers the quotations and borrowings from *The Importance of Being Earnest* that Tzara, Joyce and Carr's younger self consistently act 'in character', enabling him to create an elaborate parallel structure between his play and Wilde's. In addition to these three parallel characters (Lenin is omitted for reasons examined below), he subordinates with cheeky appropriateness the real British consul at the time, Bennett, to the rôle of Carr's manservant and invents a sister for Carr named Gwendolen and a librarian called Cecily to complete the essential cast as follows:

ALGERNON MONCRIEFF:	HENRY CARR
JOHN WORTHING:	TRISTAN TZARA
LANE:	BENNETT
AUNT AUGUSTA (LADY BRACKNELL):	JAMES JOYCE
GWENDOLEN FAIRFAX:	GWENDOLEN CARR
CECILY CARDEW:	CECILY CARRUTHERS

In this way the only true correspondence – that Carr recalls playing Algy – becomes the starting point from which Stoppard organises practically the entire course of his play along the lines of Wilde's, with Carr in romantic pursuit of Cecily and Tzara of Gwendolen. In defence of this improbable schema, two remarkable further coincidences may be cited: that Joyce was in reality mis-registered at birth as 'James Augusta' (in error for Augustine) and that the actor playing Worthing in the English Players' production was indeed named Tristan. Carr's mistakes are therefore almost plausible, enabling Stoppard to use *The Importance of Being Earnest* – with considerable ingenuity and dexterity – to furnish the audience with familiar and coherent bearings. The concept of setting characters within borrowed cultural patterns plainly owes much to Joyce, since

Ulysses – in the use it makes of the *Odyssey* – provides the archetype
for this kind of structure. Stoppard himself had earlier attempted a
similar experiment in the use to which he puts *Hamlet* in *Rosencrantz*.
Here, however, the whole point of the 'play-within-a-play' concept
is the absence of any real mutual dependence of the one on the
other. Wilde's play is thus used to provide a steadily identifiable
but essentially bogus focus, unifying the otherwise disparate strands
of Stoppard's complicated subject and creating a narrative thrust
that Carr alone cannot offer. Charles Marowitz has therefore
described *Travesties*, with some justice, as 'a play-within-a-mono-
logue',[2] neatly highlighting the patent discrepancy between Carr's
real existence in Zurich in 1917 and his fantastic representation of
it, which – as if to 'seal in' these discrepancies – is everywhere
permeated by the characters, structure and even *tone* of Wilde's play.
Even where there is no direct mimicry, one senses the way in which
Carr's account is shot through with a joyous sense of play-acting:

It is this complete absence of bellicosity, coupled with an ostentatious punctuality
of public clocks, that gives the place its reassuring air of permanence. Switzerland,
one instinctively feels, will not go away.   [p. 26]

The epithets, if not Wilde's own, bear the unmistakable stamp of
his delight in artifice and style as Stoppard cultivates for Young
Carr a tone of extravagant loquaciousness that carries as far as
possible the image of a cultivated Victorian–Edwardian world of
gentlemanly leisure – a world which Carr capriciously desires to
believe in but which, in its turn, travesties the *real* mood of 1917.

Carr's fantasy does not therefore exist merely for the pleasure its
playful variations on *The Importance of Being Earnest* undoubtedly
provide. As the central characters might suggest, both political
activity and philosophical theory – especially as reflected in artistic
theory – are major preoccupations in this play, as in *Jumpers*.
Travesties represents a further advance in Stoppard's attempt to
marry the 'play of ideas' with 'farce or high comedy'; indeed, the
presence of the 'ideas' is rather more ostentatious here, especially in
respect of the character of Lenin. Stoppard is primarily concerned
with the concepts of art and revolution and the possible relationship
between them. Inside the frame established by Carr runs a broad-
based discussion of these two subjects in which each character has
a clear-cut contribution to make. Lenin is presented as a man of
absolute commitment to action, burning with fervent determination
to implement the theories he has spent his life formulating. Joyce
demonstrates a scarcely lesser commitment to his art, and pursues
it with a passion and conviction that verge upon religious dedication.
Tzara exemplifies the artist's zealous commitment to the destruction

of the false and outmoded gods of established culture. In addition,
Lenin holds important views on art, Tzara on revolution. Between
them the three provide a wealth of possibilities and opportunities,
but without any self-evident focal point. It is Young Carr's role as
prompter and catalyst which provides this, as his trenchant and
reactionary views fuel – not to say inflame – the various stages of
the debate. Unlike *Jumpers*, the role of the central character therefore
exists both outside the action – as Old Carr, presenting his fabricated
portrait of Zurich – and within it, as Young Carr, an active
combatant in a similar sense to George in his pitched battle against
the legions of Logical Positivism. . . .

SOURCE: extract from *Tom Stoppard: An Assessment* (London and Basing
stoke, 1985), pp. 136–41.

NOTES

1. It is interesting to compare Carr's comically exaggerated self-importance with
that of Spike Milligan in *Adolf Hitler: My Part in his Downfall* (Harmondsworth, 1972),
which is also set in the chaos and passion of a World War (see, for example, p. 34).
2. *New York Times* (19 Oct. 1975), p. 1.

C. W. E. Bigsby 'Seeking a Balance between Art and History' (1976)

. . . The moral dimension of Stoppard's work appears at times to
suffer from his own commitment to farce. He seems afraid to take
himself seriously, to allow his humour to become a consistent
critique – hence his *penchant* for parody rather than satire, his
technique of building scenes through contradiction. As he once
remarked, 'I write plays because dialogue is the most respectable
way of contradicting myself.'
   It follows that he feels 'committed art' to be 'a kind of bogus
exercise'. As he has explained, 'I get deeply embarrased by the
statements and postures of "committed" theatre. There is no such
thing as "pure" art – art is a commentary on something else in life –
it might be adultery in the suburbs, or the Vietnamese war. I think
that art ought to involve itself in contemporary social and political
history as much as anything else, but I find it deeply embarrassing
when large claims are made for such an involvement: when, because

art takes notice of something important, it's claimed that the art is important. It's not.'

Travesties attempts to debate essentially this problem. As Stoppard has said, 'it puts the question in a more extreme form. It asks whether an artist has to justify himself in political terms *at all*, 'whether the words "revolutionary" and "artist" are capable of being synonymous or whether they are mutually exclusive, or something in between.' It is a play which brings together the opposite extremes of the debate in the persons of James Joyce, whom Stoppard elsewhere quotes as saying that the history of Ireland, troubles and all, was justified because it led to a book such as *Ulysses*, and Lenin, who felt that the only justification for art lay in its political utility. Mediating between the two is Tristan Tzara, drawn simultaneously in both directions; on the one hand spinning neologisms and cascades of words like Joyce, convinced that the artist constitutes the difference between brute existence and any sense of transcendence, and on the other seeing the writer as the conscience of the Revolution and justifying the brutality of its servants. However, the question is effectively begged by the form in which Stoppard chooses to conduct the debate. For the most part we see the characters only as they are refracted through the febrile imagination of a minor British consular official, Henry Carr. Just as *Hamlet*, viewed through the eyes of Rosencrantz and Guildenstern, is drained of tragic meaning, so too this clash of ideas loses much of its urgency seen from the perspective of a deluded, prejudiced and erratic minor functionary. In this context, perforce, they become mere performers in a Wildean comedy which jolts along with all the manic energy and manifest dishonesty of a bogus memoir.

In 'The Critic as Artist', Oscar Wilde remarks of memoirs that they are 'generally written by people who have either entirely lost their memories, or have never done anything worth remembering'. This proves all too accurate a description of Carr's memoirs, which tend to confuse his own fictions with those of *The Importance of Being Earnest* in which he had once scored a minor success. Indeed, apart from appropriating dialogue and even two of his characters directly from Wilde's play, he even restructures history so that it conforms to the requirements of high comedy. The title is thus an appropriate one as Stoppard, through Carr, presents a travesty of both literary styles and historical events.

Carr erroneously remembers himself as having been British Consul in Zurich during the First World War, at a time when Lenin, Joyce and Tzara were living out an expatriate existence, plotting their various revolutions in art and society. In juxtaposing these forces,

Stoppard seems to be suggesting that history is no less a fiction than Joyce's parodic constructions; that it has no more logic than Tzara's poems, which are themselves the product of pure chance. But something about this question of literary performance and *bravura* politics fails to convince. In picking Lenin as the embodiment of political fabulism, he engages not merely a historically bound figure who can be parodied as himself a none too competent role player, but also a palpable reality whose particular fictions have assumed an implacable form. There is a degree, therefore, to which Stoppard seems to have been unnerved by the ineluctable consequences of revolutionary conviction. We know, or think that we know, that the opinions expressed by the various characters in the play are those which Carr constructs. The single exception is Lenin, who stands, perhaps, as a corrective to those fictions – massive, real. The grand claims of Tzara, the self-confident assertiveness of Joyce, real or illusory, can only inhabit a world defined by the prosaic realities defined by Lenin. The massive scale of his impact on history, an impact which transcends both the banality of his life-style and his literary style, is a fact tucked away in the mind of the audience. Just as his presence seems to neutralise the play's anarchic humour, to inhibit the irresponsible contempt for social realities, so his presence in the real world does much the same. He is a materialist and the material has no time for fantasy as Dotty had realised in *Jumpers*. The details of Lenin's career, solemnly narrated by Nadya, his Russian secretary (a narration which Stoppard incautiously invites his directors to edit to taste) contrasts markedly with the anarchic frivolity of those other revolutionaries who surround him in Zurich, and whose revolutions are contained by the boundaries of artistic concern.

From his initial description of the characters through to Lenin's departure for Russia, it is the political activist alone who for the most part escapes parody. Carr's imagination makes both Joyce and Tzara perform a series of bizzarre antics. Indeed they become the chief actors in a baroque farce, likely at any moment to lapse into song and dance. Lenin remains stolidly detached. His speeches are authentic, a point which Stoppard is at pains to stress. He is the only character, in other words, who is not controlled by Carr's distorting imagination, though according to the conventions of the play he too should be moulded to fit the elderly diplomat's psychic needs. And though this is perhaps a conscious comment on the nature of the difference between the artist and the social revolutionary, a difference which makes the fusion of the two roles unlikely, it also has the effect of dislocating the play. The second act is not merely less funny than the first, containing a detailed documentary account of Lenin's career (accompanied by objectifying photographs), and also a debate about the role of the artist between Carr on the one hand and Tzara and Cecily on the other; it is also less effective. The sources for the first act are Wilde's play, *The Importance of Being Earnest*, James Joyce's *Ulysses* and the documented excesses of Dada; the source for the second is Lenin's biography. The change in mood is inevitable. The result is a curiously reverential treatment of the political leader, an approach quite at odds with the tone of a play which seems to suggest his poverty of imagination, his disregard for moral values and his misconceptions about the function of art and history. Farce drains away as Stoppard comes to the heart of his concern, and though he is careful to conceal his own commitments by refusing to resolve the contradictory views expressed by his characters, the stylistic dislocation exposes the seriousness of his concern as the play becomes at moments a genuine debate about the importance of being earnest – of adopting a humourless dedication to social realities.

Stoppard has called his distinguishing mark, an 'absolute lack of certainty about almost anything'. This detachment, though unnerving in some respects, gives him the freedom, for most of the time, to criticise the materialist inhumanity of Lenin, the spurious artistic arrogance of Joyce, the cavalier socialism of Tzara and the aristocratic hauteur of Carr. All seem squarely rooted in self-concern. But Stoppard's detachment slips once or twice. Despite his failure to locate a satisfactory mode of parody with regard to Lenin, his distrust of ideologists surfaces at moments, cutting through the comic banter which otherwise for the most part defuses any attempt at moral seriousness. Carr's rebuttal of Marxist analysis and Cecily's disingenuous justification for Lenin's inhumanity are too studied to sustain a credible commitment to ethical distance. The assumptions of farce come up against the moral presumptions of comedy, and the resulting clash disturbs not merely stylistic unity but also the momentum of the humour.

In a conflict between a materialist view of history and an approach which translates the substantial realities of human life into fictions, fantasies, and plots, there can be little doubt where Stoppard's sympathies will lie – nor, by the end, can we be in any doubt that these two views are so clearly antithetical that the notion of a revolutionary artist is a demonstrable contradiction in terms. Yet, in his own way, Carr is as dedicated to a simplistic view of reality as is Lenin. He wants to believe in a world in which he can play a central role. Language must provide a precise symbolism, the artist must be a beautifier of reality, a licenced hedonist. He resists reality with as much dedication as either Joyce or Tzara. He is, of course, in a real sense a playwright. He 'creates' the drama in which he casts himself as the central character (as, essentially, does each individual). He claims the same right to refuse social liability as he believes the true artist must do. As he remarks, 'to be an artist *at all* is like living in Switzerland during a world war'.

In this respect, also, he is close kin to Rosencrantz and Guildenstern, to George Riley and Professor Moore. Like Stoppard himself, these characters choose to respond to the bewildering vagaries of existence by creating games, plays, by remaking the world until its absurdities dissolve in simple performance. Lenin, Joyce, Tzara, Carr, all are equally pathetic and heroic as they inhabit with such apparent conviction the fictions which they choose to regard as reality. Role players all, they seek to construct plots which will make sense of their urge for personal, social or metaphysical order. Art, politics, philosophy, logic are deployed with varying degrees of conviction. But behind it all there lurks the savage joke which is implicit in the figure of the ageing Carr who reconstructs his past out of the same compulsions which led Beckett's Krapp to turn the switch of his tape recorder to replay the hopes and aspirations of his youth. It is Carr's distinction that he glimpses this truth for a moment and is still able to justify his challenge to reality. . . .

SOURCE: extract from *Tom Stoppard* (London and Harlow, 1976), pp. 24–9.

SELECT BIBLIOGRAPHY

Most of the books used in this volume contain good accounts of plays other than those excerpted here, and should be further consulted. In addition, the following are of value:

Jim Hunter, *Tom Stoppard's Plays* (London, 1982).
Felicia Londré, *Tom Stoppard* (New York, 1981).
John Russell Taylor, *Anger and After*, rev. edn (London, 1969).
John Russell Taylor, *The Second Wave* (London, 1971).
Kenneth Tynan, *Show People* (New York, 1979).

There is an extensive literature about Stoppard in critical articles. Check-lists of these are:
Randolph Ryan, 'Theatre Checklist No. 2: Tom Stoppard', *Theatrefacts*, 2 (May–July 1974), pp. 2–9.
Charles A. Carpenter, 'Bond, Shaffer, Stoppard, Storey: An International Checklist of Commentary', *Modern Drama*, xxiv (1981), pp. 546–56.

For editions of the plays, see Editor's Notes appended to the Introduction, pages 23–4, above.

NOTES ON CONTRIBUTORS

J. A. BAILEY is in the Department of Philosophy, University of Manitoba.

JOHN BARBER was for many years theatre critic of the *Daily Telegraph*.

NORMAND BERLIN teaches in the University of Massachusetts; among his publications are *Eugene O'Neill* (in the Macmillan Modern Dramatist series) and the Casebook *O'Neill*.

C. W. E. BIGSBY is Senior Lecturer in the School of English and American Studies, University of East Anglia; his many publications include books on contemporary American drama, on Dada and Surrealism, and studies of Edward Albee and Joe Orton.

TIM BRASSELL is Literature and Publicity Officer with Northern Arts in Newcastle-upon-Tyne. He is Editor of *Arts North*.

ROBERT BRUSTEIN is Dean of Drama at Yale University.

RONALD BRYDEN, theatre critic for the New Statesman (1964–66) and the *Observer* (1966–71), was appointed Play Adviser to the Royal Shakespeare Company in 1971.

VICTOR CAHN teaches at Skidmore College, New York.

RICHARD CORBALLIS is Senior Lecturer in English at the University of Canterbury, New Zealand; his publications include a study of the Machiavel figure in English literature, and he writes drama criticism for a number of journals.

G. B. CRUMP teaches at Central Missouri State University; he has published studies of R. M. Koster and Wright Morris.

JOAN FITZPATRICK DEAN is Assistant Professor of English in the University of Missouri at Kansas City; her writings include studies of Peter Shaffer and Joe Orton.

JOSEPH E. DUNCAN teaches in the University of Minnesota; among his publications is a study of archetypes in Milton.

ROBERT EGAN is Assistant Professor of Dramatic Art in the University of California at Santa Barbara; he is the author of a book on Shakespeare and of articles on Renaissance drama.

MARGARET GOLD, at the time of writing her 1978 article on Stoppard, was Assistant Professor at Touro College, New York.

GILES GORDON is a novelist, poet, short-story writer and author of children's books as well as a theatre critic.

WILLIAM E. GRUBER is Assistant Professor of English at Emory University in Atlanta, Georgia.

MEL GUSSOW is a theatre critic for the *New York Times*.

RONALD HAYMAN is a biographer, literary critic and writer on theatre; his publications include books on Pinter, Stoppard, Beckett, Osborne and Arden, and on acting techniques.

PHILIP HOPE-WALLACE (1911–79) was drama and opera critic for the *Manchester Guardian* (subsequently retitled *Guardian*).

CLIVE JAMES has a wide range of literary and media interests; he has been television critic and features writer for the *Observer* since 1972.

STANLEY KAUFFMAN has written novels, plays and film scripts. He has held Visiting Professorships in Drama at the universities of Yale and New York City, and in 1979 he became theatre critic of the *Saturday Review* magazine.

J. W. LAMBERT has held prominent positions in literary and theatrical sponsoring organisations and from 1976 to 1981 was associate editor and chief reviewer of the *Sunday Times*. His publications include books on travel and on the British theatre in the 1960s and 1970s.

JILL LEVENSON is from the Department of English in Trinity College, Toronto; among other essays she has written on *Romeo and Juliet* and on *Troilus and Cressida*.

BENEDICT NIGHTINGALE was drama critic of the *Guardian* and later of the *New Statesman*, and has subsequently become a writer and publicist on a wide range of contemporary issues.

DAVID K. ROD is in the Department of Communication Arts in Texas Lutheran College at Fort Worth.

ALLAN RODWAY was formerly Reader in English at the University of Nottingham; his numerous publications include studies on English Comedy from Chaucer to the present, and on the craft of criticism.

MILTON SHULMAN is novelist, essayist, contemporary historian and critic; he has been columnist and theatre critic for the *Evening Standard* since 1953.

IRVING WARDLE, one of the most influential voices in modern British theatre, has been drama critic of *The Times* since 1963; his publications include a book on the theatrical career and aims of George Devine.

JOHN WEIGHTMAN is a prominent literary, drama and film critic, and his publications include a study of the concept of the Avant-Garde in modern culture.

THOMAS R. WHITAKER is Professor of English in Yale University; his publications include *Fields of Play in Modern Drama*.

B. A. YOUNG was for many years drama critic of the *Financial Times*.

HERSH ZEIFMAN teaches at York University, Downsville, Ontario; he has published many articles on drama, including studies of *Macbeth* and *Waiting for Godot*.

214

ACKNOWLEDGEMENTS

The editor and publishers wish to thank the following for permission to use copyright material: J. A. Bailey, extract from article in *Michigan Academician*, XI (1979), by permission of Michigan Academy; John Barber, extract from review of *Jumpers*, 3 Feb. 1972, *The Daily Telegraph*, by permission of *The Daily Telegraph*; Normand Berlin, extracts from article in *Modern Drama*, XVI, Dec. 1973, by permission of the University of Toronto; T. Brassell, extract from *Tom Stoppard: An Assessment* (1985), by permission of Macmillan Publishers Ltd.; Robert Brustein, extracts from *The Third Theatre* (1969), by permission of Jonathan Cape Ltd.; Ronald Bryden, extract from *Rosencrantz and Guildenstern are Dead*, *Observer Weekend Review*, 28 Aug. 1966, by permission of *The Observer*; Victor Cahn, extracts from *Beyond Absurdity: The Plays of Tom Stoppard*, Fairleigh Dickinson University Press (1979), by permission of Associated University Presses; Richard Corballis, extract from *Stoppard: The Mystery and the Clockwork* (1984), by permission of Amber Lane Press; G. B. Crump, extract from article in *Contemporary Literature*, XX, No. 3 (1979), by permission of The University of Wisconsin Press; Joan Fitzpatrick Dean, extract from *Tom Stoppard; Comedy as a Moral Mix* (1981), by permission of University of Missouri Press. Copyright © 1981 by the Curators of the University of Missouri; J. E. Duncan, extract from article in *Ariel*, XII, No. 4 (1981), by permission of The University of Calgary Press. Copyright © 1981, The Board of Governors, The University of Calgary Press; R. Egan, extract from article in *Theatre Journal*, XXXI (1979), by permission of The Johns Hopkins University Press; Giles Gordon, extract from article in *Transatlantic Review*, 29, Summer 1968, by permission of the author; Margaret Gold, article in *Modern Drama*, XXI (1978), by permission of the University of Toronto; W. E. Gruber, extract from article in *Comparative Drama*, XV (1981–2), by permission of *Comparative Drama*; Mel Gussow, extract from article in *The New York Times*, 26 April 1972, by permission of The New York Times Company. Copyright © 1972 by The New York Times Company; N. S. Hardin, extract from article in *Contemporary Literature*, XXII, by permission of The University of Wisconsin Press; Ronald Hayman, extracts from *Tom Stoppard*, 4th edition (1982), by permission of Heinemann Educational Books Ltd.; and extracts from article in *New Review*, I, ix (1974), by permission of Peters Fraser and Dunlop Group Ltd. on behalf of the author; Clive James, extract from review of *Travesties*, *Encounter*, XLV, Nov. 1975, by permission of Encounter Ltd.; Stanley Kauffman, extract from review of New York production of *Jumpers*, included in his *Persons of the Drama*, Harper and Row (1976), by permission of the author. Copyright © 1976 by Stanley Kauffman; Jeremy Kingston, extracts from review of *Jumpers*, *Punch*, 9 Feb. 1972, by permission of Punch Publications Ltd.; Joost Kuurman, interview with Tom Stoppard, *Dutch Quarterly Review*, X (1980), by permission of *Dutch Quarterly Review*; Jill Levenson, extracts from article in *Queen's Quarterly*, 78 (1971), by permission of the author; James Morwood, extract from article in *Agenda*, XVIII–XIX, Winter and Spring 1981, by permission of *Agenda*; Benedict Nightingale, extract from review of *Travesties*, *New Statesman*, 14 June 1974, by permission of *New Statesman*; G. S. Robinson, extracts from article in *Education Theatre Journal*, 29 March 1977, by permission of The Johns Hopkins University Press; D. K. Rod, article in *Modern Drama*, XXVI (1983), by permission of the University of Toronto; A. Rodway, extracts from article in *London Magazine*, 16, Aug./Sept. 1976, by permission of *London Magazine*; Tom Stoppard, extract from *Contemporary Literature*, XXII (1981), by permission of The University of Wisconsin Press; extracts from 'Ambushes for the Audience', *Theatre Quarterly*, IV, No. 4 (1974), by permission of the Editors of *Theatre*

Quarterly and *New Theatre Quarterly*; and extract from 'Playwrights and Professors' in *The Times Literary Supplement*, 13 Oct. 1972, by permission of *The Times Literary Supplement*; Philip Hope Wallace, extract from review of *Rosencrantz and Guildenstern are Dead*, *The Guardian*, 12 April 1967, by permission of Jacqueline Hope Wallace; Irving Wardle, extract from review of *Rosencrantz and Guildenstern are Dead*, *The Times*, 12 April 1967, and extract from review of *Travesties*, *The Times*, 11 June 1974, by permission of Times Newspapers Ltd.; Janet Watts, extracts from article in *The Guardian*, 21 March 1973, by permission of the author; John Weightman, extracts from reviews of *Rosencrantz and Guildenstern are Dead*, *Encounter*, July 1967, xxix, and *Jumpers*, *Encounter*, xxxviii, April 1972, by permission of Encounter Ltd.; Thomas R. Whitaker, extracts from *Tom Stoppard*, 1983, by permission from Macmillan Publishers Ltd.; B. A. Young, extract from review of *Jumpers*, *Financial Times*, 3 Feb. 1972, by permission opf *Financial Times*; Hersh Zeifman, extracts from article in *Yearbook of English Studies*, ix (1979), by permission of the Editor and the Modern Humanities Research Association.

Every effort has been made to trace all the copyright holders but if any have been inadvertently overlooked the publishers will be pleased to make the necessary arrangement at the first opportunity.

INDEX

1 Stoppard's Works

2 General Index

Note: two of the plays treated in this volume present fictional accounts of real-life persons – Captain Scott, G. E. Moore, Lenin, James Joyce, Tristan Tzara, Henry Carr, etc. The index refers in every case to the historical figure, not to the fictionalised dramatic character.

The spelling of names of non-English entries is taken from Martin Banham, (ed.), *The Cambridge Guide to World Theatre*, Cambridge, 1988.

.